Critical Issues in Ecclesiology

Critical Issues in Ecclesiology

Essays in Honor of Carl E. Braaten

Edited by

Alberto L. García and Susan K. Wood

WILLIAM B. EERDMANS PUBLISHING COMPANY

GRAND RAPIDS, MICHIGAN / CAMBRIDGE, U.K.

Published 2011 by
Wm. B. Eerdmans Publishing Co.
2140 Oak Industrial Drive N.E., Grand Rapids, Michigan 49505 /
P.O. Box 163, Cambridge CB3 9PU U.K.

Printed in the United States of America

17 16 15 14 13 12 11   7 6 5 4 3 2 1

Library of Congress Cataloging-in-Publication Data

Critical issues in ecclesiology: essays in honor of Carl E. Braaten /
    edited by Alberto L. García and Susan K. Wood.
        p.   cm.
    "Bibliography of the publications of Carl E. Braaten": P.
    Includes bibliographical references.
    ISBN 978-0-8028-6671-4 (pbk.: alk. paper)
    1. Church.   2. Braaten, Carl E., 1929-
    3. Lutheran Church — Theology. I. Braaten, Carl E., 1929-
    II. García, Alberto L. III. Wood, Susan K.

    BV600.3.C75 2011
    262 — dc22

                                        2011006444

www.eerdmans.com

Contents

Contents

Abbreviations

AAS   *Acta apostolicae sedis*

ARCIC   The Anglican-Roman Catholic International Commission

BC   *The Book of Concord,* edited by Robert Kolb and Timothy J. Wengert. Minneapolis: Fortress, 2000

CD   Karl Barth, *Church Dogmatics,* edited by T. F. Torrance, translated by A. T. Mackay and T. H. L. Parker. Edinburgh: T&T Clark, 1961.

ELCA   Evangelical Lutheran Church of America

Ep   Epitome of the *Formula of Concord, The Book of Concord*

ESV   English Standard Version of the Bible

FC   *Formula of Concord, The Book of Concord*

JDDJ   *Joint Declaration on the Doctrine of Justification* by the Lutheran World Federation and Roman Catholic Church, 1999

LCMS   The Lutheran Church-Missouri Synod

LG   *Lumen Gentium, The Dogmatic Constitution on the Church,* promulgated by Pope Paul VI on November 21, 1964, at the Second Vatican Council

Abbreviations

LW   Martin Luther, *Luther's Works*, American edition, edited by Jaroslav Pelikan and Helmut T. Lehman. 56 vols. St. Louis: Concordia; Philadelphia: Muhlenberg and Fortress, 1955-1986.

LWF Lutheran World Federation

NPNF *Nicene and Post-Nicene Fathers*, 1st series, edited by Philip Schaff. Peabody, Mass.: Hendrickson, 1994 reprint.

Report *Report of the Synodical President to the Lutheran Church–Missouri Synod in Compliance with Resolution 2-28 of the 49th Regular Convention of the Synod held at Milwaukee, Wisconsin, July 9-16, 1971*

SC   *Sacrosanctum Concilium, Constitution on the Sacred Liturgy*, promulgated by Pope Paul VI on December 4, 1963, at the Second Vatican Council

SD   *Solid Declaration of the Formula of Concord, The Book of Concord*

WA   Martin Luther, *D. Martin Luthers Werke: Kritische Gesamtausgabe. Schriften*. Weimar: Herman Böhlaus, 1833-1999.

Preface

This book is dedicated to the Rev. Dr. Carl E. Braaten. His closest collaborator, the Rev. Dr. Robert W. Jenson, paints for us here a picture of the friend, colleague, and theologian that we honor in this volume. Jenson takes us to the heart of Braaten's theological legacy — his passion for catholic evangelical enterprise for the sake of the church. As a Lutheran theologian Carl has anchored evangelical vision in the gospel of our Lord Jesus Christ. This gospel is not to be hidden under a bushel but to be proclaimed to the whole world in Word and deed. For Carl, the unconditional love of God in the death of his Son Jesus Christ for the forgiveness of our sins gives impetus to the witness of the church. This Good News is present for all people in the real servant presence of our Lord in the Eucharist.

Carl Braaten, along with Robert Jenson, is a co-founder of the Center for Catholic and Evangelical Theology. The goals of the center also describe his life's work: "The Center for Catholic and Evangelical Theology is an ecumenical organization that seeks to cultivate faithfulness to the gospel of Jesus Christ throughout the churches. The Center nurtures theology that is catholic and evangelical, obedient to Holy Scripture and committed to the dogmatic, liturgical, ethical and institutional continuity of the Church. The Center challenges the churches to claim their identity as members of the One, Holy, Catholic and Apostolic Church. It affirms the Great Tradition and seeks to stimulate fresh thinking and passion for mission." In the essays that follow, the contributors to this volume reflect on the church in the light of these same themes.

Braaten's witness is fundamentally catholic in its height, depth, and breadth. In breadth, his concern is always for the well-being of the church, the community of the faithful inclusive of its ecumenical variety, the *ecclesia* that witnesses to the gospel in its life and proclamation. In depth, his theological work has been dedicated to the continuity of the church in its apostolic witness throughout generations within this "Great Tradition." In height, as an eschatological theologian, Carl grounds his vision for the church in the hope of the resurrection. This hope delineates his vision of the catholic evangelical church that lives not under a theology of glories past but — as a true son of Martin Luther — under a theology of the cross. He understands the already and not-yet character of the church's service and theological enterprise. The church lives, therefore, in a hopeful renewal of herself and her people, seeking to be a new creation under the power of the Spirit in her witness to the world. The church always seeks out her reformation in light of the eschaton.

Our common theological vision in this volume is the renewal of the church. Through the lens of reformation, various themes and faith commitments find their unified focal point. The authors pursue this common vision by engaging critical issues that the church faces in her pilgrim journey toward renewal. In this respect, this volume may be useful for theologians, pastors, and seminary students engaged in a similar labor of love for the sake of the church. As collaborators with and friends of Carl Braaten in this constructive task, we write from various confessional perspectives. While most of the contributors are Lutheran, representing both the Evangelical Lutheran Church of America and the Missouri Synod, Gabriel Fackre is a member of the United Church of Christ, Timothy George is Southern Baptist, Joseph Mangina is a member of the Anglican Church of Canada, and Susan Wood is Roman Catholic. This ecumenical diversity bears witness to the fact that critical issues face the one church of Christ across confessional differences. Whatever our tradition, we affirm the canonical Scriptures and the Apostolic tradition and are committed to the ethical integrity of our witness, right belief in terms of our doctrine, and authentic worship of God in our liturgy.

Our theological contributions pursue across denominational lines the question of what is crucial for the church today. Frank Senn explores these issues in light of the history of the Catholic, Lutheran, and evangelical cultures. James Childs rehearses this history by pinpointing the tensions and controversies among Lutherans in North America. Snapshots of this story are also taken in dealing with specific points of contention. Leopoldo Sánchez M., for example, takes another historical look at Trinitarian issues that have divided the Eastern Orthodox churches and Western Christianity by engaging in a pneumatological Christology.

Specific critical themes for an ecumenical theology of the church are also explored. Robert Jenson suggests that identifying the church as the "bride of Christ" provides a necessary correction to the image of the church as the "body of Christ." He employs this image to emphasize the audible forms of the gospel expressed in the language of anticipation joyfully erupting from the eschatological wedding consummation. James Childs examines the imperative for unity within the heated rhetoric of division occasioned by controversial issues within the church. Timothy George reflects on the relationship of evangelicals to the present ecumenical movement.

The critical issue of reconciliation and redemption for an ecumenical ecclesiology is brought forth as the keystone of several essays. Gabriel Fackre pursues this theme by affirming the need of sound doctrine for a sound ecumenism in light of the doctrine of atonement under the cross. For him, an authentically "catholic" doctrine of redemption is crucial: all traditions contribute in specific and various ways to the holistic picture of Christ's person and work, his incarnation as well as his resurrection, his cross as well as his victory, and the individual as well as communal aspects of our redemption. Joseph Mangina explores these themes within a communion ecclesiology that is cruciform in light of 1 and 2 Corinthians. He grounds the judicial aspects of Pauline theology within a redemptive framework that locates the intracommunal participation of the body of Christ within the eschatological apocalyptic vision of a new creation. This shift roots the redemptive life in an ecclesiology and Christology from below that is committed to service in the world. The servant character of our communion is what grounds our ecumenicity.

Several essays examine liturgical or doctrinal themes foundational for an understanding of the church. Susan Wood highlights the relationship between the liturgy and the church, suggesting that a retrieval of the ecclesial meaning of the Eucharist corrects an overly individualistic and privatized eucharistic spirituality. Cheryl Peterson identifies key Lutheran principles for an ecumenical understanding of the church, especially the Christological principle and the criterion of justification. Alberto García, writing from the perspective of the South American or U.S. Latino experience, underscores how particular witnesses of Christian faith are necessary for a truly catholic world ecclesiology. He reflects on the message of reconciliation in light of the faith of the people.

Several authors broach the critical issue of authority in the church. Michael Root asks provocative questions concerning authority within the church regarding the relationship of Scripture to tradition, the teaching office to the priesthood of all believers, and the function of the *sensus fidelium,* the sense of the faithful, to the church's discernment of authentic teaching. Frank Senn untangles some of the thorny issues concerning episcopal authority and ministry and offers significant points for critical dialogue.

Ecclesiology does not lack for critical issues, particularly when different faith traditions seek to mend their divisions with the aim of restoring ecumenical unity as well as witnessing to gospel values in an increasingly secular world. We hope these essays will "stimulate fresh thinking" and renew a "passion for mission" within the Great Tradition and thereby honor Carl Braaten. If so, this volume will have achieved its purpose.

Alberto L. García
Susan K. Wood

Carl

Robert W. Jenson

How am I to introduce a *Festschrift* for one who is both my best friend and my oldest collaborator? I have been blessed with many friends and many outstanding colleagues, from an amazing variety of places, callings and opinions, but with none for so long and so steadily as with Carl. In consequence I have introduced him scores of times, which becomes incrementally harder; there get to be fewer honorifics not already offered or permissible anecdotes not already told.

I could, of course, make a preface by commenting on the essays — and that may have been what the editors were expecting — but I have decided that in this case something more personal is required. I will limit my remarks about the content of our volume to noting the remarkable range of those who have been willing to devote their time and theological energies to Carl's honor.

To be sure, Carl and I were not always so friendly. The tale of our problematic early relations and their transformation has also been told once or twice, but this occasion probably demands that readers who have heard it before endure it again.

We met as divinity students at Luther Seminary in St. Paul, Minnesota. He came from St. Olaf College and I from Luther College, which in those days — the early fifties — still amounted to theological identifications: "Oles" were supposed to be philosophically sophisticated thinkers, and those from Luther dedicated — and perhaps a bit rustic — Lutheran orthodoxists. We were both academic alpha dogs, who were once described as warily circling and sniffing each other.

After seminary Carl went off to Harvard and I a little later to Heidelberg — signature destinations for each of us. When Harvard awarded him a travelling fellowship and it became known that the Braatens would spend the time in Heidelberg, some wondered if the little community of American theologians there, in a town that was itself rather cozy, could easily accommodate us both.

And indeed Heidelberg's compactness did force us together: walking one day on the *Hauptstrasse,* Blanche and I saw Lavonne and Carl coming the other way on the other side, and — as we later learned — they saw us. Carl and I each asked his wife to pretend we had not noticed, but they, more civilized than we, insisted on steering to a meeting, and in the ensuing conversation further alarmed their husbands by arranging to have supper together at our apartment. Carl and I spent the evening shouting at each other, and discovered that this was remarkably enjoyable and edifying. The meals and discourse thus begun have never stopped.

There is also no point in narrating Carl's life and works, since he has now published his memoirs — I do wish he had included a few more of his stories about growing up as a missionary child in Madagascar. I will add to Carl's account of our collaborations only that it was mostly Carl who initiated them. What I want here to emphasize is how single-mindedly his career has been dedicated to the church and her theology; I will mention three characters of that dedication.

First, he has been a reformer. The title of the institute we founded, the Center for Catholic and Evangelical Theology, is in fact a program for churchly reformation.

According to that program, the theology the American ecumene needs and often lacks is "catholic," that is, dedicated to the church's structural and dogmatic continuity, to — a favorite phrase of Carl's — the great tradition. Carl was an ecumenist with catholic convictions before he knew he was one. Thus very early in his career he became notorious by proposing, what is now common ecumenical conviction, that the universal pastorate of the bishop of Rome is an important ecumenical goal — he was denounced for this by, among others, the editors of *Christian Century,* perhaps the youngest theologian ever thus honored. And according to that same program, the theology the American ecumene needs and often lacks is "evangelical," that is, dedicated to the mission of the gospel to all people.

Mention of mission brings us to, second, Carl's unabashed affirmation of the missionary enterprise that was the context of his upbringing. His parents and their colleagues were in Madagascar to bring pagans to Christ, which for Carl remains a good thing to do, whether in Madagascar or Minneapolis. A chief object of his polemical scorn has been mainline Protestantism's re-imaging of "mission," replacing evangelism with dialogue and works of love with enabling. A church reluctant about the gospel, in the original sense of "gospel," is for him, as for Paul, no church at all.

And, third, he has been, is and will doubtless remain a specifically Lutheran thinker and churchman. For him, justification by faith, high Christology, and the real presence of Christ in the Eucharist are no mere slogans; they are axioms of a coherent whole he can recommend as "Lutheran Theology." Despite what might be read from such terminology, his sort of Lutheranism and his ecumenical commitment enforce each other — though they may occasionally have bumped a bit.

There has recently been a movement of American mainline Protestant theologians to Roman obedience, including some whose thinking and careers Carl nurtured. He is not about to join them — nor, for that matter, is he about to join any of the splinter Lutheran bodies now forming. If he is someday the last theological Lutheran standing in the officially Lutheran church to which he belongs, he will register the fact and carry on protesting.

Now he is — sort of — retired, in Arizona but not for the perhaps usual reasons. He is acclimated to heat by growing up in Madagascar and finds that the Sonoran desert provides an ideal climate. Moreover, he can play tennis outdoors most of the year — he has regularly been a champion in his age group. And that "sort of" just above is a necessary qualification: in recent years he has written two books and has just organized and carried off yet another theological conference, this time for a crowd of some 900 participants. He says it was his last, but who knows?

All this does not mean that Carl has not explored some trends of the moment. He was, after all, Paul Tillich's assistant at Harvard, and edited part of the *Nachlass*. He was a leader in introducing and explaining "the new hermeneutics" to America. He took me along to visit the Pannenbergs in Bonn — until then I knew Pannenberg only from a seminar room. He told me that I had to read *The Theology of Hope*. I never could see him as a liberation theologian, but he claims to have profited from the flirtation.

I have perhaps come to the place where I can attach a complaint:

honors such as this *Festschrift* are much overdue. It is a particular scandal that his college has not honored him, since he is arguably its most distinguished living alumnus — if distinction in theology and in service to the church still count with the church's colleges.

There is, to be sure, a possible explanation for institutional avoidance: Carl has never refrained from speaking his mind, often in politically incorrect diction and with at least adequate volume, and sometimes directly to the villains of his piece. During the years that he and I alternated in editing *Dialog,* our first and more denominational journal, we regarded headquarters-critical editorials as simply a part of our assignment. We even tried to derail or at least redirect the merger that produced the Evangelical Lutheran Church in America, since we foresaw that body's present throes. Etc. "Braaten" has been and is controversial.

The life of every one of us is directed and shaped by converse with the rest of us. But to what is surely an unusual degree, Blanche's and my life has been energized and shaped by over fifty years' friendship and shared labors with LaVonne and Carl. We are grateful for that.

The Bride of Christ

Robert W. Jenson

I have a text, Ephesians 5:31-32. Paul — or some brilliant Paulinist whom I will in this essay be content to call Paul — quotes Genesis 2:24: "Therefore a man will leave his father and mother and be joined to his wife, and the two will become one flesh." Then he interprets: "This passage tells a deep mystery; now I read it of Christ and the church" (my translation). Is Paul interpreting the mystery of sexual union by the relation of Christ and the church, or the mystery of Christ and the church by sexual union? He seems to be doing both at once. The foregoing passage has been about the proper relation of husband and wife, founded in the mystery of bodily union and modelled on Christ's relation to the church; but here he interprets the mystery more directly of Christ and the church. My text is thus appropriate for an essay in this volume, since on the one hand Carl and Lavonne are a notable instance of husband and wife as indeed one flesh — so that perhaps I should say ". . . Carl-and-Lavonne is a notable . . ." — and on the other hand the theme of our volume is ecclesiology.

I have also a personal reason for writing on this matter. At a 2008 session of the Karl Barth Society, Joseph Mangina, in the course of a splendid paper, gently complained that the ecclesiology of my *Systematic Theology* so concentrates on the church as the *body* of Christ as to ignore the biblical and traditional talk of the church as the *bride* of Christ. Thereby, he said, I so emphasize the unity of Christ and the church as to obscure their distinction. I accepted the first part of his criticism, and indeed will shortly confess further sins of omission, but maintained that the second did not follow. Accordingly I claimed that I could appropriate the bridal language, and exploit the way it posits the distinction, without redoing anything I had said about the identity of Christ and church as one body. This brief essay will be an attempt to make good on that claim.

I must first review what is in the systematics. It is on account of Paul that we speak of the church as the body of Christ; therefore it is Paul whose lead we should follow when using this language — or at least that is what I have thought I should do. A first and vital step in appropriating Paul is to note that his fundamental use of "body," whether with respect to the church or the Eucharist — or in the verses preceding our text — is not metaphorical — though when some conceptual predications are once in place he can exploit them metaphorically. In Paul's general conceptual discourse, a person's body is that person's own self *as* he is available to others: it is his visibility and audibility and tangibility. To understand Paul we must always remember that in his use, "body" does not necessarily or even most properly refer to a biological organism. In Paul's language, to say that the church is the body of the risen Christ is straightforwardly to affirm that the church is his availability in and for the world. Would you now see Christ? View this gathering called the church — and blessed is he who is not offended by what he sees. Would you now come to him? Join them.

The identity of the church as the risen body of Christ is not, however, undialectical. A necessary second step is to note the peculiar logic of Paul's arguments in 1 Cor. 10 and 11. In discussing the limits of meal fellowship in 1 Cor. 10, Paul adduces the way in which the church is a particular single body because our assembling to share the bread and cup makes us sharers in the one body of Christ. Later, in ch. 11, he turns to the disunity of the Corinthian church precisely in that assembly. He charges that by their selfish behavior toward one another at the meal some Corinthians profane the body of Christ. And he enforces this, upsetting what we expect, by citing the narrative of institution, to the effect that the bread and cup are the body of Christ. According to Paul, by the Corinthians' violation of their unity as a church-body the Corinthians violate the bread and cup-body. It would surely have been simpler simply to accuse the Corinthians of lovelessness, but Paul has heavier metal to hurl.

Paul's use of the institution-narrative to convict the Corinthians of sin works if and only if the church and the sacrament are both the body of Christ and indeed the same body of Christ, so that a sin against either is a sin against the other. Yet there is also some priority, even causality between the two. The church is a body at all *because* it assembles around the bread and cup. And it is profanation of the bread and cup-body that *defines* the Corinthians' sin, even though the object of their profanation is the body they themselves are. This structure laid out, it surely does seem that Paul's appropriation and interpretation of Genesis 2:24 ought to fit into it somehow. For the mystery he finds in Genesis is precisely the mystery of two bodies making one body; and he reads this of Christ and the church.

So how can I join the two discourses? To enable that, I have to acknowledge two further deficiencies in the systematics. First, since I claim that the church is the body of Christ in and for the world *because* the sacrament is the body of Christ in and for the church, I should more have probed the nature of this causality.

Second, something prominent elsewhere in the systematics should have been prominent here also: not only is the sacrament a "visible word" of the gospel, the proclamation of the gospel is what we might call an audible sacrament, and the two are not separable. Thus the embodied presence of Christ in and for the church is constituted not only by the sacramental objects but also by the proclamation of the gospel, and so is not a silent body. The Christ available in and for the church is available not only as he is seen and touched but also as he is heard. It may be apparent what I am preparing the way for. In our text from Ephesians heterosexual union is a supreme instance of a fundamental ontological mystery, of two personal entities making one body. Marriage, the God-ordained *way* of such union, thus offers itself as a metaphor for the way in which the body of Christ in the church and the church as the body of Christ are one body — and indeed the metaphor has appeared throughout the tradition. And then, for the nature of the causality operative within this unity, we may perhaps take our lead from a passage in which Paul speaks specifically, and metaphorically, of the church as the bride of Christ: "I promised you in marriage to one husband, to present you as a chaste virgin to Christ" (2 Cor. 11:2). Here Paul casts himself as a traditional matchmaker-chaperone, supervising an engagement. If then we notice the relation between Christ and church posited by this image, we may think of Christ's action over against the church as *courtship,* of the kind that intervenes between proposal and union: Christ embodied for the church and pledged to the church *woos* the church to be "one flesh" with him.

It is, to be sure, a courtship that cannot fail; the bread and cup of the Eucharist are now in fact and not in mere potentiality the body of Christ for the church, and the church at the Eucharist is now in fact and not in mere potentiality the body of Christ for the world. Whether and how the Lord's wooing can finally fail with individuals has been controversial among Christians. But that the opposition to the Lord's wooing cannot prevail with the one holy church is ecumenical conviction. Nor, I think, is this essay the place to engage a second mystery, the one that underlies all analogies or metaphors of divine persuasion: it is precisely a divine will which cannot fail that enables creaturely freedom — indeed, nothing short of such a will could do so unlikely a thing. We will here be content with the metaphorical suggestions of "courtship."

A proper courtship is not one-sided: the one who woos will solicit and wait for response. But he will also often suggest the text of the desired response: "Please say 'I love you'." We may here think of the Psalms as such a provision by the divine wooer. Or again, no courtship is without the suitor's moral intention for the one who is courted: if the suitor does not tell the beloved what he hopes for from her, he is either an automaton, a dolt, or a sophisticated tyrant. The Lord provides his beloved with the Torah.

Thus we can press our image of courtship one more step — perhaps, indeed, to the brink of becoming a concept. An engagement is the anticipation of a wedding, and anticipation is in some recent theology, including mine, an ontological concept. The identity of Christ embodied for the church with Christ embodied as the church is constituted in that the one embodiment anticipates itself in the other. Thus Paul's bridal metaphor is eschatological: what is now is the engagement and Paul's care for its success, the wedding itself is the consummation to come. In this, he joins the Revelation, where the Old Testament's discourse of Israel as the Lord's bride massively resurfaces, but now in unambiguously eschatological context: the final event of the Revelation's drama is "the marriage of the Lamb," for which "his Bride has made herself ready" (Rev. 19:7). This prepared bride is then revealed as the heavenly Jerusalem (Rev. 21:2, 9-10), the eschatological version of the church — itself here conceived as an eschatological version of Israel.

Yet this does not mean that the identity of the church as the body of Christ is not a present reality; for in the Bible's metaphysics what a creature — here the church — will be at the end is what it truly is now. This essay is not — again I have to enter such a disclaimer — the place to develop the Bible's drastic alternative to our inherited metaphysics; the whole of the systematics is my attempt. It will suffice to assert: in Scripture my "being" — what it means to me for me to be something — is not my persistence in what I am from the beginning and so am timelessly, à la the great Greek pagan thinkers from whom we inherit so many deep questions, so much insight and so much theological trouble. In Scripture, for me to be is to be drawn forward to what I will be when fulfilled in God, it is being *in via* à la Paul.

And then a final observation. The Old Testament's discourse of Israel as the Lord's bride achieves its grandest development and force in Hosea's and Ezekiel's depictions of old Israel as the Lord's *faithless* bride, indeed his whoring bride (Hosea 1; Ezekiel 16). No prophet proclaims the Lord's sheer nullification of his marriage with Israel; but short of that, old Israel's near-mortal troubles are routinely identified by the prophets as the proof and fruit of her unfaithfulness. There is food for churchly thought here.

Ecumenism and Atonement:
A Critical Issue in Ecclesiology

Gabriel Fackre

In a prescient "Opinion" piece in the third year of the journal Carl Braaten helped to found, *Pro Ecclesia,* he writes of the developing theological renewal movements in mainline Protestantism kindred to his own passion for recentering the Churches beset by fast-eroding core beliefs. A sentence at the close of the article points to the doctrine at the heart of the matter:

> Meanwhile, we may proceed in this unsettled world, as my teacher, George Florovsky advised in calling for a renewal of the patristic tradition within Orthodox theology, "with the sign of the cross in one's heart and the prayer of Jesus in one's mind."[1]

So Lutheran Braaten cites the wisdom of Orthodox Florovsky in the journal of the Center for [both] Catholic and Evangelical Theology, "with the sign of the cross and the prayer of Jesus" grounding the call for theological integrity and the unity of the Church. Interestingly, this alliance of cross, sound doctrine and ecumenism recurs in the book edited by Center founders, Carl Braaten and Robert Jenson, and entitled with the biblical phrase, *In One Body Through the Cross,*[2] the conjunctive thesis developed therein by a group of "sixteen theologians and ecumenists" gathered by the Center for three years of study.

---

1. Carl E. Braaten, "Renewal in Theology for the Church," *Pro Ecclesia* 3, no. 2 (1994): 140.

2. Carl E. Braaten and Robert W. Jenson, eds., *In One Body Through the Cross: The Princeton Proposal for Christian Unity* (Grand Rapids: Eerdmans, 2003).

What would the relationship of sound doctrine and sound ecumenism look like vis-à-vis a theology of the cross? Or, putting the cross at the center of where it belongs, is there a relationship between the fulness of a doctrine of the Work of Christ with the wholeness of the Body of Christ? Is it any accident that we have no ecumenical consensus on the doctrine of the atonement concomitant with absence of a church ecumenical? It is the thesis of this chapter that a full doctrine of the at-one-ment is inseparable from the at-one-ment of the Church.[3]

Some personal history on all this, first. Carl Braaten and his lifelong theological comrade, "Jens" Jenson, speak of themselves as "evangelical catholic." The same partnership is reflected in the aforementioned Center which sees the state of the church as ecumenical inseparable from the state of the faith as full. And no accident that the writer, out of a parallel tradition, the "evangelical catholicity" of the Mercersburg theology, discovered kindred spirits in this pair and their ventures. Indeed, as one of the founders of the Mercersburg Society, I urged that company to invite Carl to speak to its annual meeting in 1987 on the commonalities of the "evangelical catholicism" of Mercersburg mentors John Williamson Nevin and Philip Schaff and the "evangelical catholic" movement in Lutheranism, a gathering appropriately held at Philadelphia Lutheran Seminary and featuring Carl Braaten. These companion movements both bring Christology to high profile, and both struggle against what Mercersburg calls "the sect spirit." Thus each is ardent about ecumenism. And each contests the excitable fragmentations of the day.

Reconciliation

The heart of the gospel is the Word and Act of reconciliation. "In Christ God was reconciling the world to himself" (2 Cor. 5:19). Therefore it follows, God "has given us a ministry of reconciliation . . ." (2 Cor. 5:18). The two are inseparable. Ecclesially considered, can the meaning of the first be fully discernible without the latter being fully realizable?

---

3. Following up a programmatic paragraph in the *Festschrift* for colleague Robert Jenson, "The Lutheran Capax Lives," in *Trinity, Time, and Church: A Response to the Theology of Robert W. Jenson*, ed. Colin Gunton (Grand Rapids: Eerdmans, 2000), p. 100.

The doctrine of reconciliation is the articulation of the deed God has done in Christ to bring together the alienated partners to the divine purposes. It is the at-one-ing of the Creator and creation severed by the No we have said to God's Yes. At the center of the biblical story that runs from Genesis to Revelation — from creation to consummation — is that reconciling Work of Christ, at-one-ment, atonement.

> The term "atonement" is English in origin, appearing in Elizabethan literature as the bringing of concord between persons or groups. In the Geneva Bible (1560) the word is used interchangeably with "reconciliation" in association with the root *kpr* (Lev. 23:28; Num. 15:28), though the latter is more often translated in its cultic context as "expiation." In both the Genevan and the King James (1611) version its single NT appearance is in Rom. 5:10-11 *(katallassō; katallagē)* where "reconciliation" and "atonement" are used synonymously. In theological discourse its equivalents in both non-English and English traditions are "the work of Christ," the "office of Mediator," "the work of reconciliation (redemption, salvation)," and objective soteriology.[4]

Our inquiry here is the question of the relation of "objective soteriology" to the "ecclesiology of ecumenism." Is there a connection between our reading of the doctrine of reconciliation and our practice of the ecclesial ministry of reconciliation? Is there a correlation between the yet-to-be-reached ecumenical agreement on the Work of Christ and our yet-to-be-achieved ecumenical goal of "one fully committed fellowship, holding one apostolic faith, preaching the one Gospel, breaking the one bread . . ."?[5]

Perspectives on Reconciliation

A case can be made that the varied interpretations of the doctrine of atonement that have emerged in Christian history can be identified as

4. Gabriel Fackre, "Atonement," in *Encyclopedia of the Reformed Faith,* ed. Donald K. McKim (Louisville: Westminster/John Knox, 1992), p. 13.
5. Assuming the historic consensus in the church catholic on the broad outlines of the doctrines of the Person of Christ and the Trinity, while division continues on the doctrine of the atonement.

four "models" of the Work of Christ, those models associated with comparable New Testament images of the same, correlated also with differing problematics appearing in Scripture.[6] Thus the plight of mortality is addressed by the Incarnation itself conceived as Atonement, the entry of the eternal One into our world, the realm of Life transforming the reign of Death; the issue of ignorance and error resolved by the appearance of Light overcoming the Night in the knowledge of God given in the inspiring life, teachings and healings of Jesus; our sin removed and guilt forgiven in the blood shed by Jesus on Calvary that appeased the wrath or satisfied the offended honor of God; our conflict with, and suffering caused by, the powers of evil overcome through the victory achieved and announced by the resurrection and rule of Jesus.

The four models can be correlated with phases of Jesus' career: birth, life, death, resurrection (and ascension). They also tend to be associated with traditions, streams of history, and, yes, Churches, although not simplistically, given the permeability of boundaries, and the historic interactions and mutual teachability of the charisms in the Body of Christ seen and sought early on by Paul in his counsel to the Corinthian congregation (1 Cor. 12-14). Thus the Eastern Churches and tradition focus on the at-one-ing of God and the world at Bethlehem to bring immortality to our transiency, the presence of Deity among us offering deification; the Work done by the teacher and example of Galilean ministry giving us the needed knowledge and inspiration for good works finds recurring pride of place in streams Abelardian, liberal Protestant, Roman Catholic liberation theology; the Jesus of passion and Calvary offering a suffering and death that satisfy the offended divine honor or appeasing the divine wrath comes to the fore in pieties medieval, Reformation and evangelical; the Jesus of Easter gives confidence to those who view our redemption as victory over malignant Forces and thus power to contest them, an atoning accent discernible from patristic to pentecostal traditions and in times of ecclesial and political strife. These "ideal types" obscure, of course, the richness of a given tradition that may well, arguably, have more than one soteriological accent or be associated with several phases in Jesus' career. Thus the Eastern tradition is often associated with Easter as well as Bethlehem, or the former rather than the latter.

Interestingly, Carl Braaten has expressed a similar view on the im-

---

6. So argued in Gabriel Fackre, *The Christian Story: A Narrative Interpretation of Christian Doctrine*, Vol. 1, Revised Edition (Grand Rapids: Eerdmans, 1996).

portance of acknowledging the gifts of the various streams of Christian history and faith and the need to bring them to the ecumenical table:

> Anglicans bring a theology of Incarnation, Lutherans a theology of the Cross, Orthodoxy an Easter Theology of the Resurrection, Calvinists a focus on the Ascension, charismatic churches see things in the light of Pentecost, and the Adventist groups call our attention to the future Parousia. All these salvation historical events are essential in a complete christological narrative faithful to the church's Scripture, Creeds and liturgy, but when the unity of the church is shattered, theology also reflects the marks of division.[7]

Given the broadness of these typological categories, there is intercourse between and among them. For all that, profiles in atonement are distinguishable in the history of Christian thought, and are with us today in marking and shaping our ecclesial diversity.

The Healing of the Body of Christ and the Wholeness of the Work of Christ

The New Delhi vision of "one Body" has profound implications for doctrine as well as polity. Ecumenism in "order" is the way to catholicity in "faith." Surely this is the import of Paul's disquisition on the Body of Christ. Each organ is necessary for anatomical integrity. "The eye cannot say to the hand, 'I have no need of you,' . . ." (1 Cor. 12:21a). The organs described are not only constituencies in the early church, but ones with construals about what is important in Christian witness. And each, asserts Paul, is a charism integral to the wholeness of both the church and its faith. How is this not a Word to us today about both a church ecumenical and a faith catholic? And, in our present inquiry, a doctrine of the Work of Christ not fragmented but whole?

Those on the ecumenical path have a mandate to quest for a holistic understanding of the work of Christ. What would such a full-orbed understanding of the atonement look like in a church that receives the charisms of varied present divided parts of the Body of Christ? Insofar as each of the models suggested earlier foci on one or

---

7. Carl E. Braaten, *That All May Believe: A Theology of the Gospel and the Mission of the Church* (Grand Rapids: Eerdmans, 2008), p. 155.

another phase in the journey of Jesus — birth, life, death, resurrection and rule — it would have to find a place for every step along the way. A church ecumenical would welcome the perspective of each tradition/ Church. Indeed, it would recognize that those accents might well have grown from particular historical contexts that brought them to the fore at the inception of that entity. Further, it would acknowledge that there may be times and places when such an accent is rightly bold while other accents in the Work of Christ are bashful. A powerful (yes "powerful," as this particular dimension of the Work of Christ requires in time of conflict just this victorious Word of power) expression of such single-accent *kairos* is Karl Barth's *Letter to Great Britain* in 1941 when the Nazi assault was most perilous, for all of his more full-orbed development of the doctrine of reconciliation:

> Just as Christ, according to the teaching of the whole New Testament, has already borne away sin and destroyed death, so also has He already (according to Col. 2:15) completely disarmed those "principalities and powers" . . . in order finally to tread them down under his feet on the day of his coming again (1 Cor 15:25). It is only as shadows without real substance and power that they can still beset us. We Christians of all people, have no right whatsoever to fear and respect them . . . we should be slighting the resurrection of Jesus Christ and denying His reign at the right hand of the Father, if we forgot that the world in which we live is already consecrated, and if we did not, for Christ's sake, come to grips spiritedly and resolutely with these evil spirits.[8]

This was not the only arrow in Barth's large quiver of teaching on the doctrine of reconciliation, but it was the right Word for the right time.

However, we are here looking for the fullness of that case to be carried by the wholeness of that Body. If it were only the resurrection that constituted the act of reconciliation, the Work would be incomplete, the doctrine would be reductionist and the Body would be judged by Paul accordingly: "If the whole body were an eye, where would the hearing be? If the whole body would be hearing, where would the sense of smell be? . . . If all were a single member, where would the body be?" (1 Cor 12:17, 19).

8. Karl Barth, *A Letter to Great Britain from Switzerland* (London: The Sheldon Press, 1941), p. 10.

Gabriel Fackre

In the search for fullness of the doctrine of Christ and the wholeness of the Body of Christ, do we have a hint of how and what that
could be in the earlier quest for both around the doctrine of the Person
of Christ? Consider the constituencies and allied perspectives that appeared in the first four centuries of the church's life, each dimension of
the Person being accented in reductionist fashion with increasing so-
phistication as the centuries proceeded: Ebionites, on the one side, and
Docetists on the other; Adoptionists and Modalists juxtaposed; Arians
and Apollinarians, Nestorians and Monophysites contesting one another. Then the ecumenical consensus of an undivided church in the
Chalcedonian Formula of 451 that continues authoritative to this day
in the church catholic: One Person, both fully human and fully divine.[9]
Why not, similarly, a Church of the future undivided challenging the
reductionisms of the Work, yet honoring their offerings finally united
in an understanding of the fullness of the work of Christ? And why not
ecumenists now pointing toward what that doctrine might look like?
Here we attempt such.

Bethlehem

Fundamental to any full doctrine of the Work of Christ is its integration with the doctrine of the Person of Christ, the inseparability of the
Incarnation from the Atonement. That means a welcome of the contribution of the historic tradition that associates, even identifies, the Incarnation with the Atonement. Whether the Eastern Churches, as here
presupposed, or the Anglican tradition as cited by Braaten, the linkage
of the former with the latter has implications for what transpired in
Galilee, at Calvary and on Easter morning, as well as what took place in
Bethlehem. That is, the Work of Christ was done by the one Person,
fully divine as well as fully human And that enfleshment was of the
Word, the Son of the Father, singular within the triune Life Together,
and once-happened, the turning point in our history. Whatever is
claimed to be of a piece with the "at-one-ment" of the world with God

9. A dated and oversimplified account (as compared to the detailed research of
J. N. D Kelly, Aloys Grillmeier and Jaroslav Pelikan), but still a helpful sifting and sort-
ing along these lines of the early christological controversies is Bjarn Skard, *The Incarnation: Christology of the Ecumenical Creeds,* trans. Herman Jorgensen (Minneapolis: Augsburg, 1960).

in the events of an example and teacher, a death on a cross or a resurrection entailed the fact that "in Christ, *God* was reconciling the world to himself" (2 Cor 5:19).

Standing alone — the Incarnation *as* the Atonement — such an understanding prompted by the problematic of temporality alone, does not deal sufficiently with the enemies of error, sin and Evil. However, as the presupposition of the contesting of those foes in a fuller doctrine of the Atonement, the Incarnation plays a fundamental role with a profound effect on how the counterpart aspects of the career of Jesus are construed. We examine the meaning of each, and in doing so alter conventional readings regularly found in the accents on one or another of the historic models of the atonement.

A clue concerning how that role alters our understanding of the conventional models is the hard-won affirmation of the Chalcedon Definition: "... Mary the Virgin, *Theotokos*...." At Bethlehem, the birth of Jesus Christ from the womb of Mary has to do not only with temporality invaded by eternity, but also eternity disclosed as *vulnerability*. From conception to birth we have to do with "God's weakness that is stronger than human strength" (1 Cor 1:25). No Oriental potentate coming from heaven with Mars-like legions but Deity entering our realm in the vulnerability of manger babe and virginal Jewess. In this stable birth and this mother, we begin to see the character of the divine nature mothered by Mary that is to be lived out in all of the subsequent vulnerabilities of finitude.

Galilee

The Work of Christ includes Jesus' Galilean ministry as an example and teacher of the love of God and neighbor, a construal brought to the fore by the earlier mentioned traditions, indeed, a Work too often reduced by them to these proportions. Yes we need a knowledge in its purity of the *Agape* of God and an inspiration and mandate to follow "in his steps." Yet, as God was *in* Christ at Bethlehem, Mary, the mother of God continues to be so in Galilee.

Mary mothered this God in the days of his flesh which "increased in wisdom and stature..." (Luke 2:52 KJV). How could the vulnerabilities of maturation toward adolescence not have attended this growth at home, in school, in the carpenter shop when a hand cut by a saw made

Jesus bleed like any other? Yet in this same Person, we have to do with a "wisdom" displayed in the temple to his elders. Thus the processes of human growth with the exposure to its vicissitudes did not preclude a mysterious power inseparable from the same.

From boyhood we jump over the intervening years to his baptism, on the one hand, a humble act of "baptism of repentance for the forgiveness of sins" (!), but yet, something far more, the Spirit descending on him in a voice from heaven proclaiming, "You are my Son, the Beloved . . ." (Mark 1:11). Then the beginning of Jesus' ministry, and with it again the divine vulnerability in the form of the three great temptations . . . but something else along with them. Each temptation, in its own way, is the invitation to be the conventional over-powering One. Yet, while he was "tempted as we are," he was "without sin" (Chalcedon). Again the God-Man of Galilee is vulnerable, yet in victorious vulnerability, the power of powerlessness.

And the ministry of Jesus? Here we find the prophet of a coming Kingdom, one already breaking in with the prophet. But how different a Kingdom and King from the world's ways of the potentate! The God of vulnerable, unconditional, unmerited love receiving assaults and not returning blows in kind, in both teaching and behavior. And with the teaching and its embodiments there is the healing. Why healing? Sickness is the condition that displays our human weakness in its extreme. What better way to demonstrate the power of powerlessness than in the work of Christ the healer?

In that ministry there is the praying of Jesus. The "Lord's Prayer" has counsel for our praying, but words of Jesus' own . . . to be with us/ not lead us into temptation. Then also, as Bonhoeffer reminds us, Jesus "prayed the Psalms."[10] And a refrain throughout?

> Hear my prayer, O Lord,
> Let my cry come to you . . .
> For my days pass away like smoke,
> And my bones burn like a furnace. . . . (Psalm 102:1, 3)

The one Person — divine and human — and thus also God's "bones"? "Burning"? A God in the flesh (John 1:14), for all that, and Mary mother of the same. Does Jesus get sick like the rest of us? Why not the

---

10. Dietrich Bonhoeffer, *Life Together,* trans. with Introduction by John Doberstein (New York: Harper and Bros., 1954), pp. 46-50.

"sickened God" as well as "the crucified God"? Is the One Person in both natures excluded from these vulnerabilities? *How* this could be is unimaginable to our finite, feeble minds, "unsearchable" (Romans 11:33), but the unity of the one Person is *Who* he is.

We approach now the endings. First a "triumphal entry" to Jerusalem, a king coming! But what kind? Again, the transvaluation of values: not arrival with conquering legions but jogging into town on a donkey.[11] And the denouement — brought before court, charged as a criminal, flailed and led to an execution hill, the absolute vulnerability, nails, spear, blood and scorn, and the cry of dereliction itself, the "weakness of God."[12] Is it "stronger than men"?

What has been sketched here of the Jesus of Galilee is to be contrasted with a conventional interpretation of the one Person in two natures. Indeed, it makes its appearance even in Leo's Tome, critically assessed and rightly so by Robert Jenson.[13] Thus each nature is assigned actions of Jesus that purport to represent the divine or human dimension of the Person. Acts and conditions of power (miracles, healings) embody the former and acts otherwise (temptations, frailties, sufferings) reflect the human nature. But we have to do in Galilee with the *one* Person, and therefore no exclusion of the vulnerabilities from the divine nature. Power, yes, but the power of powerlessness, their paradoxical unity, a genuine "communion of the attributes." Mary remains the "mother of God" at every point in Jesus' journey, indeed, into the next as well, already introduced, the Jesus of Calvary.

---

11. So Dale Allison's description of Matthew's Jesus: "While Jesus fulfills the Davidic covenant, at the same time he rewrites popular notions of kingship. He enters Jerusalem on a donkey." Dale Allison, Jr., "The Embodiment of God's Will: Jesus in Matthew," in Beverly Roberts Gaventa and Richard B. Hays, *Seeking the Identity of Jesus: A Pilgrimage* (Grand Rapids: Eerdmans, 2008), p. 122. Interestingly, he adds, "But maybe Matthew's Jesus encourages us to think of God's apparent passivity and silence as manifestations of an uncircumscribed love. 'Love is long-suffering,' or as the King James Version has it, love 'beareth all things [and] endureth all things' (1 Cor 13:7). Simone Weil once urged that 'love is abdication'" (123).

12. For a disquisition on "The Defenseless Superior Power" that God is, see Hendrikus Berkhof, *Christian Faith: An Introduction to the Story of Faith,* trans. Sierd Woudstra (Grand Rapids: Eerdmans, 1986), pp. 140-47.

13. Robert Jenson, *Systematic Theology,* volume 1: *The Triune God* (New York: Oxford University Press, 1997), pp. 131-33.

Calvary

The cross has been the central symbol of the Christian faith.[14] As such, it points to the heart of the gospel, the "good news." Here the core question of the biblical narrative that runs from creation to consummation — how does the alienation of the world from God caused by our sin move to reconciliation? — receives its answer. That answer is only grasped in its depth when Bethlehem is seen as the presupposition of Calvary.

Conventional theories of the atonement that fix upon the cross follow biblical images of Jesus paying the price, assuaging the wrath, satisfying the honor of God by his suffering and death on Golgotha. Surely these are faithful to New Testament portrayals and later interpretation of the journey of this historical figure to his agonizing end. Yet something profound is missing from this picture, when the whole sweep of the Christian story is considered, and especially so the Incarnation. As the one Person, Jesus Christ, truly divine as well as truly human, deity as well as humanity, paid the price, assuaged the wrath and satisfied the holy honor of God. In some unsearchable sense, God himself, in the Person of the Son, suffered and died on the cross, the Word was there silenced, the judgment of God rendered and received by the love of God. Karl Barth puts this enigmatic humanely unsearchable event this way:

> God *does* die in the Son. If this were not so, then we could not say: "The Son of God has died for us." Here we remember the lordship of God over life and death. Even the realm of darkness is not outside of God's power. God took our place in the realm of death, which is our realm. If we refuse to say that God dies on the cross, then there is no reconciliation.[15]

Of course, we must remember Barth's attack on anthropocentric readings of biblical language (viz. God as Father is no projection of human

---

14. *Pace* Jenson, with whom the writer agrees on so many other things. He declares, "The project of this present work does, however, remove the Crucifixion from the kind of centrality it has sometimes occupied in theology." Robert Jenson, *The Triune God*, p. 179. For something of a response, see the author's tribute to Jenson in Gunton, *Trinity, Time and Church*, pp. 94-102.

15. Karl Barth in John Godsey, editor, Karl Barth's *Table Talk* (Richmond: John Knox Press, n.d.), p. 52.

fatherhood into New Testament language). Thus "God dies on the cross" is not to be understood as the mortality of the second Person but "taking our place" in the ultimate alienation from God in which "the Judge is judged" and thus reconciliation effected. Might we say the triune God participated in, "experienced," death in the divine heart/ Son? Even as fore and aft of the cross, God did the same?

How theologians have wrestled with this enigmatic but funda-mental assertion at the "heart" of the at-one-ment of God and the world! Consider Gustaf Aulén on Luther quoting the latter's Longer Commentary on Galatians:

> Thus the curse, which is the wrath of God against the whole world, was in conflict with the blessing — that is to say with God's eternal grace and mercy. The curse conflicts with the blessing and would condemn and altogether annihilate it, but it cannot. For the bless-ing is divine and eternal, therefore the curse must yield. For if the blessing in Christ could yield, then God Himself would have been overcome. But that is impossible. Christ who is God's power, righ-teousness, blessing, grace and life, overcomes and carries away these monsters, sin, death and the curse.[16]

Aulén, here, is contesting the "'Latin theory of the Atonement' in which the demand of God's justice is satisfied by compensation paid by Christ from man's side . . . ,"[17] the theory we have also been challenging, one that fails to see the Incarnation as the presupposition of the Atonement. What else could match the infinite accountability of our sin before the Infinite, than an act of the Infinite himself (the question behind all puzzlements about the equivalency of the death of One to the judgment deserved by the many)?

---

16. Gustaf Aulén, *Christus Victor,* trans. A. G. Hebert (New York: The Macmillan Company, 1951), pp. 105-106 and repeated with emphases, 114. Luther strikes the same note elsewhere as in WA 50:590 cited by Jürgen Moltmann in *The Crucified God,* trans. R. W. A. Wilson and John Bowden (London: SCM Press, 1975), p. 235. "In his nature God cannot die. But now that God and man are united in one person, when the man dies, that is rightly called the death of God, for he is one thing or person with God." The Good Friday hymn by Johann Rist reflects this Lutheran refrain, formulated as the *communicatio idiomatum:* "O Great distress, God himself lies dead, He died upon a cross. . . ." (It is said that Nietzsche found his phrase "God is dead" from the hymn-writer.)

17. Moltmann, *The Crucified God,* p. 115.

Building upon this Incarnation/Atonement conjunction, Moltmann and others have sought to frame the divine vulnerability in Trinitarian terms with socio-ethical and cultural concerns in the background — the experience of abandonment of sufferers and the protest of atheism. Thus Christ's cry of dereliction is evidence, not of divine violence or absence but of a divine solidarity through co-suffering with both victims and protesters. Contra a theopaschitism which assumes God's incapacity to deal with involuntary suffering, the cross is God's voluntary suffering. Contra patripassianism, it is the Son who suffers, although the Father suffers vicariously, as the triune God is that kind of love, and speaking to the more current defense of the impassibility of God.[18] Finding the cry of dereliction key — "My God, My God, why have you forsaken me?" (Mark 15:34), Moltmann views the cross as the event of godforsakenness, the Son abandoned by the Father, a rift within the divine being itself in which Christ suffers.[19]

This conjunction of Bethlehem and Calvary with regard to the passion of God in the passion of Jesus runs athwart historic, and now current as well, assertion of the divine impassibility.[20] Yet, the intrusion of philosophical premises about the nature of an invulnerable God borrowed from cultures past and present is not difficult to discern in this separation of the natures on Calvary, and thus the denial of divine vulnerability. However, there is a legitimate concern also in the protests against trends since the 19th century in affirming the divine passibility, and anticipations of it in the heresies of the early centuries. Yes, God, finally, *is* invulnerable in the execution of the divine purposes. But the

18. As in David Bentley Hart's brilliant work *The Beauty of the Infinite: The Aesthetics of Christian Faith* (Grand Rapids: William B. Eerdmans Pub. Co., 2003). In this volume Hart does an extensive critique of (his friend) Robert Jenson, defending the divine impassibility against what he believes are Jenson's views (160-166). We await Jenson's response to that and other critics, explored in a recent Providence College conference and soon to be published as part of a collection of essays from that conference.

19. Robert Jenson has a point here when he says about Moltmann's interpretation of Gethsemane and his thesis that God the Father abandoned God the Son: "I am always tempted by such dramatic excess but cannot persuade myself that it is here justified by Scripture as a whole." "Identity, Jesus and Exegesis," in Gaventa and Hays, eds., *Seeking the Identity of Jesus: A Pilgrimage,* p. 54. The writer believes that Moltmann's overall defense of the teaching of the suffering of God does not rest on the exegesis of this one text, and is reconcilable with Jenson's more encompassing view of "God's narrative time."

20. As in Hart, *The Beauty of the Infinite,* pp. 156-67.

"finally" is crucial. When Christian faith is conceived as a "story," with the freedom of God allowing for the resistance of the other, a plot unfolds, recorded honestly in Scripture, with the pain of a "long-suffering" God, patiently pursuing us to an End when God's Yes triumphs over our No and victory and vulnerability coincide.[21]

Easter

What does Bethlehem mean for Easter? The resurrection has to do with Jesus Christ, the Son of the Father as well as the son of Mary, one Person in two natures. The empty tomb has been the symbol of theories of the atonement that fix upon the defeat of the powers of evil by the risen Jesus. So the "conflict and victory" model. But what of the counterpart when the rising of Jesus from the dead is thought through with Bethlehem inextricable from Easter, the Incarnation undergirding Atonement? As there is suffering and death in the divine Word and Son coterminous with the pain and death of Jesus of Nazareth, so there must be joy and life in the Word and Son inextricable from the resurrection of Jesus of Nazareth.

The humiliation of the one Person, Son of God and human son, is followed by the exaltation of the Son of God and human son. Dare we think of the exaltation as the exultation in the heart of God on the third day? One that overcomes the broken heart of God on Calvary? Thus we must say that the path of resurrection passes through the heart of God now emptied of death as surely as was the tomb. The exaltation/exultation of the Son of the Father by the power of the Holy Spirit has to do with the defeat of all the enemy powers, "sin, death and the devil."

21. The long-suffering but eschatologically victorious story of the triune God from creation to consummation writ large is of a piece with the story of Jesus writ small from conception to resurrection and ascension. There are ethical issues implied in the stress on the divine vulnerability. Surely they entail Christian solidarity with the vulnerable, as in Bonhoeffer's "participation in the sufferings of God in the world." But does that solidarity with, and care for, the suffering other always decline the use of less than vulnerable means and thus the pursuit of a consistent pacifism? Bonhoeffer did not think so, as in his participation in the plot against Hitler. In our fallen world with the ambiguities entailed in Christian decision-making (Reinhold Niebuhr), the assessment of what best serves the interest of the vulnerable may require acts short of mirroring the divine vulnerability, and thus the sin alone coverable by the mercy displayed and enacted on the cross of vulnerability.

So speaking we trace the journey of Jesus to a resurrection not without Incarnation. And as the ascension of the risen Jesus of Nazareth to the right hand of the Father to rule the world, so there is a corresponding joy in the heart of Heaven that accompanies this reign.

Joy, yes, but sorrow too. The battle was won by the sword of a cross, not a weapon in the hands of a tyrant. A victory in vulnerability means no coterminous Easter and Eschaton, but a long-suffering and patient outworking of the Deed done, a struggle, a "story" with the push and pull that goes with narrative trajectory toward the "sure and certain" End. Milton puts the "in-between" this way:

> The Old Dragon underground,
>   In Straighter limits bound,
>   Not half so far casts his usurped sway,
>   And wroth to see his Kingdom fail,
> Swinges the scaly horror of his tail.[22]

In speaking of divine sorrow and joy, of course, simplistic anthropomorphisms are out of order. Who can penetrate the hidden depths of deity and their unsearchable riches? Yet are there not "vestiges of the Trinity" to be discerned in our world, as Augustine argued? Our frail analogies are not even disallowed when we follow Jesus in speaking of the divine love and justice. Can we follow him here too by taking up one of his parables that can be read as anticipating his cross and resurrection as an act of the one Person in both natures? Thus a thought experiment that does not explain but does seek to explore our thesis that the Incarnation must be presupposed at every step along the path of the Atonement, a Work wrought by the one Person.

I read the prodigal son story from the perspective of a Semite — in this case a half Arab (Arabs are Semites too) with an immigrant Lebanese father who fell in love with his *Mayflower*-descended social worker. So seen, the "waiting father" in the parable surely shared the rigorous standards by which the acts of a wayward son are to be judged in Semitic cultures. Failed expectations would be met by anger and the demand for accountability. Where did the wrath and judgment of the father go in this New Testament tale? They did not descend on the prodigal for the father rushed to welcome the son even before he knew

---

22. John Milton, "On the Morning of Christ's Nativity."

that the return might mean a penitence that would be its own punishment. Here was an *agapē* of unconditional, unmerited love. Just an indulgent parent then, in the vernacular a "sloppy agapē"? Not possible for an enraged Semitic father holding such an offspring to account. Where else could the judgment have gone but into the father's own heart? And who is at that heart but the son himself, as the Son is at the heart of the Father? A broken heart here was more than crushed expectations; it was the pain of the mercy taking into itself the wrath, the Blessing receiving the Curse (Luther), the satisfaction of the justice by the judge himself, the anticipation by the brokenness in the heart of this father of the soon-to-be cross in the heart of God.[23]

But what of the resurrection? Is it anticipated in this story also? If there is a cross in the being of God, is there also a resurrection in the being of God? We have spoken of the joy in the heart of God. A hint of what that might mean is surely the joy in the heart of the father at the return of the son, so seen by his call for celebration. But that feasting signifies "welcome"! Thus the resurrection event in the prodigal son story is the open arms of the father receiving unconditionally the errant offspring. In analogy and anticipation, does such an event tell us something of what "resurrection in God" might mean correlative to the historical happenings on Easter morning? The cross in the heart of God coterminous with the cross on Golgotha is followed by the joyful heart of God manifest in the unconditional welcome home of the sinner. And more, the welcome of the world to the path of final reconciliation for which it is now destined, with the defeat of all the enemies that have made for alienation. "Jesus is risen" thereby reflects a history in and of Deity as well as the event of the empty tomb.

---

23. I sense something similar to this construal in Helmut Thielicke's memorable homilies on the prodigal son story. Thus: "You see that God 'so' loved the world that he delivered me, his Son to these depths, that it cost him something to help you, that it cost the very agony of God, that God had to do something contrary to his own being to deal with your sin, to recognize the chasm between you and himself and yet bridge it over.... How do you know there is a God who, indeed, suffers because of me ...? The ultimate theme of this story is not the prodigal son, but the Father who finds us. The ultimate theme is not the faithfulness of men, but the faithfulness of God." Helmut Thielicke, *The Waiting Father: Sermons on the Parables of Jesus,* translated with an Introduction by John Doberstein (New York: Harper & Bros., 1959), pp. 28-29.

Gabriel Fackre

Conclusion

A full understanding of the doctrine of reconciliation waits upon a Church reconciled, each tradition bringing its charism to the wholeness of the body of Christ, both ecclesially and pedagogically. And the prospect for such? Distant at best, given the present parlous state of ecumenism. For all that, the Holy Spirit lives even in the Church divided. And the evidence of hints of fullness/wholeness is sometimes discernible. What of the remarkable 1999 Joint Declaration on the Doctrine of Justification by the Roman Catholic Church and the World Lutheran Federation? Not the atonement doctrine as such, but not without implications for it when separated traditions can bring their accents kindred to the imperatives of a Galilean Christ to the indicatives of a Calvary Christ. And what of the dialogue between the Finnish school of interpreting Luther on justification and the Eastern Church's exponents of deification? Subjective soteriology, yes, but not without import for the relation of the Atonement to the Incarnation. And what of the formula with appearances as early as Eusebius, Jerome and Augustine, explored in detail by such as Calvin and Barth, with ecumenical references from Bulgakov to the Vatican II Decree on the Apostolate of the Laity — the threefold ministry of Christ, a *munus triplex* presupposing a pluriform Work of Christ, which if accomplished by the one Person captures something of what has been argued here.[24] And what of that struggle for the conjunction of Catholic and Evangelical to which the one honored here has given his life? To be continued — the reaching out of one historic tradition, ecclesial and doctrinal, to another, a hint and hope of a wholeness to come.

24. For earlier probes of some aspects of the same see the writer's "Atonement," in *Encyclopedia of the Reformed Faith,* pp. 13-16; *The Christian Story,* Vol. 1: *A Narrative Interpretation of Basic Christian Doctrine: A Pastoral Systematics,* Third Edition (Grand Rapids: Eerdmans, 1996), pp. 134-51; *The Christian Story,* Vol. 4: *Christology in Context* (Grand Rapids: Eerdmans, 2006), pp. 211-36.

"Rome, Reformation, and Reunion" Revisited

Frank C. Senn, STS

In 1966 a young Carl Braaten caused quite a stir with the publication of a brief essay in *Una Sancta,* a journal devoted to liturgical renewal, Christian unity, and Christian social responsibility edited by the then-Lutheran pastor Richard John Neuhaus.[1] This short piece entitled "Rome, Reformation, and Reunion" was Braaten's own abridgement of a longer essay that had appeared in the summer 1965 issue of *The Record* of the Lutheran School of Theology at Chicago Maywood Campus (the former Chicago Lutheran Theological Seminary).[2] Braaten later admitted that if he had published the entire essay, it might not have caused the stir that it did. But it was the *Una Sancta* version, perhaps lacking the qualifications included in the original essay, that was picked up by the Religious News Service (RNS), which reported that Professor Braaten was urging a Protestant "return to Rome" and calling on his "fellow Protestants to look upon the reformation as an event in history which, having accomplished the reforms it set out to bring about, must now become past history." The *New York Times* entitled its version of the RNS story, "Lutheran Favors Unity With Rome; Braaten Says Reformation Has Accomplished Aims." Horrified, *The Christian Century,* a

---

1. Carl E. Braaten, "Rome, Reformation, and Reunion," *Una Sancta* 23, no. 2 (Pentecost 1966): 3-8.

2. The original paper was based on a lecture Carl Braaten had given to a group of Lutheran pastors in Illinois. See Carl E. Braaten, *Mother Church: Ecclesiology and Ecumenism* (Minneapolis: Fortress, 1998), chapter 1. This "brouhaha" occurred during my first year as a seminarian at the Lutheran School of Theology at Chicago, Maywood campus, where Carl Braaten was my professor of systematic theology.

bastion of mainline Protestantism at the time, ran an editorial entitled "Protestant Hara-Kiri," and judged Braaten's thesis to be "odious, perhaps dangerous."[3] Editor Neuhaus, who never tired of chanting the mantra about "healing the breach of the sixteenth century," ran a symposium in the 1966 "Michael and All Angels" issue of *Una Sancta* featuring responses to Braaten's article by Albert C. Outler, Warren A. Quanbeck, George A. Lindbeck, and Robert McAfee Brown, with a reply from Carl Braaten entitled "Reunion, Yes; Return No."[4]

It was undoubtedly the opening parable in Braaten's essay that focused the attention of the media and Braaten's critics. (Yes, parables can be dangerous!) Braaten compared the Protestant Reformation with the French forces under Charles deGaulle, which went into exile in England during the Vichy government in order to rally support and return with the Allied forces to replace the illegitimate Nazi regime with a legitimate French government. Protestants, said Braaten, went into exile from the Roman Church, but settled down without giving a thought of returning. That was the point of Braaten's parable. (Parables should have one point and other details shouldn't be pushed too strongly.) Protestants have gotten used to the idea of living apart from the Roman Catholic Church instead of doing what is necessary to return — to healing the breach of the sixteenth century, as Neuhaus put it. The editor of *The Christian Century* rejected the whole idea of Protestants as "exiles," preferring to identify them instead as "emigrés" leaving the old world to settle in the new.[5] No thought is given to "returning."

This essay does not intend to rehearse that particular controversy of 1966. But the issue of "Rome, Reformation, and Reunion" has lingered with me over the years and may have been in the background when I helped to draft *The Rule* of The Society of the Holy Trinity (STS = *Societas Trinitatis Sanctae*) in 1996, to which I have subscribed. *The Rule* states:

> . . . the Lutheran ecumenical vocation is the unfinished business of the sixteenth century Reformation. Together with our forebears at Augsburg in 1530, we long for that reunion of Christians in which the Gospel might have free course and for that unity for which Jesus prayed (cf. John 17). Therefore, this ministerium is dedicated to

3. "Protestant Hara-Kiri," *The Christian Century*, June 22, 1966.
4. See *Una Sancta* 23, no. 3 (1966): 12-23.
5. "The Braaten Brouhaha," *The Christian Century*, October 26, 1966.

the Lutheran vocation of reform of the Church and the Lutheran ecumenical destiny of reconciliation with the bishop and church of Rome" (*The Rule*, VIII, 3-4).

> We are aware that Western Christianity as a whole is in a crisis of faith and that there are movements and orders in other ecclesial traditions organized for the confessional and spiritual renewal of their churches (i.e. the churches of the Reformation as well as the church of Rome). We will make contact with these movements and orders and invite them to chapter retreats and special meetings. (*The Rule*, VIII, 2)

This commitment in *The Rule* reflects the Preamble to the Augsburg Confession, to which all Lutheran pastors subscribe, which says that "we on our part shall not omit doing anything, insofar as God and conscience allow, that may serve the cause of Christian unity."[6]

I will deal with the problem of schism and reunion as follows. First, I will review the religious and theological context at the time Professor Braaten made his proposal — a context that also informed my own hopes. Second, I will revisit the historical situation in the sixteenth century to establish the ecclesiastical reality that underlies the schism. Third, I will assess the prospects of reunion on the basis of some fundamental differences in Lutheran/Protestant and Roman Catholic religious cultures. Fourth, I will join a few other Lutherans in recognizing the need for a universal pastoral office in the global Church today and propose that the Bishop of Rome is the most likely candidate to fill it. Finally, I will suggest an evangelical catholic agenda for Lutheran congregations that can help lay the groundwork for thinking about the possibility of reunion.

I. Evangelical Catholic Hopes in the Mid-Twentieth Century

The 1960s were heady days for advancing ecumenical hopes. Carl Braaten developed his proposal for reunion in 1965, just as the Second Vatican Council was ending. Officially named the twenty-first Ecumenical Council of the Catholic Church, Vatican II, as it has been pop-

---

6. "Preface to the Augsburg Confession," *The Book of Concord*, ed. Theodore G. Tappert (Philadelphia: Fortress, 1959), p. 26.

ularly called, opened under Pope John XXIII on October 11, 1962 and closed under Pope Paul VI on November 21, 1965. While the Second Vatican Council technically concerned only the renewal of the Catholic Church, the presence of Protestant observers at the Council who participated freely in the discussions opened up the relevance of the Council's decisions to other Christian bodies.

Perhaps the most influential product of the Council was the Dogmatic Constitution on the Church, *Lumen Gentium.* In its first chapter, "The Mystery of the Church," is the famous statement:

> the sole Church of Christ which in the Creed we profess to be one, holy, catholic and apostolic, which our Saviour, after His Resurrection, commissioned Peter to shepherd, and him and the other apostles to extend and direct with authority, which He erected for all ages as "the pillar and mainstay of the truth." This Church, constituted and organized as a society in the present world, subsists in the Catholic Church, which is governed by the successor of Peter and by the bishops in communion with him (*Lumen Gentium,* 8).

But the document immediately adds: "Nevertheless, many elements of sanctification and of truth are found outside its visible confines."[7] Statements like this, as well as the whole Decree on Ecumenism, *Unitatis Redintegratio,* demonstrated an official willingness on the part of the Catholic Church to be in dialogue with others and to work toward the restoration of unity among all Christians. The Roman Catholic Church, after the Second Vatican Council, implemented a previously-unimaginable reform and showed an unprecedented openness to the "separated brethren" and to other religions.

At the same time, a new self-understanding had been taking hold of Lutheranism during the course of the nineteenth and twentieth centuries that disposed at least some Lutherans to think about the possibility of reunion with the Roman Church. This was the view that "evangelical catholicity" is an appropriate description of classical Lutheranism. The roots of this self-understanding are found in nineteenth-century Germany and in early-twentieth-century Sweden.

The German ecclesiastical situation had been shaken up by the territorial redistribution that took place during the Napoleonic Era

---

7. Translation from *The Documents of Vatican II,* ed. Walter M. Abbott, S.J. (New York: Herder and Herder, 1966), *Lumen Gentium,* no. 8.

and at the Congress of Vienna in 1815. In a situation in which, for the most part, each region had the religion of its ruler *(cuius regio cuius religio)*, the redistribution of territory meant that Protestant Churches came under the jurisdiction of Catholic regimes, and vice versa. Thus, the Catholic Kingdom of Bavaria acquired Lutheran Franconia, and the Protestant (Lutheran/Reformed) Kingdom of Prussia acquired Catholic territories in the Rhineland. This situation required a reassessment of confessional identity among the Churches.

In Bavaria Pastor Wilhelm Löhe of Neuendettelsau wrote *Three Books About the Church* (1844) in which he argued that the Church is one, but it is divided into many denominations, and the Church with the clearest confessional witness to the truth of Scripture is the truest Church. He, of course, identified the truest confession with Lutheranism and situated the Lutheran Church between the Roman and Reformed Churches.[8] While Löhe might seem to be privileging "the word of God alone" above the catholic tradition, in fact he recovered in practice historic orders of liturgy in his Agenda for Lutheran congregations in the American Midwest served by the missionary pastors sent from his mission school,[9] and he established a deaconess community at Neuendettelsau, thus broadening the understanding of ordered ministry and providing a Lutheran religious community.

In the Rhineland around 1850, Professor Johann Peter Lange of Bonn used the concept of "evangelical catholicity" as a part of a Hegelian-inspired dialectic of church history to define the confessional situation of the Rhenish *Landeskirche*. The thesis of Catholicism and the antithesis of Protestantism (the Evangelical Church) would be replaced by the synthesis of evangelical catholicity.[10]

At the same time, two conservative Lutherans, Ernst Ludwig von Gerlach and Heinrich Leo, used the concept of "evangelical catholicity" to steer the Prussian Church Union (a union of Lutheran and Reformed confessions) in a more Catholic than a Reformed direction.[11]

8. Wilhelm Löhe, *Three Books About the Church*, trans. with an Introduction by James L. Schaaf (Philadelphia: Fortress, 1969).

9. See Wilhelm Löhe, *Agenda für christliche Gemeinden des lutherischen Bekenntnisses* (Nördlingen: Beck, 1988).

10. Johann Peter Lange, *Die gesetzlich-katholische Kirche als Sinnbild der Freien evangelisch-katholischen Kirche im Zusammenhange mit der Grundformen der symbolischen Religionsweise* (Heidelberg, 1850).

11. Lutherans in Brandenburg-Prussia had been smarting under the Reformed

Frank C. Senn, STS

Coming out of the tradition of the "Prussian Union," Paul Tillich articulated the concept of evangelical catholicity in a way that transcended the Reformation divide, and he later developed the dialectic between "Catholic substance" and "Protestant principle."[12] Justification by faith is the "Protestant principle" that critiques the whole theological system, but it can never stand alone; it depends on the context of "Catholic substance." Evangelical catholicity is the synthesizing ideal, although it can never be completely realized in the Church. Nevertheless it stands as a corrective of both empirical Catholicism and empirical Protestantism. (We note that Paul Tillich was Carl Braaten's *Doktorvater* at Harvard Divinity School and that during the mid-1960s Carl was editing Tillich's lectures on church history.)[13]

Jaroslav Pelikan used this Tillichian understanding to apply "Catholic substance" and "Protestant principle" to Luther's Reformation. He applied evangelical catholicity in a constructive way as the principle that critiques both Protestant principle and Catholic substance but also expresses a program of its own. Pelikan saw the program of evangelical catholicity especially manifested in the liturgical renewal movements of the twentieth century.[14] To take but one example: Catholic substance affirms that there is no public worship of God without forms, and even the divine revelation assumed external, visible forms in the incarnation of the Word and the institution of sacraments as "visible words." But Protestant principle holds that the actual forms of worship are not laid down in Scripture and are matters of indifference *(adiaphora)* because they have nothing to do with our salvation; therefore uniformity in rites and ceremonies should not be legalistically imposed (Augsburg Confession, Article 7). The evangelical catholic approach would make decisions about forms within the cultural

---

rule of the Hohenzollerns since 1613 when Margrave Ernst openly embraced the Reformed confession, and they fought back by embracing the most "Catholic" elements in Lutheranism, as, in fact, had the Elector Joachim II in the conservative 1540 Mark Brandenburg Church Order. See Bodo Nischan, *Prince, People, and Confession: The Second Reformation in Brandenburg* (Philadelphia: University of Pennsylvania Press, 1994).

12. Paul Tillich, "The End of the Protestant Era," *Student World* 30 (1937); *The Protestant Era* (Chicago: University of Chicago Press, 1957).

13. Paul Tillich, *Perspectives on 19th and 20th Century Protestant Thought.* Edited with an Introduction by Carl E. Braaten (New York: Harper and Row, 1967); *A History of Christian Thought.* Edited by Carl E. Braaten (New York: Harper and Row, 1968).

14. Jaroslav Pelikan, "Luther and the Liturgy," in *More About Luther,* Martin Luther Lectures, Vol. 2 (Decorah, IA: Luther College, 1958), pp. 3-62; see especially pp. 43-62.

context in which the Church lives. As Pelikan suggested already in 1958, the American cultural context might suggest giving more attention to the heritage of Christian liturgical forms as a way of shoring up Christian dogma *(lex orandi, lex credendi).*[15] Pelikan also saw evangelical catholicity as a challenge to Protestant theologians to take more seriously the Great Tradition (i.e. the canon of Scripture, the ecumenical creeds, the dogmas promulgated by ecumenical councils, and even the biblical commentaries of the church fathers) as they engage in the conserving as well as the critical tasks of theology.[16]

Evangelical catholicity also became an ecumenical identifier. It was the way the Church of Sweden understood itself within the ecumenical family of churches. Archbishop Nathan Söderblom posited evangelical catholicity within the "branch theory" of Christianity that included Greek Catholicism, Roman Catholicism, and Anglo-Catholicism. "Catholicity" is compromised in every tradition by a modifier, including "Roman" Catholicism. Söderblom saw the Church of Sweden as the premier example of evangelical catholicity because of its confessional commitment to the Lutheran doctrine of justification by faith through grace while retaining historic orders of ministry (including bishops in apostolic succession) and historic orders of worship. He put evangelical catholicity in opposition to "Romanism," with its hierarchical authoritarianism and canon law, and "Protestant reductionism," with its negative attitude toward the church's historic forms that results in discontinuity with tradition.[17] Bishop Gustav Aulén held that the Lutheran Reformation's affirmation of Catholic substance is evident in the references to the ecumenical councils and church fathers in its Confessions and the inclusion of the three ecumenical creeds in *The Book of Concord.*[18]

Friedrich Heiler carried the idea of the catholicity within Lutheranism a step further. He held that it was not Luther's intention to create a new Church but to remain within the Catholic Church and reform it. "Luther and his friends wished, as they were never tired of

---

15. Jaroslav Pelikan, *Obedient Rebels: Catholic Substance and Protestant Principle in Luther's Reformation* (New York: Harper and Row, 1964).

16. Pelikan, *Obedient Rebels*, pp. 170-206.

17. See Sven-Erik Brodd, *Evangelisk Katolicitet. Ett studium av innehåll och funktion under 1800- och 1900-talen* (Lund: CWK Gleerup, 1982), pp. 101-34.

18. Brodd, *Evangelisk Katolicitet*, pp. 135-59. See Gustaf Aulén, *Reformation and Catholicity*, trans. Eric H. Wahlstrom (Philadelphia: Muhlenberg Press, 1961).

emphasizing, to be and to remain Catholic."[19] In his analysis of the Reformation and catholicity Heiler avoided the question of whether something was true or false and asked instead if it was helpful or a hindrance in church life. He found episcopal order, sacramental liturgy, private confession, and religious community good for the church, but curialism, liturgical legalism, and forced conformity bad. Further, he held that the Augsburg Confession is an evangelical catholic confession that both criticizes Roman authoritarianism and guards against Protestant reductionism.[20]

There was hope in the period after World War II leading up to the 450th anniversary of the Augsburg Confession in 1980 that the Roman Catholic Church might, in some way, recognize the Augsburg Confession. In Germany Max Lackman and the League for Christian Reunion proposed the formation of a uniate Evangelical Catholic Church in communion with the Roman See that Rome would recognize on the basis of the Augsburg Confession.[21]

Of course, the heart of the Augsburg Confession is Article IV on justification by faith alone. This is the great "Protestant principle." This is the theological basis of the Confession's evangelical critique of the "Catholic substance" of the Church. The Smalcald Articles, drawn up in response to the call of Pope Paul III for an ecumenical council to resolve the religious controversies tearing apart the Church and the Empire, hold that "Nothing in this article can be given up or compromised."[22]

Eric W. Gritsch and Robert W. Jenson wrote a study of the Lutheran Confessions that proposed that the Augsburg Confession's article on "justification by faith alone, without the works of the law" was "an ecumenical proposal of dogma" to the Western Church as a way of resolving the lingering issue of Pelagianism in the Western Church.[23]

19. Friedrich Heiler, "The Catholic Movement in German Lutheranism," in *Northern Catholicism: Centenary Studies in the Oxford and Parallel Movements,* ed. N. P. Wilson and Charles Harris (London: SPCK, 1933), p. 478.

20. See Friedrich Heiler, "Evangelische Katholizität," in *Gesammelte Aufsätze und Vorträge,* I: *Der Wesen des Katholizismus* (Munich, 1920), pp. 92-115.

21. See Max Lackman, *Katholische Einheit und Augsburger Konfession* (Graz, 1960); English trans. by Walter R. Bouman, *The Augsburg Confession and Catholic Unity* (New York: Herder and Herder, 1963).

22. *The Book of Concord,* p. 293.

23. Eric W. Gritsch and Robert W. Jenson, *Lutheranism: The Theological Movement and Its Confessional Writings* (Philadelphia: Fortress, 1976).

The very way the article on justification is presented in the Augsburg Confession shows that it is a theological implication of established church dogma. Articles 1, 2, and 3 deal respectively with the doctrines of God, of original sin, and of the saving work of Christ. The implied argument is that if God is as holy as the doctrine of the Trinity affirms, if original sin is as virulent as the Augustinian tradition holds, and if Christ is as necessary for salvation as the christological doctrines imply, then the only way to talk about the human relationship to God is to hold with St. Paul that "we are justified by faith apart from the works of the law" (Roman 3:28). Luther would add "justified by faith *alone*" in his German translation of the Bible.

The great ecumenical breakthrough, after years of Lutheran-Roman Catholic dialogue, was the adoption of the Joint Declaration on the Doctrine of Justification by Faith by the Vatican and the Lutheran World Federation on October 31, 1999. While not embracing everything that Lutherans or Roman Catholics would want to say about justification and sanctification, the Declaration solidly affirmed: "Together we confess: By grace alone, in faith in Christ's saving work and not because of any merit on our part, we are accepted by God and receive the Holy Spirit, who renews our hearts while equipping and calling us to good works."[24] Surely if agreement has been reached on this article on which the Lutheran Confessions hold that "the church stands or falls," the possibilities of reconciliation and reunion must be on the horizon.

II. The Schism in the Catholic Church in the Sixteenth Century

Well, not so fast! The subtitle of Gritsch and Jenson's book on *Lutheranism* is "The Theological Movement and Its Confessional Writings." Evangelical catholics have held that Lutheranism was a confessional movement for the reform of the Catholic Church in the West. Richard John Neuhaus stated this tirelessly in the pages of the *Lutheran Forum Letter,* which he edited before transferring to the Roman Catholic Church. It is an attractive understanding of Lutheranism because it implies that the natural home of this confessional movement is the

---

24. The Lutheran World Federation and the Roman Catholic Church, *Joint Declaration on the Doctrine of Justification* (Grand Rapids: Eerdmans, 1999).

Catholic Church. What has not been appreciated as well is the socio-logical as well as the theological reality of the schism of the Catholic Church in the sixteenth century.

I wrote this last sentence intentionally. As far as Lutheranism is concerned, what was produced by the Reformation was not a new Prot-estant Church but a schism in the Catholic Church of the West. At the end of the day the result of Luther's reform movement was a division in the Catholic Church between those who continued under the papacy of Rome and those who did not. By way of comparison, Reformed Churches clearly set out to create a new Church. Lingering catholic ele-ments of church life were tolerated only until a more complete reform could be achieved (and some Reformed Churches ended up being more reformed than others). Lutheranism expressed no desire to depart from the Catholic Church or the catholic tradition. This was stated twice in the Augsburg Confession: once at the conclusion of the doc-trinal articles and again at the conclusion of the practical articles. "There is nothing here that departs from the Scriptures or the Catholic church or the Church of Rome, insofar as the ancient church is known to us from its writers."[25] "Only those things have been recounted which it seemed necessary to say in order that it may be understood that nothing has been received among us, in doctrine or in ceremonies, that is contrary to Scripture or to the church catholic. For it is manifest that we have guarded diligently against the introduction into our churches of any new and ungodly doctrines."[26]

There was no effort to found a new Church, but there was schism in the one Catholic Church of the West. It is well known that in the Holy Roman Empire especially, territorial rulers played the role of bish-ops in appointing priests. Lords of manors appointed priests in cha-pels on their lands. Kings played a role in selecting bishops and abbots of prestigious monasteries. Ottonian emperors before Pope Greg-ory VII and the Investiture Controversy even selected popes. It is not surprising that princes within the Empire would continue to exercise this episcopal role after the Reformation by choosing the confession of the Church in their territory. This applied to both Lutheran and Ro-man Catholic territories (and after the Peace of Westphalia in 1648, to Reformed territories as well). The Augsburg Confession was signed by

25. *The Book of Concord*, p. 47.
26. *The Book of Concord*, p. 95.

princes and mayors of free cities and the Confutation was authorized by the Emperor. These confessions were political as well as theological documents.

The process by which the free cities considered the Reformation is interesting. In places like Nürnberg, Zurich, Strassburg, and Regensburg, reform-minded preachers were called by the city council to the great church of the city. The preacher preached for reform. This provoked controversy. The city council held a public disputation between the reformers and the papalists and declared for the reformers. The extent of the reforms enacted by the city council varied from place to place. Reforms enacted in Nürnberg in 1524, the first city to embrace Luther's reformation, were moderately conservative, as can be seen in the Brandenburg-Nürnberg Church Order of 1533 prepared by Osiander.[27] Reforms in Zurich under Zwingli's leadership were more radical,[28] and reforms in Strassburg under Bucer's leadership were moderate.[29] The city of Regensburg adopted the Lutheran Confession in 1542, and its City Council remained entirely Lutheran until the incorporation of the city into the Principality of Regensburg in 1803. A minority of the population remained Roman Catholic but were excluded from civil rights ("Bürgerrecht"). But although this Imperial city had adopted the Reformation, the city remained the seat of a Roman Catholic bishop and several Catholic abbeys.

The armed conflict of the Smalcald War (1546-1548) and the unsatisfactory Interims that followed did nothing to end the stalemate. Emperor Charles V was becoming weary of the conflict and abdicated in favor of his brother Ferdinand in 1554 and retired to a monastery. Ferdinand convened a Diet at Augsburg in 1555 and wanted to press for unification, but the electors insisted on a truce. The Peace of Augsburg gave equal standing to the Lutheran and Roman Catholic confessions within the Empire. Ecclesiastical jurisdiction of Catholic prelates over adherents of the Augsburg Confession was suspended and medieval laws regarding heresy were rescinded. Catholic and Lutheran estates received the right to determine the religion of their sub-

---

27. See "Nuremberg," in *The Oxford Encyclopedia of the Reformation,* ed. Hans J. Hillerbrand (Oxford: Oxford University Press, 1996), 3: 160-62.

28. See Ulrich Gäbler, *Huldrych Zwingli: His Life and Work,* trans. Ruth C. L. Gritsch (Philadelphia: Fortress, 1983), pp. 63-90.

29. See Lorna Jane Abray, *The People's Reformation: Magistrates, Clergy, and Commons in Strasbourg, 1500-1598* (Ithaca, NY: Cornell University Press, 1985).

jects. (The principle, "Ubi unus dominus ibi una sit religio," was expressed in the seventeenth century by the pithy phrase *cuius regio cuius religio* — "whoever the ruler, his religion.") Ecclesiastical leaders (e.g. bishops) did not possess the right of the temporal rulers to determine the confession of their jurisdiction; they were free to embrace the other confession, but would then have to give up their office. Subjects were free to retain their religion, but if it conflicted with the religion of the territory in which they lived they would have to emigrate elsewhere in order to practice it. Citizens of free cities that had adherents of both confessions before 1555 were free to exercise their religion.[30] Thus, within the Holy Roman Empire of the German Nation the one Catholic Church divided into two confessions that were granted equal recognition and protection.

In Scandinavia the Lutheran movement was embraced by national Churches. At the time of the Reformation Sweden had just won independence from Denmark, and Finland was under Swedish administration. Norway and Iceland remained united administratively to Denmark. The Swedish war for independence from Denmark and the Union of Kalmar brought Gustav Vasa to the throne (reigned 1523-60), who championed the work of the reformers in the Church largely because it served the purpose of filling the empty royal treasury. (He appreciated good preaching of the Word, being an able stump politician himself.) His need for legitimacy as an elected monarch in a conservative country argued for retaining the bishops in place. Before the royal wedding in 1531, he set aside the rights of the Uppsala cathedral chapter and convened a synod of the whole national Church to elect a new archbishop since there were already two elected Catholic archbishops of Uppsala contending for their old position. The synod chose Laurentius Petri, younger brother of Sweden's leading reformer Olavus Petri (both had studied in Wittenberg). Gustav compelled the papal nuncio to consecrate Laurentius as archbishop (he served from 1531 until 1573) without waiting for papal confirmation, thus creating an autocephalous Church.[31] But through Laurentius Petri the apostolic succession continued in the increasingly Lutheran Church of Sweden,

30. See Herbert Immenkötter, "Augsburg, Peace of," in *The Oxford Encyclopedia of the Reformation* 1: 91-93.

31. See Theodor van Haag, "Die apostolische Sukzession in Schweden," *Kyrkohistorisk årsskrift* 44 (1944): 1-168.

and the Swedish Church Order of 1571 deemed the episcopal office a useful historical development under the guidance of the Holy Spirit.[32]

In Denmark, the overthrow of the Catholic King Christian II in 1536 brought the Lutheran Frederick of Holstein to the throne. With the assistance of the Wittenberg reformer Johannes Bugenhagen, on loan from the Elector of Saxony, a Danish Church Order was prepared in 1537. The new king and queen were crowned that year with Bugenhagen officiating. The seven Catholic bishops were incarcerated and seven new superintendents were appointed. However, two of the new superintendents in Norway were actually duly-elected Catholic bishops who had never been consecrated. There was a brief armed struggle in Iceland between the Catholic bishop of Holar and the new Lutheran bishop of Skálholt appointed by King Frederick, in which the Catholic bishop and his two sons lost their lives. Thus, there was more discontinuity than continuity in church order under the Danish regime in comparison with the Swedish, but in ordinary church life little was changed in any of these countries.[33]

Thus, Luther's movement was embraced by territorial and national Churches which implemented it into law in church ordinances and severed communion, intentionally or by default, with the bishop of Rome, the patriarch of the West. The traditions of these Churches have passed into Lutheran denominations in North America and other countries. There are now more than a hundred Lutheran church bodies around the world. Since Lutheranism lacks a world-wide organization that embraces all Lutherans (the Lutheran World Federation comes close, but it is not itself a church; it is a communion of churches), the issue of whom the Roman Catholic Church would reach out to remains problematic. Lutheran church bodies would probably have to make the overtures to Rome. But apart from the fact that denominations seek self-preservation above all things, there remain significant impasses between Lutherans and Roman Catholics.

32. *Den svenska Kyrkoordningen 1571*, ed. Sven Kjöllerström (Lund: Håkan Ohlsson, 1971), 98; Conrad Bergendoff, "The Unique Character of the Reformation in Sweden," *Symposium on 17th Century Lutheranism* (St. Louis: Concordia, 1962).

33. On the lingering use of Latin in liturgy see Frank C. Senn, "The Mass in Sweden: From Swedish to Latin?" in Karin Maag and John D. Witvliet, eds., *Worship in Medieval and Early Modern Europe: Change and Continuity in Religious Practice* (Notre Dame, IN: University of Notre Dame Press, 2004), pp. 63-83.

Frank C. Senn, STS

III. Continuing and New Impasses to Reunion

It is beyond the scope of this essay to trace the theological and ecclesiastical developments in Lutheranism and in Roman Catholicism since the Reformation. It is enough to point out that there have been subsequent developments which involved a hardening of confessional positions in the Formula of Concord and the Canons and Decrees of the Council of Trent. Lutheranism has experienced further theological development in the periods of orthodoxy, pietism, rationalism, as well as liberalism, neo-orthodoxy, liberation theology, etc., in the last two centuries. Roman Catholicism has experienced its own complex historical development as well as the promulgation of three further dogmas that pose new hurdles to reunion, those of papal infallibility (First Vatican Council, 1871), the Immaculate Conception of Mary (Pope Pius IX, 1854), and the Assumption (Pope Pius XII, 1950). In spite of remarkable convergences in theological understanding brought about by patient bilateral theological dialogues, it is ultimately whole church bodies that must be reunited, and this entails dealing with ecclesiastical institutions and church cultures as well as theology. The breach of the sixteenth century cannot be healed just by going back to the sixteenth century!

Social historians have pointed to a profound change in church culture and popular piety that occurred as a result of the Reformation's rejection of the doctrine of purgatory, which had been held in the Western Church for nearly a thousand years. Once the Greek view of the immortal soul was imported into early Christian anthropology, the question of what becomes of the soul when the body dies was inevitably raised. The dead body awaits resurrection when Christ comes again to judge the living and the dead. Where is the soul in the meantime? It was reasoned that very few souls existed in a pure enough state to immediately behold the beatific vision in heaven. Neither were most souls deemed evil enough to be consigned to hell. The Western Church, beginning with St. Augustine and St. Gregory the Great, established the theological underpinnings on which the intermediate other world was based.[34] Augustine introduced the notion of a purgatorial time while Gregory contributed to the imagery of purgatory on the basis of recorded apparitions and visions.[35]

---

34. See Jacques Le Goff, *The Medieval Imagination,* trans. Arthur Goldhammer (Chicago: The University of Chicago Press, 1988), pp. 67-75.

35. Later theologians drew upon such texts as 2 Maccabees 12:41-46 (the sacrifice

Popular piety was already offering prayers for the dead before a doctrine of purgatory was developed. Requiem masses were offered for the souls of the dead on the third and thirtieth days and on the yearly anniversary. Families of the deceased arranged for perpetual votive masses for the deceased by endowing chantries. During the late Middle Ages, especially during the time of widespread plagues, confraternities were organized, which paid for votive masses for their deceased members. So great were the requests for votive masses for the repose of the souls in purgatory that priests called altarists were ordained who did no pastoral work but only offered votive masses paid for by mass stipends. Indulgences could be earned which, along with prayers and masses offered for the deceased, reduced the time departed souls had to spend in purgatory. The special plenary indulgence granted by Pope Leo X to raise money for building St. Peter's Basilica in Rome, peddled in Germany by Albrecht of Brandenburg (archbishop of both Magdeburg and Mainz), which occasioned Martin Luther's *Ninety-Five Theses,* allowed the pious to buy full remission of sins for their deceased loved ones in purgatory. "As soon as the coin in the coffer rings, so quickly the soul from purgatory springs," enthused the Dominican peddler John Tetzel. All this passed for what John Bossy called "charity for the dead."[36] The medieval world was one in which there was a strong sense of communion between the living and the dead.

Luther's attack on the sale of indulgences, then on the very concept of penance that supported indulgences, and finally on the biblical foundation of purgatory on the basis of the justification of the sinner who in faith appeals to the merits of Christ alone, resulted, in the words of Edward Muir, in "a forceful rejection of the ritual industry of death with all its expensive commitments to priestly intervention."[37] The extent of Luther's awareness of this whole ritual industry of death and its economics can be seen in The Smalcald Articles, Article II on the Mass, in which he connected the "dragon's tail" of the mass (by

---

ordered by Judas Maccabeus to redeem the sins of soldiers fallen in battle), Matthew 12:31-32 (the remission of sins in the other world), I Corinthians 3:11-15 (the purification of sinners after death "as if by fire"), and Luke 16:19-31 (the parable of the rich man and Lazarus) to provide a biblical basis for the doctrine of purgatory.

36. John Bossy, *Christianity in the West 1400-1700* (Oxford and New York: Oxford University Press, 1985), pp. 61-62.

37. Edward Muir, *Ritual in Early Modern Europe.* New Approaches to European History (Cambridge: Cambridge University Press, 1997), p. 52.

which he meant the votive mass) with purgatory, the apparition of evil spirits, pilgrimages, fraternities, relics, and indulgences. A telling accusation is this:

> They were so occupied with requiem Masses, with vigils, with the weekly, monthly, and yearly celebrations of requiems, with the common week [the week following St. Michael's Day when many requiem masses were offered], with All Souls' Day, and with soul-baths [paying the poor to pray for the donor's salvation] that the Mass was used almost exclusively for the dead although Christ instituted the sacrament for the living alone.[38]

The abolition of votive masses, burial fraternities, chantries, and other aspects of the ritual industry of death had the effect of severing the communion of the living and the dead. Christian funerals were concerned to bring comfort to the living by teaching the faithful to rely on the promises of Christ. The dead sleep in Jesus until the resurrection and the last judgment.[39]

In response to these developments, Chapter II of the Decrees of the Council of Trent on the Mass affirmed that the mass, "according to the tradition of the apostles, is rightly offered not only for the sins, punishments, satisfactions, and other necessities of the faithful who are living but also for those who have died in Christ and have not yet been fully purified."[40] The Council of Trent reformed abuses in the system of votive masses, but insisted that the Eucharist gathers the living and the dead in one communion of grace. David N. Power, O.M.I., has suggested that the practices behind the Tridentine decree "offered an integral and coherent social and cultural persuasion and a Christian identity to peoples and institutions."[41] As I wrote in *Christian Liturgy — Catholic and Evangelical,*

---

38. *The Book of Concord,* pp. 294-95.

39. See the hymn of Martin Schalling (1532-1608), "Lord, Thee I Love with All My Heart," stanza 3, with which J. S. Bach concluded his *St. John Passion.*

40. *The Canons and Decrees of the Council of Trent,* trans. H. J. Schroeder, O.P. (New York: Herder and Herder, 1946), p. 146.

41. David N. Power, O.M.I., "The Sacrifice of the Mass: A Question of Reception and Re-reception," *Ecclesia Orans* 1 (Rome 1985), p. 74. This view is more fully developed, along with its ecumenical implications, in David N. Power, *The Sacrifice We Offer: The Tridentine Dogma and Its Reinterpretation* (New York: Crossroad Publishing Company, 1987).

The sacrifice of the mass was an integral part of a religio-cultural system which the Catholic reformers wanted to keep, freed from an overlay of superstition and popular ignorance, but which the Protestant reformers wanted to dissolve in the name of salvation through the merits and work of Christ alone. The clash between Tridentine and Reformation theologians was between a religio-cultural system and a recovered biblical principle that was challenging that system and establishing a new one. Transcending a confessional impasse becomes even more difficult if a whole worldview and community identity are at stake.[42]

Catholic church culture has a lively sense of the communion of the living and dead that is not expressed in Lutheran church culture.

Pope Benedict XVI, in his 2007 Encyclical, *Spe Salvi (In Hope We Were Saved),* related the recent views of some theologians "that the fire which both burns and saves is Christ himself, the Judge and Saviour. The encounter with him is the decisive act of judgment. Before his gaze all falsehood melts away. This encounter with him, as it burns us, transforms and frees us, allowing us to become truly ourselves." The Pope does not provide any alternative explanation to these theologians' ideas, nor does he refute them. This is surely not by accident. Such a statement must have the intention, therefore, of opening up dialogue on the understanding of purgatory.

As intractable as this cultural-religious impasse is, involving contrasting views of the state of the dead, an equally intractable cultural-religious impasse has emerged in the twentieth century involving contrasting views of human sexuality. As Mary Eberstadt has noted in a recent article, one by one mainline Protestants in Western Europe and North America (many Lutherans among them) have jettisoned traditional Christian sexual ethics regarding divorce, contraception, abortion, and homosexual behavior.[43] Against the rising tide of sexual liberation in Western secular society, the Roman Catholic Church has held the line on traditional Christian sexual teachings, most famously in the 1968 encyclical of Pope Paul VI, *Humanae Vitae (On Human Life).* In this encyclical the Pope re-affirmed the traditional teaching of the Catholic Church regarding abortion, contraception, and other issues

42. Frank C. Senn, *Christian Liturgy: Catholic and Evangelical* (Minneapolis: Fortress, 1997), p. 466.

43. Mary Eberstadt, "Christianity Lite," *First Things* 200 (February 2010): 21-27.

pertaining to human life. As abortion has become a political issue in Western democracies, the Catholic Church has drawn a line in the sand, encouraging its members to resist and roll back the legalization of abortion. A statement of comparable gravitas has not addressed homosexuality, although conferences of Catholic bishops have opposed gay marriage legislation.

However, a more positive approach toward dealing with sexual ethics was developed by Pope John Paul II in his theology of the body.[44] This theology was developed in a series of 129 addresses to general audiences early in his pontificate. As I understand the general thrust of this theology, by focusing on the beauty of God's plan for the union of the sexes, John Paul II shifts the discussion from legalism ("How far can I go before I break the law?") to liberty ("What is the truth that sets me free to love?"). As a Christian humanist, John Paul II asked what it means to be human and how to live life in a way that brings true happiness and fulfillment. While the theology of the body focuses on sex and marriage and celibacy as a special calling, it is really wider than that. It provides a whole worldview. In the Pope's theology, the body reveals the mystery of God. And that mystery, which has been fully revealed in Jesus Christ, is that God is love. God is love in the relationship of Father, Son, and Holy Spirit. The theology of the body means that our bodies somehow reveal the mystery of divine love in the world through the mystery of sexual difference and the call of the two to become one flesh. In other words, in the mystery of marital union we have a sign here on earth of the eternal mystery of love found in the Trinity.

The vast implications of this theology are only now being explored in books, conferences, and institutes. This theology opens up the possibilities of theological dialogue. More than that, however, Pope John Paul II addresses in a magisterial way the issues of human sexuality that have been among the most church-dividing of the late twentieth/early twenty-first centuries — in much the same magisterial way that Pope Leo the Great addressed the christological issues that were tearing apart the Church in the fifth century. Not all Eastern Christians accepted Pope Leo's Tome at Chalcedon, just as not all Western Christians (including many Roman Catholics) will accept John Paul II's theology of the body. But in both cases, there is a sense that "Peter has spoken."

---

44. John Paul II, *Man and Woman He Created Them: A Theology of the Body* (Boston: Pauline Books, 2006).

IV. Toward Recognizing a Universal
Pastoral Office for the Global Church

How disappointing that denominations like my own Evangelical Lutheran Church in America stumble around on issues of human sexuality without a sense of the biblical and theological foundations that papal teaching could have provided. The highest legislative authority in my Church is a churchwide assembly that, according to our own Confession, lacks the qualifications to exercise teaching authority, since laity comprise 60 percent of the churchwide assembly. Article 14 of the Augsburg Confession states, "It is taught among us that nobody should publicly teach or preach or administer the sacraments in the church without a regular call."[45] So where do Lutherans turn for teaching authority?[46]

In his debate with Johannes Eck at Leipzig Martin Luther contended, "popes and councils can err" (so also churchwide assemblies that do not place themselves under the word of God). But on issue after issue the modern popes since John XXIII have served as the voice of the Gospel to the world, exercising a magisterial (teaching) office with which leaders of other Churches cannot compete. Standard Roman Catholic claims for the papal office — that Christ founded his Church on Peter, that Peter was the first pope, that Peter continues to speak in the popes, as the Council of Chalcedon affirmed — remain difficult for Protestants to accept. The dogma of papal infallibility requires a lot of theological spin to bring it into the orbit of dialogue. The claim of universal jurisdiction is equally problematic for all non-Roman Churches. But in his remarkable 1995 encyclical, *Ut Unum Sint (That They May All Be One)*, Pope John Paul II insisted that "the Bishop of Rome must ensure the communion of all the Churches" and must therefore be "the first servant of unity" (94). He recognized the obstacle that the papal primacy erects for Christian unity, and invited the Orthodox and Protestants "to seek — together, of course — the forms in which this ministry may accomplish a service of love recognized by all concerned" (95).

This is an invitation too important to turn down. Can the papal office serve the cause of Christian unity rather than be a major barrier

---

45. Augsburg Confession, 14; *The Book of Concord,* p. 36.
46. See Frank C. Senn, "A Magisterium for Lutherans," *Lutheran Forum* 40, no. 2 (2006): 50-57.

to it?[47] Lutherans have a minority report that opens the door to recognizing the service that the papal office can render to Christian unity, and that may prepare the way to possible reunion. In the Smalcald Articles, Luther rejected papal leadership of a proposed ecumenical council and even called the pope the Antichrist since he will not permit Christians to be saved except by his own power, which is neither established nor commanded by God. Philipp Melanchthon, however, in a codicil to the Articles took exception to Luther's vehemence and added after his signature, "concerning the pope I hold that, if he would allow the Gospel, we, too, may concede to him that superiority over the bishops which he possesses by human right, making this concession for the sake of peace and general unity among Christians who are now under him or who may be in the future."[48]

Building on Melanchthon's codicil, the Common Statement in the Lutheran–Roman Catholic Dialogue, *Papal Primacy and the Universal Church,* provides a functional view of the papal office. It states, "This Petrine function of the ministry serves to promote or preserve the oneness of the Church by symbolizing unity, and by facilitating communication, mutual assistance or correction, and collaboration in the Church's mission."[49] I second David Yeago's motion that we should move toward consideration of what the role of a universal pastor might entail rather than tackle head-on such issues as papal infallibility and primacy.[50] It might be possible to ease into those more difficult issues after positive experience of papal leadership.

V. Establishing an Evangelical Catholic Identity in the Parish

Reunion of Lutherans and Roman Catholics seems a long way off, perhaps longer than when Carl Braaten wrote about "Rome, Reformation, and Reunion" in the mid-1960s. Successes in ecumenical dialogue, such

47. See Carl E. Braaten and Robert W. Jenson, eds., *Church Unity and the Papal Office: An Ecumenical Dialogue on John Paul II's Encyclical Ut Unum Sint* (Grand Rapids, MI: Eerdmans, 2001).

48. *The Book of Concord,* pp. 316f.

49. *Lutherans and Catholics in Dialogue V: Papal Primacy and the Universal Church,* ed. Paul C. Empie and T. Austin Murphy (Minneapolis: Augsburg, 1974), p. 11.

50. See David S. Yeago, "The Papal Office and the Burdens of History: A Lutheran View," in *Church Unity and the Papal Office,* pp. 98-123.

as the Joint Declaration on the Doctrine of Justification, are set back by policy decisions made by both Lutheran and Roman Catholic Churches. Moreover, rank-and-file Lutherans are by no means ready for reunion with the Roman Catholic Church, even if, under some model such as full communion or a Lutheran rite in communion with the Bishop of Rome, they can retain their Lutheran cultural identity.

However, if Lutheran parishes worked on securing their own evangelical catholic identity just because, as Friedrich Heiler suggested, it is a good thing to do, the way toward reunion might be paved at the grass roots level. Elements of evangelical catholic parish life would include the celebration of Word and Sacrament on Sundays and other holy days using the order of Mass provided in the historic liturgy, regular opportunities for individual confession and absolution, and use of the daily prayer offices of the Church. To these I would add giving greater attention to the communion of saints, including celebration of the faith of the saints and of the Mother of God, the Blessed Virgin Mary, by observing the commemorations listed in the church year calendar, and by remembering the faithful departed on anniversaries of their entrance into the Church Triumphant.

Finally, I would suggest that when the Bishop of Rome addresses significant theological and moral issues in encyclicals, these should be studied in Lutheran synods, districts, conferences, and parishes as diligently — maybe more diligently — as they are studied in Roman Catholic dioceses and parishes. And the Bishop of Rome should be included in the intercessions in the liturgy along with Lutheran bishops and church leaders. If we begin to act as though we were one Church, prayer might presage reality.

Evangelicals and the Present Ecumenical Moment

Timothy George

On July 29, 1928, a young evangelical pastor began his sermon on St. Paul's discourse on the Body of Christ in 1 Corinthians 12 with these words:

> There is a word that, when a Catholic hears it, kindles all his feeling of love and bliss; that stirs all the depths of his religious sensibility from dread and awe of the Last Judgment to the sweetness of God's presence; and that certainly awakens in him the feeling of home; the feeling that only a child has in relation to its mother, made up of gratitude, reverence, and devoted love; the feeling that overcomes one when, after a long absence, one returns to one's home, the home of one's childhood. And there is a word that to Protestants has the sound of something infinitely commonplace, more or less indifferent and superfluous, that does not make their heart beat faster; something with which a sense of boredom is so often associated, or which at any rate does not lend wings to our religious feelings — and yet our fate is sealed, if we are unable again to attach a new, or perhaps a very old, meaning to it. Woe to us if that word does not become important to us soon again, does not become important in our lives. Yes, the word to which I am referring is "Church" the meaning of which we propose to look at today.[1]

---

1. Cited in Eberhard Bethge, *Dietrich Bonhoeffer* (New York: Harper and Row, 1970), p. 42. An earlier version of this essay was presented at Princeton Theological Seminary in 2005 at a conference organized by the Center for Catholic and Evangelical Theology on "The Princeton Proposal for Christian Unity." I am pleased for this essay to appear in a

These words were spoken by Dietrich Bonhoeffer to a small German-speaking congregation in Barcelona, Spain. Admittedly, Bonhoeffer was an "evangelical" of a rather distinctive type, but his warning about the need for a more considered ecclesiology is as urgently important today for the worldwide family of Christian believers known as evangelicals as it was, and still is, for the wider Protestant family of faith. The fact is, evangelicals have not been particularly concerned about the church, being more preoccupied with other theological themes such as biblical revelation, religious epistemology, and apologetics. In fact, evangelicals have not merely ignored ecclesiology in the interest of these other themes, many of them have seen it as a downright hindrance to more important priorities such as evangelism, missions, and church planting. One evangelical scholar has put it like this: "We are too busy winning people to Christ to engage in something which seems to us like navel-gazing."[2] No doubt, many evangelicals would agree with the statement by missiologist J. C. Hoekendijk who once observed that "in history a keen ecclesiological interest has, almost without exception, been a sign of spiritual decadence."[3]

All the while, evangelicals are writing best-selling books about the church: Leith Anderson's *A Church for the 21st Century* and Rick Warren's *The Purpose-Driven Church* (which preceded his even more gigantic bestseller, *The Purpose-Driven Life*), to name just two.[4] Another popular book on the church, though not written by a self-professed evangelical, reflects the kind of ecclesiology found in abundance on the shelves of many Christian bookstores. Some chapter titles are: "The Church as a Helpful Service Organization," "The Church as an Insurance Policy,"

---

volume offered in honor of Carl E. Braaten. During the past fifty years Carl Braaten has modeled with fidelity and clarity what it means for a serious churchly theologian to be committed to Christian unity on behalf of the Gospel of Jesus Christ. Through his friendship and collegiality he has encouraged my own vocation as an ecumenical theologian. He has also helped to open wide the door to ecumenical engagement for many other North American Evangelicals.

2. D. A. Carson, "Evangelicals, Ecumenism and the Church," in *Evangelical Affirmations*, ed. Kenneth S. Kantzer and Carl F. H. Henry (Grand Rapids: Zondervan, 1990), p. 355.

3. J. C. Hoekendijk, "The Church in Missionary Thinking," *The International Review of Missions* 41 (1952): 325.

4. See Leith Anderson, *A Church for the 21st Century* (Minneapolis: Bethany, 1992); Rick Warren, *The Purpose-Driven Church* (Grand Rapids: Zondervan, 1995); and *The Purpose-Driven Life* (Grand Rapids: Zondervan, 2002).

"The Church Serves My Special Interests," and "The Church Rescues Me in Times of Crisis."[5] This kind of low, functionalist ecclesiology, which is more concerned with individualistic therapeutic spirituality than with churchly Christianity, was epitomized for me when I drove by an evangelical church in Kentucky with a flamboyant sign inviting people to the services with these words: "The Church that asks nothing of you"! This seems a long way from the church of the apostles and martyrs which asked everything of you!

Within the past twenty years, the dearth of serious evangelical reflection on the church has begun to change, and this is very good news indeed. Still, no work comparable to the classic studies of Yves Congar, Avery Dulles, Henri de Lubac, G. C. Berkouwer, or Georges Florovsky can be cited among evangelicals in North America. We have only begun to give serious systematic reflection to the theme "What makes the church one?" Still, evangelicals, including Pentecostals, have been invited to participate in consultations, symposia, and dialogues committed to the quest for Christian unity. Evangelicals have something to contribute, as well as a great deal to learn, from this kind of ecumenical encounter. If nothing else, such an experience can be an antidote to the two besetting diseases of contemporary evangelicalism: amnesia — we have forgotten who we are; and myopia — whoever we are, we are glad we are not like "them"! With this in mind, this essay will pursue a three-fold strategy: first, to examine what evangelicals can bring to the question "What makes the church one?" by suggesting a broader than usual definition of the evangelical church; then, by looking at some of the reasons why evangelicals have found participation in ecumenical ventures problematic; and finally, to suggest, at least tentatively, what a faithful evangelical response to the classic vision for Christian unity articulated at New Delhi in 1961 might look like today.

Four Streams of Evangelical Faith

Wolfhart Pannenberg once predicted that evangelicals, along with Roman Catholics and Orthodox believers, would constitute one of the three ascendant, most resilient forces within world Christianity as it en-

5. Barbara Brown Zikmund, *Discovering the Church* (Philadelphia: Westminster, 1983).

tered the third millennium.[6] But who are these evangelicals? Taxonomies and definitions abound, including this one drawn largely from an overview article by Alister McGrath: Evangelicals are a worldwide fellowship of Bible-believing Christians whose faith and life emphasize four things: (1) the authority and sufficiency of Holy Scripture, the only normative rule of faith and practice for all true believers; (2) the uniqueness of redemption through the death of Christ upon the cross, the benefits of which are imputed to believers who are justified by faith alone; (3) the necessity of personal conversion, wrought by the Holy Spirit through personal repentance and faith and issuing in a life of obedience and growth in Christ; and (4) the priority and urgency of evangelism and missions in fulfillment of the Great Commission of Christ himself.[7]

It is possible, of course, to define evangelicalism in other ways as well: sociologically, demographically, or even anecdotally, as in Dr. Bob Jones, Sr.'s famous quip that an evangelical is a person who says to a liberal, "I'll call you a Christian if you'll call me a scholar!" Jerry Falwell once said that a fundamentalist is just an evangelical who is mad at somebody! It is relatively easy to say who a Roman Catholic is: A Roman Catholic is a person who belongs to a church whose bishop is in communion with the bishop of Rome. Likewise, Orthodox believers can be fairly easily recognized by certain creedal commitments and liturgical practices, as well as by national and ethnic loyalties.

But evangelicalism is a movement of bewildering diversity, made up of congregations, denominations, and parachurch movements whose shared identity is not tied to a particular view of church polity or ministerial orders. Evangelicalism has been fed by many diverse rivulets and tributaries, including Puritanism, Pietism, and, most vigorously in the last hundred years, Pentecostalism. For our present purposes, how-

6. For further elaboration of this theme, see Timothy George, "The Unity of the Faith: Evangelicalism and 'Mere Christianity'," *Touchstone* 16 (2003): 8-66. Material in this section was originally presented at the conference "Christian Unity and the Divisions We Must Sustain," in November 2001 at the University of Saint Mary of the Lake in Mundelein, Illinois.

7. Alister McGrath, *The Blackwell Encyclopedia of Modern Christian Thought* (Cambridge: Blackwell, 1993), p. 183. J. I. Packer has given a more expansive list of Evangelical essentials in seven points. See his "Crosscurrents among Evangelicals," in *Evangelicals and Catholics Together: Toward a Common Mission,* ed. Charles Colson and Richard John Neuhaus (Dallas: Word Publishing, 1995), pp. 150-152. For a trenchant analysis and lament of "the changing face of Western Evangelicalism," see D. A. Carson, *The Gagging of God: Christianity Confronts Pluralism* (Grand Rapids: Zondervan, 1996).

ever, I would like to propose a new definition: Evangelicalism is a renewal movement within historic Christian orthodoxy, a movement that has been shaped diachronically by four historical complexes or "moments," which continue to shape evangelical theology and identity today.

1. The Trinitarian and Christological Consensus of the Early Church

Evangelicals accept without hesitation what Anglican theologians used to refer to (perhaps some of them still do) as the *consensus quinque-saecularis*. That is to say, we worship and adore the one and only and true and living God who has forever known himself as the Father, the Son, and the Holy Spirit. We further believe that this triune God of love and holiness became incarnate in Jesus of Nazareth, the Son of Man of the four canonical Gospels. We confess that Jesus Christ is the one and only Lord of heaven and earth. Jesus Christ is the only begotten Son of God, Light from Light, true God from true God. This one, we say, who is the Lord of the Church was miraculously conceived by the Holy Spirit and born of the Blessed Virgin Mary. He lived a sinless life, died a sacrificial and substitutionary death on the cross, was buried, is risen, ascended, and he is coming again as the King and Judge of all who are, ever were, or ever shall be. Evangelicals, no less than Roman Catholics and Orthodox believers, thus stand in fundamental continuity with the 318 fathers of Nicea, the 150 fathers of the First Council of Constantinople, and the canons of Ephesus (431), including the affirmation of Mary as Theotokos and the condemnation of Pelagianism, as well as the Definition of Chalcedon (451).

From time to time evangelicals have explicitly stated their agreement with the historic creeds of the church. For example, there is an English Baptist confession, known as "The Orthodox Creed," published in 1679 — and an Arminian one at that — which reproduced the Apostles', Nicene, and Athanasian Creeds *in toto* commending all three as worthy to be thoroughly

> received and believed . . . for they may be proved by most undoubted authority of Holy Scripture and are necessary to be understood of all Christians; and to be instructed in the knowledge of them by the ministers of Christ, according to the analogy of faith,

recorded in sacred Scriptures, upon which these creeds are grounded and catechistically opened and expounded in all Christian families, for the edification of young and old which might be a means to prevent heresy in doctrine and practice. These creeds contain all things in a brief manner that are necessary to be known, fundamentally, in order to our salvation.[8]

So much for the hypothesis that Baptists are not a creedal people!

More recently, at the opening meeting of the Baptist World Alliance in London in 1905, Dr. Alexander Maclaren asked the entire assembly to rise and confess in unison the Apostles' Creed, as a way of expressing Baptist solidarity with the orthodox Christian faith, and this same affirmation was repeated in 2005 in Birmingham, England at the centennial celebration of the Alliance's founding. In the year 2000, some 12,000 evangelical Christians from 210 countries around the world, more than belonged to the United Nations at the time, gathered in Amsterdam at the invitation of Dr. Billy Graham to pray, reflect, and renew their commitment to world evangelization. Out of this assembly emerged "The Amsterdam Declaration" which again echoes the language of the Trinitarian faith of the church. "God in his own being is a community of three co-equal and co-eternal persons, who are revealed to us in the Bible as the Father, the Son, and the Holy Spirit. Together they are involved in an unvarying cooperative pattern in all God's relationships to and within this world. God is the Lord of history, where he blesses his own people, overcomes and judges human and angelic rebels against his rule, and will finally renew the whole created order."[9]

2. The Protestant Reformation

Evangelicals are also Reformational Christians in that we affirm both the formal and material principles of the Protestant Reformers. The formal principle, sometimes referred to by the slogan *sola scriptura,* was set forth with clarity by Martin Luther is his famous debate with Johannes Eck at Leipzig in 1519 and reiterated in classic form ten years

8. Timothy and Denise George, eds., *Baptist Confessions, Covenants, and Catechisms* (Nashville: Broadman and Holman, 1996).

9. Amsterdam Declaration, see Appendix C in J. I. Packer and Thomas C. Oden, *One Faith: The Evangelical Consensus* (Downers Grove, IL: Intervarsity Press, 2004), p. 196.

later at the Second Diet of Speyer which also gave us the word "Protestant," understood not merely in the sense of "protest against" but also "witnesses on behalf of" *(pro-testantes)*.

> We are determined by God's grace and aid to abide by God's Word alone, the holy Gospel contained in the biblical books of the Old and New Testaments. This word alone should be preached, and nothing that is contrary to it. It is the only Truth. It is the sure rule of all Christian doctrine and conduct. It can never fail us or deceive us. Who so builds and abides on this foundation shall stand against all the gates of hell, while all merely human additions and vanities set up against it must fall before the presence of God.[10]

As I have argued elsewhere, neither Luther nor any other of the mainline Reformers, read Scripture in isolation from the community of faith.[11] For them, *sola scriptura* did not mean *nuda scriptura!* Overwhelmingly, the Reformers saw themselves as part of the ongoing Catholic tradition, indeed as the legitimate bearers of it. They read the Bible in dialogue with the exegetical tradition of the church. That is to say, the Scriptures were seen as the book given to the church, gathered and guided by the Holy Spirit. While the Reformers could never accept what the Council of Trent seemed to say (though some recent Catholic theologians have challenged this interpretation), namely, that Scripture and Tradition were two separate and equable sources of divine revelation, or as Vatican II would later say in a somewhat softened form, "Both sacred tradition and sacred Scripture are to be accepted and venerated with the same sense of loyalty and reverence" (DV 9), still the Reformers did believe in the coinherence of Scripture and Tradition. The Evangelicals and Catholics Together statement, "Your Word Is Truth," attempts to address this historically divisive issue in a way that is both faithful to the formal principle of the Reformation and yet recognizes a proper evangelical awareness of tradition:

> Together we affirm that Scripture is the divinely inspired and uniquely authoritative written revelation of God; as such it is normative for the teaching and life of the church. And we also affirm

10. On the Diet of Speyer, see E. G. Léonard, *A History of Protestantism* (Indianapolis: Bobbs-Merrill Co., 1968), pp. 122-28.
11. See Timothy George, "An Evangelical Reflection on Scripture and Tradition," *Pro Ecclesia* 9 (2000): 184-207.

that Tradition, rightly understood, is the faithful transmission of the truth of the Gospel from generation to generation through the power of the Holy Spirit. As Evangelicals and Catholics fully committed to our respective heritages, we affirm together the co-inherence of Scripture and Tradition: Tradition is not a second source of revelation alongside the Bible but must ever be corrected and informed by it, and Scripture itself is not understood in a vacuum apart from the historical existence and life of the community of faith. Faithful believers in every generation live by the memories and hopes of the *actus tradendi* of the Holy Spirit: This is true whenever and wherever the Word of God is faithfully translated, sincerely believed, and truly preached.[12]

Evangelicals also embrace justification by faith alone as the logical and necessary consequence of the ecumenical orthodoxy affirmed by Catholics and Protestants alike. Philipp Melanchthon cited references to *sola fides* in patristic sources while others claimed to find the essence, if not the exact wording, of the Reformation doctrine of justification in the liturgy of the church and the prayers of the saints, especially those of Bernard of Clairvaux, a favorite writer of both Luther and Calvin. In the early twentieth century, the Lutheran New Testament theologian, Adolf Schlatter, claimed that Jesus himself was the creator of the formula *sola fides,* as it was he who said "Only believe"![13] While Schlatter's exegesis here may be debatable, there is no doubt that the first Protestants saw themselves in doctrinal continuity with the early church when they set forth the material principle of the Reformation. Jaroslav Pelikan has summarized well the essence of their argument:

> If the Holy Trinity was as holy as the Trinitarian dogma taught; if original sin was as virulent as the Augustinian tradition said it was; and if Christ was as necessary as the Christological dogma implied — then the only way to treat justification in a manner faithful to the best of Catholic tradition was to teach justification by faith.[14]

---

12. The full statement, along with several related essays, have been collected in Charles Colson and Richard John Neuhaus, eds., *Your Word Is Truth: A Project of Evangelicals and Catholics Together* (Grand Rapids: Eerdmans, 2002), p. 5.

13. Adolf Schlatter, *Der Glaube im Neuen Testament* (Stuttgart: Calver Verlag, 1896 or 1963 [5th ed.]), p. 103.

14. Jaroslav Pelikan, *Obedient Rebels* (New York: Harper and Row, 1964), pp. 50-51.

3. Evangelical Awakenings

While the patristic and Reformational roots of evangelicalism are more often assumed than explicitly acknowledged, the spiritual awakenings of the eighteenth and nineteenth centuries produced many of the forms and modalities of evangelicalism we still recognize today. The Awakenings were international, transatlantic movements of ecclesial and spiritual renewal embracing pietism in Germany, Methodism in Great Britain, and revivalism in the American colonies. Only in the light of these various awakenings can we understand what historian Timothy L. Smith called "the kaleidoscopic diversity of our histories, our organizational structures, and our doctrinal emphases."[15]

Not only did the Awakenings bring new life into some of the older denominational structures producing, for example, New Light Congregationalists, New Side Presbyterians, and New Connection Baptists, it also produced a variety of brand new movements including Adventist, Holiness, Restorationist, and Pentecostal churches. Looking back from the perspective of two centuries later, we can see that the Awakenings decisively shaped the future of evangelicalism in three important ways.

First, a new kind of interdenominational cooperation arose based on a distinctively evangelical version of mere Christianity. Without ever denying the doctrinal fundaments of the wider catholic and Reformational heritage (except in some bizarre cases as when a few Baptists became universalists), evangelicals put primary emphasis on the preaching of the Gospel and the call to personal conversion. In other words, they emphasized the inward work of the Holy Spirit to bring about the new birth and to transform the regenerate into the likeness of Christ. They taught the necessity of personal repentance and faith in Christ, and they understood the church as the universal Body of Christ which incorporates all true believers, and all of its members as called to ministry — "the priesthood of all believers."

This emphasis led to the blurring of old denominational alignments and even some theological distinctives. Two quotations from the two leading lights of this period, John Wesley and George Whitefield, illustrate this point. They disagreed sharply with one another on the

15. See Timothy L. Smith, "An Historical Perspective on Evangelicalism and Ecumenism," *Mid-Stream* 22 (July–Oct. 1983): 308-25.

controverted doctrine of predestination, Wesley following a more Arminian approach and Whitefield adhering to the Calvinist understanding. Despite this difference, the two evangelists remained friends and worked together in their revival efforts. On one occasion, Wesley said this:

> I . . . refuse to be distinguished from other men by any but the common principles of Christianity. . . . I renounce and detest all other marks of distinction. But from real Christians, of whatever denomination, I earnestly desire not to be distinguished at all . . . dost thou love and fear God? It is enough! I give thee the right hand of fellowship.[16]

On another occasion, Whitefield, while preaching from a balcony in Philadelphia, looked up to heaven and cried out these words:

> Father Abraham, whom have you in heaven? Any Episcopalians? No! Any Presbyterians? No! Any Independents or Methodists? No, No, No! Whom have you there? We don't know those names here. All who are here are Christians. . . . Oh, is this the case? Then God help us to forget party names and to become Christians in deed and truth.[17]

This kind of mere Christian appeal spawned a host of interdenominational ministries including orphanages, Bible societies, publication boards, colleges and academies and, above all, an evangelical missionary movement of global proportions.

The world Protestant missionary movement began humbly enough when an English Baptist shoemaker turned small-town pastor, William Carey, encouraged his fellow Calvinistic Baptists to establish a society for "the propagation of the Gospel among the heathens." By 1793 Carey had arrived in India to begin his remarkable career which included the planting of churches, the building of schools, the organization of an agricultural society, the establishment of India's first newspaper, and the translation of the Scriptures into some forty languages and dialects. Carey was a Baptist, indeed a rather strict one, but from

16. See Winthrup S. Hudson, *American Protestantism* (Chicago: University of Chicago Press, 1961), p. 33.

17. Hudson, *American Protestantism*, p. 33.

the beginning of his mission work in India, he saw the importance of working closely with non-Baptist evangelicals including the Anglican missionary Henry Martyn. The school he established at Serampore was interdenominational, although all professors were required to embrace the essential evangelical doctrines such as the deity of Christ and his substitutionary atonement. And, in what has been called the "most startling missionary proposal of all time," he called for a coordinated strategy for world evangelization:

> Would it not be possible to have a general association of all denominations of Christians, from the four quarters of the world, held once in about ten years? I earnestly recommend this plan, let the first meetings be in the year 1810, or 1812 at the furthest. I have no doubt but that it would be attended with many important effects.[18]

Precisely one hundred years after Carey had proposed such a gathering, the first international mission conference convened in Edinburgh in 1910.

The Awakenings also gave rise to numerous evangelical movements for social reform including, in England, a call for the end of the slave trade, and, on this side of the Atlantic, the abolition of slavery itself. In recent years, evangelicals have joined forces with Roman Catholics and other persons of faith to uphold the sanctity of human life and oppose the culture of death. In doing so, they stand in a worthy evangelical lineage of those who from Carey onward have prayed and worked for justice and peace in an admittedly fallen and even desperately lost world.

4. The Fundamentalist-Modernist Controversy

It is impossible to understand contemporary evangelicalism, especially in North America, without reference to the seismic divide between Fundamentalists and Modernists which took place in the first three decades of the twentieth century. By my reading, the key leader of post-Fundamentalist evangelicalism par excellence was Harold John

---

18. Letter of William Carey to Andrew Fuller, 15 May 1806. Cited in Timothy George, *Faithful Witness: The Life and Mission of William Carey* (Birmingham: New Hope Press, 1991), p. 163.

Ockenga. It is hardly an exaggeration to say that Ockenga single-handedly created evangelicalism. It was he who founded the National Association of Evangelicals in 1942, who persuaded evangelist Charles Fuller to found Fuller Theological Seminary and then served as its first president (albeit in absentia much of the time), who promoted Billy Graham and encouraged him and his father-in-law, L. Nelson Bell, to found *Christianity Today* as a counter-voice to the *Christian Century,* and who fought tirelessly to position conservative Protestant Christians in North America over against compromising liberalism on the one hand and separatistic Fundamentalism on the other. At the heart of Ockenga's agenda was a commitment to mere Christianity: He wanted to affirm the classic fundamentals of the faith while transcending the intellectual ghettoization and cultural disengagement that had be-fallen much of conservative Protestantism in the decades between J. Gresham Machen and Carl F. H. Henry.

The original motto for the National Association of Evangelicals was "cooperation without compromise." From time to time evangelicals have debated among themselves as to whether or not it is possible to be faithful to the Gospel, faithful to the Fundamentals, and still practice the kind of cooperation Ockenga called for and Billy Graham has modeled. The late James Montgomery Boice was one of the foot soldiers in that effort and shortly before his death he expressed to me his sense of disillusionment of a dream gone awry. Iain Murray has made a similar case with reference to British evangelicalism, sharply criticizing Billy Graham, John Stott, and J. I. Packer.[19] Although he does not put it this way, Iain Murray might agree with those who say that it is precisely the evangelical preoccupation with "mere Christianity" that has led to a compromise of the Gospel and a kind of inclusivism not far distant from the attenuated, liberal Christianity from which true evangelicals must always distance themselves. While the dust from the Fundamentalist-Modernist disputes has receded into history, the lingering effects of those earlier debates continue to fuel evangelical suspicions about ecumenical initiatives.[20]

19. Iain Murray, *Evangelicalism Divided: A Record of Crucial Change in the Years 1950-2000* (Edinburgh; Carlisle, PA: Banner of Truth, 2000).

20. See the discussion in Timothy George, ed., *Pilgrims on the Sawdust Trail: Evangelical Ecumenism and the Quest for Christian Identity* (Grand Rapids: Baker Academic, 2004).

Timothy George

Evangelicals at the Ecumenical Table

Before turning to the New Delhi statement on the church's unity, it will be helpful to say a brief word about evangelical engagements with ecumenical discussions. If evangelicalism is best understood as a renewal movement within historic Christian orthodoxy, it was also clearly a renewal movement set *over against* some other so-called Christian tradition or emphasis. To be a Protestant meant *not* to be a Roman Catholic. To be a Methodist, or "enthusiast," to use Ronald Knox's pejorative term, was to oppose deism, formalism, and latitudinarianism. To be a Baptist meant not to be anything else: as frontier Baptist preachers frequently reminded their congregations, the New Testament does not speak of John the Presbyterian, or John the Methodist, but John the Baptist! Modern American evangelicalism was forged against both separatist fundamentalism on the right and accommodating liberalism on the left. Thus what might be called the contrarian character of the evangelical ethos has made evangelicals more than a little wary of entangling alliances and ecumenical initiatives which threatened to undermine traditional boundaries and definitions.

It would be a mistake, of course, to imagine that evangelicals have inhabited a *cordon sanitaire* uncontaminated by contact with the ecumenical world. Indeed, as we have seen, it was an evangelical missionary pioneer, William Carey, who first envisioned the kind of ecumenical missionary conference that was actually held at Edinburgh in 1910. "The evangelization of the world in this generation" was the motto of the Student Volunteer Movement, one of several of para-ecclesiastical streams which contributed to the earliest structures of the modern ecumenical movement. The World Student Christian Federation was another such organization, and its motto was taken directly from John 17:21: "That they all may be one." As Geoffrey Wainwright has noted, in one direction unity among Christians appeared as an aid, even a requirement, for evangelistic mission, while, in the other direction, the very spread of the faith throughout the world constituted an invitation, which indeed came to be understood as a mandate, to seek universal Christian unity.[21] Evangel-

21. Geoffrey Wainwright, "The Global Structures of Ecumenism," in *The Ecumenical Future: Background Papers for* In One Body through the Cross: *The Princeton Proposal for Christian Unity,* ed. Carl E. Braaten and Robert W. Jenson (Grand Rapids: Eerdmans, 2004), pp. 11-28.

ical leaders were in the thick of this dynamic movement which to a great extent both reflected and contributed to the exuberant optimism that pervaded the western world before the guns of August 1914 forever shattered the myth of inevitable progress and innate benevolence.

While evangelicals were not much involved in the developing ecumenical structures between the two world wars, it is worth noting that the Southern Baptist Convention did send a delegation to the 1937 World Conference on Faith and Order at Edinburgh. However, numerous evangelical groups worldwide did participate in the International Missionary Council which had been founded in 1921 and which seemed more congruent with evangelical concerns than either the movements for Life and Work or Faith and Order. Indeed, one of the concerns voiced by Max Warren and Lesslie Newbigin about the integration of the IMC into the World Council of Churches in 1961 was that this merger could result in the marginalizing of the missionary dimension within the WCC and the further alienation of evangelicals from the entire ecumenical movement. While both of these leaders supported this merger, Newbigin with more enthusiasm than Warren at the time, they were not silent about their apprehensions. In the case of Newbigin, these misgivings grew stronger and more vocal in subsequent years. In his typically blunt way of putting things, Newbigin declared that the WCC was in danger of becoming "a mere global sectarianism" without a strong focus on world missionary and evangelistic initiatives.[22]

To move from the early sixties to the mid-seventies is to witness the emergence of a maturing, self-conscious world evangelical movement which came to be seen in some sense as a counter-movement to what we may now begin to call mainline Protestant ecumenism. Building on the momentum and success of the 1966 World Congress on Evangelism, with Dr. Billy Graham as its honorary chairman, some 2,700 people from around the globe converged on Lausanne, Switzerland in July 1974 for the International Congress on World Evangelization. Lausanne was not chosen by accident. This beautiful city had been the scene of the first World Conference on Faith and Order in 1927 and was just across Lake Leman from the WCC base in Geneva. It

---

22. David J. Bosch, "'Ecumenicals' and 'Evangelicals': A Growing Relationship?" *Ecumenical Review* 40 (1998): 461. See the helpful analysis of M. E. Brinkman, *Progress in Unity? Fifty Years of Theology Within the World Council of Churches, 1945-1995* (Louvain: Peeters Press, 1995), pp. 145-66.

was natural that many should think of the Lausanne Congress as an embryonic global organization set up in opposition to the WCC. But this scenario was never seriously considered, not least because some sixty percent of the delegates who came to Lausanne were members of churches represented in the WCC! Lausanne was a movement, not a church, nor even a council of churches. The real counterpart to the WCC in terms of churchly structures was on the far-right fringe of the Protestant movement, the International Council of Christian Churches led by the indomitable Carl McIntyre. And McIntyre was an equal-opportunity picketer. He protested as vigorously against Lausanne and the NAE as he ever did against the WCC.

Still, the lines were drawn rather firmly in the sand by the Lausanne Congress. This became evident in the following year when the premiere statesmen of the Lausanne movement, Dr. John R. W. Stott, gave a public response to a plenary address presented by Bishop Mortimer Arias at the Fifth Assembly of the World Council of Churches in Nairobi (November 27, 1975). While affirming Bishop Arias's plea for evangelism as an essential, primary, normal, permanent, and costly task of the churches, Stott evoked the memory of John Mott who at Edinburgh in 1910 had estimated the number of unevangelized people in the world as about one thousand million and referred to this fact as a "longstanding reproach to the church." "I wonder what he would say if he were here today?" asked Stott.[23] He then listed five concerns which seemed to go to the heart of the growing evangelical-ecumenical divide.

First, a recognition of the lostness of human beings: "This assembly is listening with great sensitivity to the cry of the oppressed, and rightly so," Stott noted. "But are we also listening to the cry of the lost?" He also quoted Bishop Stephen Neill: "The primary factor in humanization is the knowledge of God revealed in Jesus Christ. No man is fully human until he has come to know God and himself in the searchlight of Jesus Christ."

Stott's second and third points were explicitly doctrinal: confidence in the Gospel of God and conviction about the uniqueness of Christ. The former is being undermined, Stott claimed, by "the church's loss of confidence in the truth, the relevance and the power of

---

23. John Stott, "Response to Bishop Mortimer Arias," *International Review of Mission* 65 (1976): 30-34.

the Gospel." To affirm the sole sufficiency of Jesus Christ as the only way of salvation for all persons everywhere, he argued, is not to deny that there is also truth in other religions for we affirm general revelation and common grace. But it is to oppose theologies of uncritical pluralism and syncretism against which Visser 't Hooft had warned so presciently in his 1963 book, *No Other Name: The Choice Between Syncretism and Christian Universalism.*

Stott next turned to the sense of urgency about evangelism. He applauded Bishop Arias for calling for a "holistic approach" to mission and evangelism but wondered whether this rhetoric was matched by the reality of WCC programs. "If justice means the securing of people's rights, is not one of their most fundamental rights the right to hear the Gospel?" And, finally, Stott called for a renewed personal experience of Jesus Christ on the part of both ecumenical leaders and evangelicals.

While there was a clear polemical edge to Stott's comments at Nairobi, he also called for evangelical repentance and supported the kind of irenic bridge building called for by Arthur Glasser, another prominent evangelical voice at the time:

> I feel that as an evangelical I should not speak darkly of ecumenical plots, of conspiracies to sow seeds of doubt, stab at true faith, and sabotage all those who accept the Bible as the Word of God. I should be willing to initiate efforts to bridge these gulfs that separate evangelicals from the conciliar movement. I should seek to listen and learn as well as bear witness and serve.[24]

It was this spirit, rather than more raucous tones, which characterized the Lausanne Covenant. One is struck by the prominence given to the church in this document:

> We need to break out of our ecclesiastical ghettos and permeate non-Christian society. . . . World evangelization requires the whole church to take the whole Gospel to the whole world. The church is at the very center of God's cosmic purpose and is his appointed means of spreading the Gospel. But a church which preaches the cross must itself be marked by the cross. . . . We affirm that the church's visible unity in truth is God's purpose. Evangelism also

24. Arthur Glasser, cited in David J. Bosch, "'Ecumenicals' and 'Evangelicals': A Growing Relationship?" *Ecumenical Review* 40 (1998): 461.

summons us to unity, because our oneness strengthens our witness, just as our disunity undermines our gospel of reconciliation. We pledge ourselves to seek a deeper unity in truth, worship, holiness, and mission.[25]

These themes were echoed and further expanded at a second International Congress on World Evangelization held in Manila in 1989. More recently, the Amsterdam Declaration (2000) defined the church as "the people of God, the Body and the Bride of Christ, the temple of the Holy Spirit. The one, universal church is a transnational, transcultural, transdenominational and multi-ethnic family, the household of faith." In the widest sense, "The church includes all redeemed of all the ages, being the one Body of Christ extended throughout time as well as space. Here in the world, the church becomes visible in all local congregations that meet to do together the things that according to scripture, the church does. Christ is the head of the church. Everyone who is personally united to Christ by faith belongs to his body and by the spirit is united with every other true believer in Jesus." The Amsterdam Declaration also contains a separate article on Christian unity which acknowledges that one of the great hindrances to evangelism worldwide is the lack of unity among Christ's people, a condition made worse when Christians compete and fight with one another rather than seeking together the mind of Christ. This article concludes with a commitment: "We pledge ourselves to pray and work for unity and truth among all true believers in Jesus and to cooperate as fully as possible in evangelism with other brothers and sisters in Christ so that the whole church may take the whole gospel to the whole world."[26]

Two additional developments need to be mentioned in order to round out the picture, one quite discouraging, the other much more promising. In 1995 Dr. Konrad Raiser, then secretary-general of the World Council of Churches, spoke to the Joint Working Group between the Roman Catholic Church and the World Council of Churches. Speaking at a meeting in Rome, he called for an "urgent reordering of the ecumenical agenda away from old doctrinal disputes and unresolvable arguments of the past toward more urgent contemporary issues such as justice, peace, and concern for the environment."

25. J. I. Packer and Thomas C. Oden, *One Faith: The Evangelical Consensus* (Downers Grove, Ill.: InterVarsity Press, 2004), p. 179.

26. Packer and Oden, *One Faith*, pp. 196-208.

This so-called paradigm shift in ecumenical discourse has had a chilling effect not only on evangelical-ecumenical relations but also within other sectors of the world Christian community. A significant realignment could be seen taking place at the Seventh Assembly of the WCC at Canberra in 1991 as both Orthodox and evangelical participants responded to issues regarding the relationship of gospel and culture. In rather different language both of these constituent groups, which might be seen to occupy polar opposites within the *oikumenē*, expressed their disquiet and deep concern over what appeared to be the loss of theological substance and Christocentric commitment. The Orthodox declared:

> We must guard against a tendency to substitute a 'private' spirit, the spirit of the world or other spirits for the Holy Spirit who precedes from the Father and rests in the Son. Our tradition is rich in respect for local and national cultures, but we find it impossible to invoke the spirits of 'earth, air, water and sea creatures.' Pneumatology is inseparable from Christology or from the doctrine of the Holy Trinity confessed by the church on the basis of divine revelation.[27]

The evangelical participants also called for the development of "criteria for and limits to theological diversity," considering there to be "insufficient clarity regarding the relationship between the confession of the Lord Jesus Christ as God and Savior according to scripture, the person and work of the Holy Spirit, and legitimate concerns which are part of the WCC agenda."[28] If a new conference on Faith and Order in North America is to succeed on its fourfold aim of issuing a common declaration of Christian truth, helping the churches engage in mission together, preparing a new generation of church leaders, and helping bring new partners into the movement toward Christian unity, then the witness of dissent offered boldly by the Orthodox believers at Canberra, and somewhat more tentatively by the evangelicals there, must be taken into account.

Much more promising is the renewed contact and serious engage-

27. "Reflections of Orthodox Participants" in *Signs of the Spirit: Official Report Seventh Assembly,* ed. Michael Kinnamon (Geneva: WCC Publications, 1991), p. 281.
28. "Evangelical Perspectives from Canberra" in *Signs of the Spirit: Official Report Seventh Assembly,* ed. Michael Kinnamon (Geneva: WCC Publications, 1991), p. 282.

ment between evangelicals and Roman Catholics. In 1928, the year of
Bonhoeffer's sermon in Barcelona, Pope Pius XI issued his encyclical
Mortalium animos in which he forbade Catholic theologians to partici-
pate in ecumenical discussions and stated that "the unity of Christians
can come about only by furthering the return to the one true church of
Christ of those who are separated from it."[29] If this papal encyclical by
Pius XI marks one bookend in this development, then surely *Ut Unum
Sint* (That All May Be One), the twelfth encyclical released by Pope John
Paul II, represents the other end. Building on the earlier conciliar documents *Lumen Gentium* and *Unitatis Redintegratio,* this document underscores the importance of interconfessional dialogue as well as patterns
of practical cooperation in the ongoing quest for Christian unity.
Christians belonging to the churches of the Reformation, no less than
believers in the East, can rejoice that *Ut Unum Sint* gives more prominence to the priority of prayer than to the primacy of Peter. Interlaced
throughout *Ut Unum Sint* is this constant theme reiterated by Pope
John Paul II:

> Love for the truth is the deepest dimension of any authentic quest
> for full communion between Christians. The unity willed by God
> can be attained only by the adherence of all to the content of re-
> vealed faith in its entirety in matters of faith; compromise is in con-
> tradiction with God, who is truth. In the body of Christ, the Way,
> and the Truth, and the Life, who could consider legitimate a recon-
> ciliation brought about at the expense of truth?[30]

During the Reformation the great humanist scholar Erasmus believed that the way to peace in the church was to define the smallest
number of doctrines possible, and to hold them as lightly as one could.
Over against Erasmus, Luther declared that there could be no Christianity without assertions. By assertions he meant "a constant adhering, affirming, confessing, maintaining, and invincible persevering . . .
in those things which have been divinely transmitted to us in the sacred writings."[31] On this score, if not indeed in all particulars, faithful

29. Pius XI, "Mortalium Animos," *The Papal Encyclicals 1903-1939,* ed. Claudia
Carlen (Ann Arbor: Pierian Press, 1990), pp. 313-19.
30. John Paul II, *Ut Unum Sint,* 1995.
31. *Luther and Erasmus: Free Will and Salvation,* ed. E. G. Rupp and P. S. Watson
(Philadelphia: Westminster Press, 1969), p. 105.

Roman Catholics, consistent evangelicals, and Orthodox believers alike are the spiritual heirs of Luther, not Erasmus.

Among the various bilaterals and other initiatives that have taken place over the past two decades, four discussions between Roman Catholics and evangelicals are particularly significant. The first is ERCDOM, the Evangelical–Roman Catholic Dialogue on Mission, carried out between 1977 and 1984. To some extent, this dialogue was prompted by the Lausanne Conference and John Stott was a principal participant in it. Perhaps the most important fact about this dialogue was its role in identifying issues which required further discussion, thus providing a basis on which further dialogue could be undertaken. The second, and even more remarkable, exchange, has taken place between Roman Catholics and Pentecostals. The full reports from the Pentecostal–Roman Catholic Dialogue (1976, 1982, 1989, 1997) are indeed remarkable both for their durability and their substance. In particular, the document "Evangelicalization, Proselytism, and Common Witness," issued in 1997, constitutes something of a breakthrough on the controverted themes of proselytism, evangelism, and religious liberty.[32] The third project is the ongoing discussions of Evangelicals and Catholics Together, convened by Richard John Neuhaus and Charles Colson. The ECT project began in 1992 with a conference occasioned by growing and often violent conflicts between Catholics and evangelical Protestants in Latin America. The initial ECT statement, "Evangelicals and Catholics Together: The Christian Mission in the Third Millennium," was released in March 1994.[33] The signers of the statement referred to one another as "brothers and sisters in Christ," and pledged to support one another both in the task of evangelization and the need to confront the pressing moral and cultural threats of the time. Despite an initial flurry of controversy, largely from a sector within the evangelical community, the ECT collaborators have continued their work, producing in fifteen years six additional joint statements on issues of traditional disagreement between evangelical Protestants and Roman Catholics, including salvation/justi-

32. See "Evangelization, Proselytism and Common Witness," the report from the fourth phase of the International Dialogue 1990-1997 between the Roman Catholic Church and some Classical Pentecostal Churches and Leaders posted on-line in *Cyberjournal for Pentecostal-Charismatic Research* at http://www.pctii.org/cyberj/cyberj4/rcpent97.html. Accessed on 07.21.2010.

33. See Charles W. Colson, "Evangelicals & Catholics Together: The Christian Mission in the Third Millennium," *First Things* 43 (May, 1994): 15-22.

fication, Scripture and Tradition, the communion of saints, and the role of the Virgin Mary in the plan of redemption.[34] Finally, a report of the International Consultation between the Catholic church and the World Evangelical Alliance, which took place between 1993 and 2002, was released in 2003 as "Church, Evangelization, and the Bonds of *Koinonia.*"[35] While this report breaks little new ground, it does provide a good summary of evangelical and Roman Catholic discussions over the past decade, acknowledging the many things these two Christian communities share in common such as the Holy Scriptures, the Lord's Prayer, the classic creeds, a high Christology, the gospel call to conversion and discipleship, and the common hope of Christ's return. At the same time, this document frankly acknowledges differences as well as convergences and concludes with a stirring call to conversion — a turning away from the prejudices and stereotypes of the past, and a fresh turning toward one another in Christian charity. "On the basis of our real but imperfect communion, we ask God to give us the grace to recommit ourselves to having a living personal relationship with Jesus as Lord and Savior and deepening our relationship to one another."

Back to New Delhi

This is a moment of extraordinary ecumenical promise, and evangelicals are called to a stewardship of engagement in the ongoing quest for Christian unity. This engagement needs to be undertaken both with humility, acknowledging the shortcomings and blind spots of our own tradition, and boldness, that is, boldness in the New Testament sense of *parrēsia,* the boldness that comes from the imperative of the gospel itself. In retrospect, it seems that the Third Assembly of the World Council of Churches at New Delhi in 1961 represented both a great op-

34. Each of these statements has been printed in *First Things.* For "The Gift of Salvation" see issue 79 (January 1998): 20-23; for "Your Word Is Truth" see issue 125 (August/September 2002): 38-42; for "Communion of Saints" see issue 131 (March 2003): 26-33; for "A Call to Holiness," see issue 151 (March 2005), 23-26; for "That They May Have Life," see issue 166 (October 2006): 18-25; for "Do Whatever He Tells You: The Blessed Virgin Mary in Christian Faith and Life," see issue 197 (November 2009): 59.

35. World Evangelical Alliance — Pontifical Council for Promoting Christian Unity, "Church, Evangelization and the Bonds of *Koinonia,*" *Origins* 33, no. 19 (16 October 2003): 310-20.

portunity for ecumenical advance and the beginnings of a fissure that would issue in our present ecumenical malaise. While one cannot unravel the mistakes of the past four and one-half decades, it may be helpful to revisit the vision of Christian unity set forth with such clarity in the New Delhi report:

> We believe that the unity which is both God's will and his gift to his Church is being made visible as all in each place who are baptized into Jesus Christ and confess him as Lord and Savior are brought by the Holy Spirit into one fully committed fellowship, holding the one apostolic faith, preaching the one gospel, breaking the one bread, joining in common prayer, and having a corporate life reaching out in witness and service to all and who at the same time are united with the whole Christian fellowship in all places and all ages in such wise that ministry and members are accepted by all, and that all can act and speak together as occasion requires for the tasks to which God calls his people.[36]

An evangelical commentary on this classic text would require consideration of at least the following seven items: the visibility of the church, baptism, the content of "the one apostolic faith," the priority of preaching, the Eucharist, prayer, and Christian ministry.

Looking briefly at only the first of these items, evangelicals will want to bring to the table a distinction which seems to have played little role in recent ecumenical texts, namely, the Augustinian distinction between the church visible and invisible. A classic definition of the invisible church can be found in the Second London Confession, a Calvinistic Baptist statement of faith (first published in 1677 and reissued in 1689), which echoes the language of the Westminster Confession:

> The Catholic or universal Church which with respect to the internal work of the spirit, and truth of grace, may be called invisible, consists of the whole number of the elect, that have been, are, or shall be gathered into one, under Christ, the Head thereof; and is the spouse, the body, the fullness of Him, that filleth all in all.[37]

---

36. The Third Assembly of the World Council of Churches 1961, *The New Delhi Report* (New York: Association Press, 1962), p. 116.

37. Timothy and Denise George, eds., *Baptist Confessions, Covenants, and Catechisms* (Nashville: Broadman and Holman, 1996), pp. 84-85. In 1742 this same confession was

The church, in this sense, is the Body of Christ extended throughout time as well as space consisting of all persons everywhere who have been placed in vital union with Jesus Christ through the ministry of the Holy Spirit. As Georges Florovsky used to say, the church is characterized by a temporal as well as a spacial catholicity, a catholicity not reducible to, nor strictly verifiable by, historical continuity, numerical quantity, or geographical extent.[38]

While emphasizing the priority of the invisible church as the Spirit-sustained reality that brings believers "in all places and all ages ... into one fully committed fellowship," as New Delhi puts it, evangelicals will be aware of how the concept of the invisible church has often been distorted into a kind of ecclesiastical docetism according to which the earthly and historical form of the church has been negated and its mission in the world reduced to a "spiritualized" fellowship with no more gravity than a discussion group or social club. Already in the sixteenth century, the Reformers were aware of this criticism and vigorously denied the charge that by the church they meant only a *civitas platonica*. Indeed, they sought to reconstruct a purified form of Catholic Christianity, a real life and blood community of faith that would bear the "marks of the true church" *(notae verae ecclesiae)*. The *notae* do not replace the traditional Nicene attributes *(una, catholica, apostolica, sancta)*, but they rather call into question the unity, catholicity, apostolicity, and holiness of every congregation which claims to be a church, thus subjecting it to an outward, empirical examination. In this way, as Calvin says, "the face of the church" emerges into visibility before our eyes *(Institutes* 4.1.9).

Evangelicals will also be sensitive to another similar, but not identical, distinction in ecclesiology, namely, the distinction between the church local and the church universal. The principal framer of the New

---

published in America, with slight alterations, as the Philadelphia Confession of Faith. The visible/invisible church distinction is mentioned in the document "Towards a Common Understanding of the Church (1984-1990)," in William G. Rusch and Jeffrey Gros, eds., *Deepening Communion: International Ecumenical Documents with Roman Catholic Participation* (Washington, D.C.: United States Catholic Conference, 1998), pp. 175-229, from the Reformed–Roman Catholic Dialogue where the point is to affirm the indissoluble link between the two "sides" of the one ecclesial reality.

38. Georges Florovsky, "The Catholicity of the Church," in G. Florovsky, *Bible, Church, Tradition: An Eastern Orthodox View* (Belmont, MA: Nordland Publishing, 1972), pp. 39-42.

Delhi call to Christian unity, Lesslie Newbigin, addressed this very issue in his 1976 essay, "What Is a Local Church Truly United?"[39] In his explanation of the expression from New Delhi, "all in each place," Newbigin insisted on understanding "place" in a wider, Christological sense. As the church is the sign, instrument, and foretaste to the reign of Christ, "place" cannot be related solely to geography. Indeed, it must include every realm of human endeavor — language, culture, politics, economics, ethnicity, etc. However, there are two dangers in emphasizing the visibility and localness of the church in this way: first, where the local church never becomes truly inculturated and so reflects the language, worship, and witness of another "place"; and second, where the local church becomes so conformed to its particular "place" that it simply echoes the environing culture becoming not inculturated but acculturated and thus forfeiting its witness to the sovereign judgement and mercy of God. As Newbigin recognized, the challenge for each local church is to be so rooted in the being of the Triune God that universality neither cancels out the particularity of each distinctive "place," nor does locality deny universality, for the full flowering of the life of Christ must be present in each local church. For evangelicals the visibility of the church must always be interpreted in light of the mission of God. For this, ultimately, is the gospel imperative for Christian unity — "that they may all be one; even as thou, Father, art in me and I in thee, that they may also be in us, so that the world may believe that thou hast sent me" (John 17:21).

---

39. See *The Ecumenical Movement: An Anthology of Key Texts and Voices*, ed. Michael Kinnamon and Brian E. Cope (Geneva, Grand Rapids: WCC Publications, Eerdmans, 1997), p. 114.

The Cross-Shaped Church: A Pauline Amendment to the Ecclesiology of *Koinōnia*

Joseph L. Mangina

In a splendid recent collection of essays, *That All May Believe,* Carl Braaten links the cardinal Lutheran doctrine of justification by faith alone with that of the Church. Cautioning that consensus on justification will not, by itself, bring about Christian unity, Braaten writes:

> What stands in the way [of unity]? "It's the church, stupid!" It's ecclesiology. Catholics and Lutherans must go on to explore the connection between the doctrine of justification and the church. . . . The church is a fundamental article of faith: "We believe in the church." What is meant by this? The church is a congregation of saints in communion with the Triune God and therefore also in communion with each other. The concept of *koinōnia/communio* is central in ecclesiology today, but its far-reaching implications are still to be worked out.[1]

Braaten here not only confirms the thought of his teacher Paul Tillich, who famously sought to unite "Protestant principle" with "Catholic substance";[2] he also aligns himself with the ecumenical ecclesiology of *koinōnia.* Over the past few decades communion ecclesiology has come into its own as a kind of ecumenical *lingua franca.* No less than Pope Benedict XVI has called this teaching the heart of the Second Vatican Council's distinctive teaching about the

---

1. Carl Braaten, *That All May Believe: A Theology of the Gospel and the Mission of the Church* (Grand Rapids: Eerdmans, 2008), p. 58.
2. Braaten, *That All May Believe,* pp. 61-69.

church.[3] The centrality of *koinōnia* for ecclesiology has been underscored by the recent *Harvesting* document, in which the Pontifical Council for Promoting Unity has sought to gather the fruits of decades of ecumenical labor.[4]

Different churches may have different reasons for embracing Communion ecclesiology. For the Eastern Orthodox, the *koinōnia*-concept serves as a way of affirming the church's unity and historic structure, while avoiding submission to Rome. For Roman Catholics, communion ecclesiology elevates the mystical and sacramental aspects of the church over its institutional expression. In the famous formula of Henri de Lubac: "The Eucharist makes the church" — not the Pope or the hierarchy in the first instance, but Christ himself. This recognition has had profound consequences for ecumenism. It means that *koinōnia* can be participated in to varying degrees, thus opening the door to acknowledging the (real but imperfect) ecclesiality of non-Roman communities.[5] Protestants have welcomed communion ecclesiology for its robust Trinitarianism and for the check it provides against their own temptation towards individualism. In all this, Protestants, Catholics, and Orthodox are but tracing a very real thread that runs throughout the apostolic testimony. As Paul writes at the opening of his first letter to Corinth: "God is faithful, by whom you were called into the fellowship [*koinōnia*] of his Son, Jesus Christ our Lord" (1 Cor. 1:9).[6]

Paul's affirmation displays the unity between justification and ecclesiology rightly noted by Carl Braaten. God is faithful — here is grace, divine action, the "rightwising" of the sinner. And yet the sinner is not justified so that he or she may remain in the same place. Justification means being set on a new path of life — here is gift, human transformation, membership in Christ's body. "Protestant principle" thus meets "Catholic substance." Later in this same letter, Paul will show just how far he is willing to press the theme of *koinōnia*. To break the bread of the Eucharist, to share the cup of blessing is to participate in the body and blood of Christ.[7] To betray this fellowship

3. "Die Ekklesiologie des Zweiten Vatikanums," *Communio* 15 (1986): 44.

4. Walter Kasper, ed., *Harvesting the Fruits: Basic Aspects of Christian Faith in Ecumenical Dialogue* (London: Continuum, 2009); see especially sections 34-40, 74.

5. A theme explored in Douglas M. Koskela, *Ecclesiality and Ecumenism: Yves Congar and the Road to Unity* (Milwaukee: Marquette University Press, 2008).

6. All Scripture quotations are from the English Standard Version (ESV).

7. 1 Cor. 10:16-21.

— by making the Lord's Supper the private possession of an "in" group, by treating the poor in the church as second-class citizens — is to incur God's judgement. Make no mistake, warns Paul. The Eucharist can kill you.[8]

This sequence of thought reaches a climax in Paul's teaching on spiritual gifts. *Koinōnia* means more than simply the banal idea that gifts are complementary, and that all have different roles to play. Any management consultant could have said as much. No, it means deference by the "strong," the group with which Paul himself identifies, to the community's weaker members. It means refraining from exercising one's rights if it means offending a brother or sister. For that person is a member of *one's own body,* and deserves the care and respect that the eye, ear, hand et al. owe each other.[9] After establishing the general principle, the apostle drives the point home with existential force: "Now you are the body of Christ and individually members of it" (1 Cor. 12:27). Here we see one of those indicative statements that are really imperatives. "You Corinthians are — really are! — the body of Christ; it is high time you started acting like it."

Ecclesial ontology, then, implies ethics. Without the ontology, the ethics Paul commends seems to float in mid-air, becoming little more than scattered bits of Hellenistic wisdom teaching. And yet the converse is also true. Without the ethics, without solicitude for the "weaker member," ecclesial ontology tends to become abstract and triumphalist, even as (rather ironically) it is deprived of the transformed behavior that would render it visible. As Nietzsche scornfully remarked, "The redeemed ought to look more like the redeemed."

Yet what the redeemed "should look like" is precisely what so horrified Nietzsche: a life that is cross-shaped, a following in the way of the Crucified. This is a note one misses in much of the literature surrounding communion ecclesiology.[10] It is an emphasis that must, however, be

---

8. 1 Cor. 11:28-32.

9. 1 Cor. 12:14-26.

10. There are exceptions, of course. J. M. R. Tillard's classic *Église d'Églises: L'ecclésiologie de communion* (Paris: Les Éditions du Cerf, 1987) contains a brief discussion of martyrdom, although it is not well integrated into the work as a whole. Tillard also notes that communion is "always fragile, always being put to the test," a nod to the struggles and conflict that mark the life of the church, especially in its disunity (pp. 52-66). In other treatments of communion ecclesiology, such as Dennis Doyle's *Communion Ecclesiology: Vision and Versions* (Maryknoll, NY: Orbis Books, 2000) and Lorelei Fuchs's

retrieved if we are to think the movement's ontological claims to the end. The church shares in the communion of the holy and blessed Trinity — yes, but it does this not through some abstract participation in the divine nature, but through its unity with the incarnate Son. The church is Christ's body — but then unavoidably his body as humiliated and suffering. An ecclesiology without the cross floats above the surface of history, failing to penetrate into the human flesh inhabited by Jesus himself. My thesis is that ecclesial *koinōnia* can only be cruciform, and that if it lacks this character it cannot be the *"koinōnia* of [God's] Son, Jesus Christ our Lord"* (1 Cor. 1:9).

To develop this claim more fully, let us turn to Paul's second letter addressed to the church at Corinth.[11] After the greeting, which notably identifies the readers as "those made holy in Christ Jesus, called to be holy ones," and the bestowal of "grace and peace to you from God our Father and the Lord Jesus Christ," Paul opens with an unusual doxology:

> Blessed be the God and Father of our Lord Jesus Christ, the Father of mercies and God of all comfort, who comforts us in all our affliction, so that we may be able to comfort those who are in any affliction, with the comfort with which we ourselves are comforted by God. For as we share abundantly in Christ's sufferings, so through Christ we share abundantly in comfort too. If we are afflicted, it is for your comfort and salvation; and if we are comforted, it is for your comfort, which you experience when you patiently endure the same sufferings that we suffer. Our hope for you is unshaken, for we know that as you share in our sufferings, you will also share in our comfort. (2 Cor. 1:3-7)

God is, of course, to be blessed at all times: here Paul is simply being a good Jew. But the blessing also has a more particular occasion. God is specifically blessed as the source of comfort, comforting "us" (an "apostolic plural"), so that Paul may comfort others in turn. Especially striking here is the mesmerizing repetition of the word "comfort," both as noun and as verb *(paraklēsis/parakaleō),* alongside the words for "affliction" and "afflict" *(thlipsis/thlibō).* Though the passage

---

Koinonia and the Quest for an Ecumenical Ecclesiology (Grand Rapids: Eerdmans, 2008), the eclipse of the cross is even more complete.

11. Second in the canonical numbering, that is. I set aside all questions concerning the integrity of 2 Cor. and the ordering of Paul's correspondence with this church.

is a brief one, words from these groups occur no fewer than thirteen times. What is going on here?

Paul's relationship to the church of Corinthian was, of course, famously troubled. From 1 Cor. we know that he had to deal with party strife and friction connected with the presence of different social classes within the community. From 2 Cor., we know that Paul had to contend not only with external opponents, the "super-apostles" mentioned at 11:5 and 12:11, but with enemies inside the community. These enemies found Paul to be all words and no action — a bully, and yet a peculiarly weak and ineffectual one. While Paul must have hoped that his own arrival on the scene would improve the situation, in fact, it only tended to make things worse. Moreover, his stubborn refusal to accept financial support from the church was apparently perceived as an insult by some. Much of 2 Cor. consists of his self-defense against such charges. When Paul insists that he is not commending himself, we sense that he protests too much.[12] At the human level the whole letter is an effort at self-commendation.

Equally human, however, is Paul's tender concern for this church, apparent in his sense of being wounded by those he loves. "We have spoken freely to you, Corinthians; our heart is wide open."[13] The apostle and his community are joined together by strong bonds of affection, love, and common purpose. We might rightly refer to such bonds as *koinōnia*. And indeed, the letter concludes with one of the more famous New Testament uses of that word: "The grace of the Lord Jesus Christ and the love of God and the *koinōnia* of the Holy Spirit be with you all."[14] This verse is regularly cited in discussions of both New Testament trinitarianism and the ecclesiology of communion.

And yet it is not the fact of communion *per se* that Paul appeals to in his opening bid for reconciliation with the Corinthian church. As I have already noted, he appeals first of all to the *comfort* that flows from God to the apostle, and from the apostle to his readers. Comfort comes from God. Shall we then say that affliction comes from the world or from Satan? While this is certainly true at one level, Paul is not hesitant to ascribe even the affliction to God himself. Thus he believes that his near-death experience in Asia was by no means accidental. It happened

12. 2 Cor. 3:1.
13. 2 Cor. 6:11.
14. 2 Cor. 13:14.

"in order that" *(hina)* Paul might be taught to rely, not on himself, but on "God who raises the dead."[15] At the ultimate level it is God who orders and supervises Paul's afflictions. It is only when human possibilities are exhausted that space is made for the display of God's lifegiving power.

Paul is not the only New Testament author for whom "affliction" functions as a basic category of Christian experience.[16] Affliction, suffering, is a mark of living in the end times. In this regard, Christianity simply inherited the widely-held Jewish belief in a period of messianic woes prior to the End. What sets Christian writers apart is the conviction, not just that the End has commenced with Jesus' death and resurrection, but that the mark of a truly messianic life is suffering the End *with* Jesus, or even "in" him. Nowhere is this theme more evident than in 2 Corinthians, with its stress on apostolic suffering:

> But we have this treasure in jars of clay, to show that the surpassing power belongs to God and not to us. We are afflicted in every way *(en panti thlibomenoi)* but not crushed; perplexed, but not driven to despair; persecuted, but not forsaken; struck down, but not destroyed; always carrying in the body the death of Jesus, so that the life of Jesus may also be manifested in our bodies. For we who live are always being given over to death for Jesus' sake, so that the life of Jesus also may be manifested in our mortal flesh.[17]

Two simple observations will serve to reconnect us with our theme of ecclesiology. First, it should be obvious that Paul here is not talking about some purely inward, spiritual dying with Christ, but about the very public life he enacts and suffers in relation to his churches, in his social environment, and not least in his own body. This point is underscored in the famous catalogue of hardships offered in 2 Cor. 11:21-33, part of the "angry" portion of that difficult letter. It is also hinted at in the cry of exhaustion and irritation that concludes the even angrier epistle to the Galatians: "From now on let no one cause me trouble, for I bear on [or 'in'] my body the marks of Jesus."[18] Bearing the cross is not simply an interior attitude. It is the very form of Paul's existence in time and the flesh.

15. 2 Cor. 1:9b.
16. Cf. Heb. 10:33; Rev. 1:9.
17. 2 Cor. 4:7-11.
18. Gal. 6:17.

Second, Paul's manifestation of the death of Jesus names a dynamic not just in his relationship to God and to Christ, but in his relationship to the Corinthians themselves. Thus the decisive concluding verse in the passage just cited reads: "So death is at work in us, but life in you."[19] The plural form of the word "you" is significant. It is the Corinthian *community* that is the beneficiary of Paul's sufferings. The apostle and his readers are bound together in a kind of "blessed exchange." Paul dies, and the Corinthians live. Nor does the exchange end there, because Paul expects the Corinthians to embody the pattern in turn. The ultimate warrant for this complex reality of shared affliction, of comforting and being comforted, is Christ himself: *"For as we share abundantly in Christ's sufferings,* so through Christ we share abundantly in comfort too."[20]

In his famous study *The Mysticism of Paul the Apostle,* Albert Schweitzer argued that at the heart of Paul's theology is not, as Protestantism would have it, the doctrine of justification by faith alone, but Paul's transforming experience of union with Christ. Schweitzer may thus be seen as a precursor to the "new perspective" that has recently come to dominate Pauline studies. Like Schweitzer, the new perspectivalists have tended to de-emphasize the juridical aspects of Paul's thought in favor of covenantal and participatory motifs. God does not declare us righteous on account of Christ's merit, it is argued. Rather, righteousness is a function of membership in God's covenant people. The new thing that has happened in Christ is simply that the covenant has opened up to include the Gentiles.

While the participationist and communal emphasis of the new perspective is welcome, it misses something important.[21] A flat reading of the new perspective might suggest that God, through Christ, has simply created a new possibility of being righteous. With the failure of Is-

---

19. 2 Cor. 4:12.

20. 2 Cor. 1:5.

21. Perhaps that is why there are calls for us to move "beyond" the static opposition between perspectives new and old. On this point see Francis Watson's *Paul, Judaism, and the Gentiles: Beyond the New Perspective* (Grand Rapids: Eerdmans, 2007; this is a revised version of an earlier work). Watson makes clear what should have been apparent all along, namely that the new perspective itself was never simply one thing, and that its advocates often disagreed among themselves. To give but one example, James Dunn has never accepted the "subjective" reading of *pistis Christou* that has been embraced by scholars like Wright, Hays, Donaldson, and Campbell.

rael and the Torah-way of salvation, the torch of covenant now passes to the church and the Jesus-way. This essentially salvation-historical view, however, fails to do justice to the reality-making power of the gospel, whose coming issues in nothing less than the dawning of a new world. The new perspective's tendency to flatten divine action requires an apocalyptic corrective. "If anyone is in Christ," Paul writes, he or she is . . . not "saved," not "inserted into the covenant," but "new creation!"[22]

Fair enough; and yet this new creation, this apocalyptic act of renewal, is precisely participatory. "If anyone is *in Christ.* . . ." Schweitzer and many who have followed him have set up a false dichotomy. Having a "high view" of church, sacraments, and the moral life does not entail having a "low view" of justification. Paul's concern is never less than the radical divine action in which God brings a new world into being through the cross. The fact that the particular juridical *language* of justification does not appear, as it admittedly does not in letters like 1-2 Thessalonians and the Corinthian correspondence, does not mean that the *force* of such language is missing, or that justification is only of secondary concern to Paul. The juridical/forensic vocabulary is rather a particular idiom that Paul employs to express the new-world-making power of God. But as the new world comes into being in Christ, a human being becomes part of that world by being joined to Messiah's body, becoming one flesh with him and so participating in his life with God.

Now we make one final step: the Messiah to whom one is joined by faith, baptism, and sacramental existence is the Crucified, as the apostle makes clear in what is perhaps the most "mystical" passage of all, Gal. 2:19-21: "I have," Paul writes, *"been crucified* with Christ." Like the event of Golgotha, the Christian's initiation into Christ happens only once. The old self is gone, drowned in the waters of baptism.[23] Yet what follows is not simply a "de-selfing" as in Buddhism, but the emergence of a new ego, a new self. If this ego is in the first instance that of Christ himself — "It is no longer I who live, but Christ who lives in me" (2:20a) — it is secondarily yet truly Paul's own "I," as new person who exists in *communion* with the risen Messiah: "And the life I now live in

---

22. 2 Cor. 5:17. The apocalyptic reading of Paul is found especially in the work of J. Louis Martyn and his school. Martyn himself is deeply indebted to the work of Ernst Käsemann.

23. Cf. Rom. 6:4.

the flesh I live by faith in the Son of God, who loved me and gave himself for me" (2:20b).

In a remarkable series of studies, New Testament scholar Michael Gorman has endeavored to show how the theme of "cruciformity" permeates every facet of the apostle's thought, from the Trinity to justification to Christian ethics.[24] Once identified, the motif can be seen everywhere. It is present in an especially potent way in the Christ-hymn in Philippians 2, which Gorman sees as being the Pauline "master story." That story describes a great downward parabola from divine to human status, from life to death — the words "death on a cross" are by scholarly consensus Paul's own contribution — and from death to exaltation. The divine figure who is the subject of all these verbs is the kenotic God, the God who is not so great that he cannot also be humble.

Paul rehearses this story, however, not as the first chapter in his Christology — though it should probably be the first chapter in ours — but to reinforce a point about the moral life. "Do nothing from rivalry or conceit," he tells his readers, "but in humility count others more significant than yourselves. Let each of you look not only to his own interests, but also to the interests of others." It is in this context that he then rehearses Christ's narrative of kenosis as the example they are to imitate, and not just to imitate, but to indwell. "Have this mind among yourselves [*en hymin*], which is yours in Christ Jesus, who. . . ." The Philippians' lives are determined by their location "in" Christ. How can they not treat each other as he treated them?

The cross so understood is not primarily a moment of negativity, as though its character were primarily determined by its association with sin and death. The cross is the fullest expression of the self-emptying love of God. Almost unbelievably, it is *God* who subordinates his own interests to that of others, Adamic humans, those who had set themselves up as God's enemies.[25] This is the great apocalyptic event that Paul proclaims. It is unrivalled, brooking no competitors: "I de-

---

24. Michael Gorman, *Cruciformity: Paul's Narrative Spirituality of the Cross* (Grand Rapids: Eerdmans, 2001); *Apostle of the Crucified Lord: A Theological Introduction to Paul and His Letters* (Grand Rapids: Eerdmans, 2004); *Inhabiting the Cruciform God: Kenosis, Justification, and Theosis in Paul's Narrative Soteriology* (Grand Rapids: Eerdmans, 2009). It is worth noting that Gorman is a Methodist who teaches at a Roman Catholic seminary. In focusing on the participatory/transformatory aspects of Paul, he is playing to both a Wesleyan and a Catholic strength.

25. Rom. 5:10.

cided to know nothing among you [*en hymin*] except Jesus Christ and him crucified."[26] Compared with God's gift of the Crucified, everything else appears to Paul as so much crap.[27]

So de-centered has Paul's ego become that, with an objectivity that is almost alarming, he can calmly deliberate on the pros and cons of his own death.[28] While Paul would personally prefer to be "with the Lord," yet it is to the Philippians' advantage that his earthly existence continue. In another letter he raises this insight to the level of a general principle: "If we live, we live to the Lord, and if we die, we die to the Lord. So then, whether we live or whether we die, we are the Lord's. For to this end Christ died and lived again, that he might be Lord both of the dead and of the living."[29]

Once again, the context in which Paul makes this assertion is that of intracommunal relations — specifically, the relation between groups that differ on matters of diet and festival observance. Paul does not deny that good arguments can be lined up on both sides of such questions. Nor is he afraid to make his own views plain. Yet the debate itself is a matter of secondary importance. Far more important to him is the scandal presented by Christians who absolutize their particular form of observance, forgetting that they belong not to this or that party but "to the Lord." Being in Christ means acknowledging the lordship of Christ, a lordship defined by a life lived on behalf of others — in the first instance one's brothers and sisters in Christ, but by extension all those who were once God's enemies.[30]

Participation in Christ's death is therefore a key not just to Paul's understanding of individual Christian existence, but to his understanding of life in the *ekklēsia*. Even in its imperfection the church exists in communion with the Crucified; perhaps we should say, *especially* in its imperfection. The "high" character of Paul's ecclesiology derives from the church's bearing the marks of Jesus in its common life, so becoming a kind of "living icon of the cross, of the crucified Messiah."[31]

In the decades since the Second Vatican Council, it has become an ecumenical commonplace to speak of the church as the "universal sac-

---

26. 1 Cor. 2:2.
27. *Skybala,* Phil. 3:8.
28. Phil. 1:20-26.
29. Rom. 14:8-9.
30. Cf. Rom. 12:20.
31. Gorman, *Cruciformity,* 367.

rament of salvation." Nothing in our exploration of Paul should cause us to question this concept. Yet notice in what this sacramental-showing forth consists: not in a vague mirroring of trinitarian *koinōnia*, but in the church's embodied witness to the love of God poured out on the world in Jesus. The Trinity itself is made known by the Son's journeying forth "into the far country," to use Barth's image. It is this divine action, and not some banal ideal of perichoretic life in community, that should shape our thinking about the church. As Ephraim Radner writes, the notion of unity-in-diversity is a theological abstraction that

> has little bearing on the actual account of Jesus' relation to the Father, and/or Spirit, and therefore even in its Trinitarian symbology is inadequate to, as it were, "the facts." For the "facts" are that the Son does only what he is told — "not my will, but thine"; and that, despite worries in the past over monothelitism . . . all talk of "diversity" of wills makes sense only if that diversity is a subjected one, a submitted and abandoned one.[32]

It is not simply that Christ loves, and is loved by, the Father in the mystery of the immanent Trinity. True enough. But we must think in the first instance "economically." In the fullness of time the Father *sends* the Son into the world, so that those whom God has predestined might receive adoption as sons, crying out "Abba! Father!" in the power of the Spirit.[33] As the Father sends the Son, so the church is sent into the lost world, enacting a kind of parable of the Son's sojourn in the far country. The church realizes itself — and just so affirms its real existence as Christ's body — by losing itself, as Christ himself was lost before being found.

All this talk about suffering, crucifixion, and death can easily be misinterpreted. It could be seen, and too often has been seen, as a fixation on weakness for its own sake. That is exactly what Nietzsche feared. Yet Christian existence is no thanatos syndrome, no romantic fascination with the power of death as such. Paul describes the Christian as participating not just in Christ's death but in his resurrection; and not just in the future, but in the present.[34] The life that embraces

---

32. Ephraim Radner, "Is Christ Divided? Locating the Possibility of the True Church," unpublished manuscript.
33. Gal. 4:4-6.
34. See Gorman's sage remarks on the hypersensitivity of most Pauline interpret-

the cross is in no way "tragic," but bears eloquent witness to the God who "gives life to the dead and calls into existence the things that do not exist."[35]

That the church embodies unity in diversity, that it mirrors the extraordinary richness of created time, place, language, culture — who would wish to deny that this is so? Yet it is not *this* that constitutes the church's existence as a communion. The key question with respect to terms like "communion" or "participation" is always, communion in what? Participation in whom? We have seen Paul's way of answering these questions: communion in Christ's sufferings, participation in the folly of the cross as the very wisdom of God. Paul says that only when he is weak is he strong, apprehended by the power of Christ.[36] This is the church's story as well.

But what, one might plausibly ask, is all this supposed to look like? Can one really specify in advance the church's existence under the cross in the form of an "ecclesiology"? Luther, we may recall, named the bearing of the holy cross as one of seven gifts bestowed by the Spirit upon the church.[37] Unlike the other six gifts Luther names,[38] it is difficult to align this one with a particular human practice. Let us suppose that the seventh gift in Luther's ordering is the climactic one, naming the end to which all the gifts/sacraments/holy things are ordered. But then it is in principle present everywhere, and just so eludes easy articulation.

This is a fair objection, one that indeed goes to the very heart of the matter. Stanley Hauerwas has spoken of Christ as "cross-shattered."[39] Just to the extent that the Spirit, blowing where he will, unites the church with *this* Christ, there can be no aspect of her life that is not cruciform, or that does not display his agony and his love. As we

---

ers to the dangers of "realized eschatology"; Gorman, *Cruciformity*, 34 n. 34. According to Rom. 6:4, Christians participate not only in Christ's death but in his resurrection.

35. Rom. 4:17.

36. 2 Cor. 12:10b.

37. Martin Luther, *On the Councils and the Church*. In *Luther's Works,* vol. 41: *Church and Ministry, III,* ed. Erich W. Gritsch (Philadelphia: Fortress, 1966).

38. The seven "holy things" *(Heligthümer)* named by Luther are the word of God, Baptism, Eucharist, ordained ministry, the exercise of the keys, public worship, and the bearing of the cross.

39. Stanley Hauerwas, *Cross-Shattered Christ: Meditations on the Seven Last Words* (Grand Rapids: Brazos, 2004).

have seen, in Paul's letters the church's cruciform character is often manifest in the tensions and quarrels that mark the lives of his congregations. When the apostle proclaims "God was in Christ, reconciling the world to himself," he is not so much formulating a doctrine of atonement as he is attempting to back up the imperative: "Be reconciled to God!"[40] And yet communal conflict is not the only ecclesial matrix for cruciformity. It can be seen in suffering occasioned by persecution and martyrdom;[41] in the church's obligation to care for the sick, the hungry, and the imprisoned;[42] and more generally in the messianic reality of "the tribulation and the kingdom and the patient endurance that are in Jesus," as attested by the book of Revelation (1:9).

When John seeks to denote the church's participation in that reality, he uses a word in the *koinōnia*-family.[43] John and his readers are *synkoinōnoi* in tribulation — companions, comrades, partisans. If, at the deepest level, this unity is given once for all in Christ, yet it is received and apprehended in time, as the Spirit works to conform the church to his cross. The church may be thought of as the death of Jesus stretched out across time, not by way of repeating or supplementing that death — the Reformers were very clear about this — but by way of attesting and confirming it.[44] The unity of the church is not an end in itself. Its particular *koinōnia* serves the larger covenant in which God is involved with the world as a whole. Thus Jesus' prayer — one of the foundational texts of the ecumenical movement — "that they may all be one, just as you, Father, are in me, and I in you, that they also may be in us, so that the world may believe that you have sent me."[45]

If the ecclesiology of *koinōnia* has generally neglected the church's cross-shattered character, this does not mean the latter has been left without witnesses. Recent theology offers several examples of writers who have sought to retrieve the mystery of the church's participation in the cross. I will conclude this essay by briefly examining just three of these. All of them manifest a spirituality of the cross that, while stressing the priority of God's action in and for the church, nevertheless does

40. 2 Cor. 5:19, 20.
41. E.g. 1 Peter 4:12.
42. Matt. 25:31-46.
43. Rev. 1:9.
44. See for example 2 Cor. 4:10, "always carrying in the body the death of Jesus, so that the life of Jesus may also be manifested in our bodies."
45. John 17:21.

not counsel passivity. To the Spirit's gift of grafting the church into the self-donation of Christ, there correspond definite human actions that seek to be faithful to this gift, actions by which the church, so to speak, may "live into" it.

The first of these examples is one with which Carl Braaten will be thoroughly familiar: the working group that produced the document *In One Body Through the Cross: The Princeton Proposal for Christian Unity.*[46] This project, sponsored by the Center for Catholic and Evangelical Theology, sought to re-ignite some of the passion that originally animated the ecumenical movement. Indeed, the proposal that emerged was in many ways a project of retrieval, celebrating the vision of unity classically expressed at the New Delhi assembly of the WCC in 1961. Perhaps it is this aspect of the proposal that has led some to regard *In One Body* as a reactionary document. I know of one Anglican theologian who dismissed the work as merely the grumblings of conservatives, prone to idealize the ecumenical past, while a Roman Catholic colleague was put off by its "too negative" tone.

In One Body certainly *is* negative in one sense: it chides the churches for their all-too-worldly clinging to their established identities. Did not the New Delhi assembly acknowledge that "the achievement of unity will involve nothing less than a death and rebirth of many forms of church life as we have known them . . . nothing less costly can finally suffice"?[47] Here, as so often, retrieval of a classic vision offers a clearer perspective on the present. Thus the signatories of *In One Body* criticize "our churches"[48] for succumbing to the temptation to "relish the special marks that distinguish our communities from others, and not to glory in the confession of the crucified Lord we share in common."[49] And while the project is certainly an act of retrieval, its authors duly note the dangers involved in certain forms of traditionalism, which can become another way of "enhancing denominational loyalty by 'boasting' of something more unique than the gospel of Jesus Christ."[50]

46. Grand Rapids: Eerdmans, 2003. Citations below refer to page numbers, not sections.

47. As cited in *In One Body*, 22.

48. It might be noted that the sixteen signatories of *In One Body* included Catholics, Lutherans, Methodists, Anglicans, Orthodox, and free church Evangelicals.

49. *In One Body*, 34.

50. *In One Body*, 35.

Nor does *In One Body* simply float free in the theological ether. It outlines a series of practical steps that could be taken, right now, to advance the cause of unity: developing forms of common teaching, a greater cooperation in witness and service, an imaginative rethinking of bureaucratic structures that foster ecclesial sclerosis. Such proposals are meant to forestall the defeatism that says that because we cannot do everything, we must therefore resign ourselves to doing nothing. The church's unity is not just a gift, but a task. This is no less true today than it was in 1910 Edinburgh or 1961 New Dehli.

Nevertheless, the deepest impulses of *In One Body* lie in a form of spiritual ecumenism, without which the practical proposals would be meaningless. Human action must be firmly grounded in divine action:

> We believe that these suggestions are realistic, not in the worldly sense of relying on human motives, but in the godly sense of relying upon the cross of Christ. For in the cross of Christ, the personal and corporate suffering entailed in giving up aspects of our denominational heritages becomes the grace of fellowship with the Son, who brings us to the Father, in the power of the Spirit.[51]

The grace of God as source of the church's unity, yes; but a grace apprehended in the form of a costly love.

As a second instance, we may cite John Paul II's 1995 encyclical *Ut Unum Sint*, which in its own way tried to rekindle commitment to the ecumenical cause. Many of the themes it sounds will be thoroughly familiar: the church's participation in the life of the triune God; the church as "inseparable sacrament of unity"; the full, though by no means exclusive, presence of this sacrament in the Roman Catholic Church. All this is fairly standard communion ecclesiology, in which one may hear echoes of the writings of then-Cardinal Joseph Ratzinger.

What makes *Ut Unum Sint* ecumenically important, however, is not the conceptual framework it lays out, but the way it sets the cross at the center of the church's existence. The point is signalled early on in the text. John Paul writes that the church "feels herself constantly called to be renewed in the spirit of the Gospel," and so "does not cease to do penance."[52] Yet in a turn that will warm Protestant hearts, the

51. *In One Body*, 50.
52. Cf. *Lumen Gentium* 8: "While Christ, holy, innocent and undefiled, knew nothing of sin, but came to expiate only the sins of the people, the Church, embracing in its

Pope goes on to assert the priority of God's grace: "at the same time, [the church] acknowledges and exalts still more *the power of the Lord,* who fills her with the gift of holiness, leads her forward, and conforms her to his Passion and Resurrection."[53]

One of the ways in which *Ut Unum Sint* develops the theme of cruciformity is in relation to martyrdom, which forms a kind of "deep background" to what he has to say about Christian unity. While the disunity of the churches is scandalous under any circumstances, it is especially so in light of the horrendous history of martyrdom in the century just past. Noting that martyrdom crosses confessional boundaries, John Paul writes that "these brothers and sisters of ours, united in the selfless offering of their lives for the Kingdom of God, are the most powerful proof that every factor of division can be transcended and overcome in the total gift of self for the sake of the Gospel."[54] The martyr abandons self in favor of Christ. How, then, can the churches cling to their received identities, rather than following obediently in the way of the cross?

Much of the hortatory force of *Ut Unum Sint* consists in its summons to Catholics[55] to practice spiritual ecumenism, especially in the form of prayer with their fellow Christians.[56] Here the Pope leads by example. He cites the many occasions on which he has made pilgrimages to other churches and prayed with their leaders. In so doing, he sees himself as carrying out a specific mandate of the Second Vatican Council.[57] The Pope is a pilgrim by the very nature of his office; thus the many miles logged by John Paul in the course of his papacy.

The most striking aspect of *Ut Unum Sint,* however, is its powerful

---

bosom sinners, at the same time holy and always in need of being purified, always follows the way of penance and renewal." From the English text of *Lumen Gentium* on the Vatican web site.

53. *Ut Unum Sint,* 3, emphasis in original.

54. *Ut Unum Sint,* 1.

55. Although the encyclical clearly has other Christians in mind, its immediate audience is Catholic bishops and clergy.

56. See "The Primacy of Prayer," *Ut Unum Sint,* §§21-27.

57. "I am very conscious that it was the Second Vatican Council which led the Pope to exercise his apostolic ministry in this particular way. Even more can be said. The Council made these visits of the Pope a specific responsibility in carrying out the role of the Bishop of Rome at the service of communion." *Ut Unum Sint,* 24, referencing John Paul II, Apostolic Letter *Tertio Millennio Adveniente* (10 November 1994), 24: *AAS* 87 (1995), 19-20.

reaffirmation of the servant-character of the bishop of Rome. A comparison with the apostle is in order here. Michael Gorman has summarized the cruciform logic of Phil. 2:5-11 as "Although [*status*], not [*selfishness*], but [*self-abasement/slavery*]."[58] But this is the encyclical's vision for the papacy: "Although the Pope is the legitimate successor of Peter and so the 'perpetual and visible principle and foundation of unity,' he is — precisely as such! — not a tyrant but the *servus servorum Dei*, the 'servant of the servants of God.'"[59] Of course, many Orthodox and Protestant Christians may feel that this ideal has all too rarely been honored in practice. Acknowledging this credibility gap, John Paul asks pardon for the "painful recollections" other Christians may harbor of himself and his predecessors: "To the extent that we are responsible for these, I join my Predecessor Paul VI in asking forgiveness."[60]

John Paul II, then, was a communion ecclesiologist, one who advanced the vision of the church promoted by the Second Vatican Council. It is to his credit that he did not ask the concept of "communion" to do too much work. At best, *koinōnia* can serve as a kind of shorthand for the complex bonds of love, forgiveness, prayer, mission, and shared suffering that make up the church's life in time. Moreover, John Paul understood that the church knows God primarily in the form of weakness. "When I am weak, then I am strong," he quotes the apostle as saying, adding simply: "This is a basic characteristic of the Christian experience."[61]

As a third example of a cruciform ecclesiology, we may look to the proposed Anglican Covenant, currently under review by the member churches of the Communion. The occasion for the Covenant was the crisis occasioned by certain actions of the Episcopal Church (USA) and the Anglican Church of Canada. For some, the origins of the document in controversy are a cause for suspicion. Surely political ends are being served here, the argument goes. Surely this is simply a ploy by conservatives to sideline or exclude the progressive forces in the church.

It would be foolish to deny that the Covenant is mired in politics. So were the ancient councils, the Reformation, and the Confessing Church! Nevertheless, the Covenant holds out the promise of a form of

---

58. Gorman, *Cruciformity*, 91.
59. *Ut Unum Sint,* 88.
60. Ibid.
61. 2 Cor. 12:10, *Ut Unum Sint,* 92.

Anglican common life that would more clearly embody the ties of affection, charity, and obligation that bind us together in Christ. It must be recalled that just a few decades ago there was no "Anglican Communion," only the Church of England and her daughter churches, the products of missionary activity and colonial expansion. Now the daughters have all grown up. Global Anglicanism has become self-conscious of itself precisely *as a communion,* and is confronted with the question of just what that means in practice.

In its ecumenical conversations with Roman Catholics and the Orthodox, the Anglican Communion is on record as having committed itself to the vision of communion ecclesiology.[62] That vision was a winsome one, but until recently existed largely on paper. Now the question arises whether the language of *koinōnia* is simply a cover for the autonomy of dioceses or national churches. On this reading communion may be important, but not *as* important as the right of local churches to act on the basis of conscience and Christian freedom. On this "weak" reading of communion, the concept is defined as mere federation or association. This is the grain of truth in the argument that the current crisis is not (whatever the media may say) mainly about human sexuality at all, but about the nature of the church.[63]

This is where the Covenant comes in. It invites the churches to affirm a form of *koinōnia* that asks more of them than federation, in which local churches, dioceses, and provincial churches are held accountable for their actions. Accountable . . . but to what, we might ask. Some evangelical Anglicans may reply: to the Bible, the Thirty-Nine Articles, or perhaps to some newly devised confession of faith. Apologists for Catholic hierarchalism may reply: accountable to some form of magisterium, Anglicans' desperate need for which has been exposed by the recent crisis.

Might it not be, however, that the Covenant embodies the way neither of Roman centralization nor of Protestant confessionalism, but something quite different, a common life at once more Anglican and more New Testament–apostolic in character? The accountability

62. See "The Church as Communion" (ARCIC Agreed Statement, Dublin 1990) and "The Church of the Triune God" (International Anglican-Orthodox Dialogue, Cyprus 2006).

63. I do not mean to imply that these issues can be neatly distinguished. Ephesians 5 is a *locus classicus* of their interconnection, articulating a kind of "depth grammar" apparent throughout Scripture.

to which the Covenant invites us is mutual care within the body of
Christ. It is accountability *to each other.* This is by no means to exclude
the need for defined doctrine, or the need for teaching and other forms
of authority. Indeed, the Covenant makes nods in both these directions.[64] Yet the peculiar genius of the Covenant is its vision of gracious
submission to one another within Christ's body. Much criticism of the
document has focused on Section 4, especially 4.2, with its outline of
procedures to follow when things go wrong. It is obvious that such procedures could become the occasion for legal wrangling, ecclesial politics of the worst sort. But it is not obvious that this must happen.
Surely the process of discernment outlined here is more evangelical,
more in the spirit of Matt. 18:15-20, than the unedifying spectacle of Anglicans bringing civil lawsuits against each other!

Yet closer to the heart of the text is Section 2, "The Life We Share
with Others," which not only affirms communion as a gift from God
and as a sign of God's reign (2.1.1), but the need to acknowledge our *fail-
ures* of communion:

> [Each church affirms] in humility our call to constant repentance:
> for our failures in exercising patience and charity and in recogniz-
> ing Christ in one another; our misuse of God's gracious gifts; our
> failure to heed God's call to serve; and our exploitation one of an-
> other. (2.1.3)

This is *koinōnia,* certainly — but with an edge to it. A church that
affirms the call to repentance is not a people that can boast of its
ecclesial or sacramental integrity. It is a misshapen and imperfect body,
a community of sinners, as was recognized also by *Ut Unum Sint.* Yet in
its very imperfection, the church is given the opportunity to participate
in the cross of Christ. The sinful church need fulfill no preconditions to
be close to Jesus, for its life in time is a constant being-conformed to his
image. If the cross, in the words of Ernst Käsemann, is the "signature of
the risen Christ," then the church is a letter that bears that signature.[65]

Finally, the Anglican Covenant joins both *Ut Unum Sint* and the
Princeton Proposal in affirming the intrinsically missionary character

---

64. Section One of the Covenant affirms such matters as the Chicago-Lambeth
Quadrilateral, the shared Anglican tradition of worship and devotion, and the mission
of the church, all within a larger trinitarian framework (1.1.1-1.1.8).

65. Cf. 2 Cor. 3:1-3.

of the church. The church that shuns the cross will just to that extent be self-protective, clinging to past privileges rather than joyfully proclaiming the gospel to the world. The Covenant invites the churches to affirm "the imperative of God's mission into which the Communion is called, a vocation and blessing in which each Church is joined with others in Christ in the work of establishing God's reign" (2.1.4). But what is a gain for the kingdom, cannot but involve loss for the established (and historically rich) churches of Britain and North America. The growing edge of the Communion has long since shifted to Africa, where most of the world's Anglicans are to be found. There is a danger here, of course. It would be a tragedy if the triumphalism of the West were to recede, only to be replaced by a new triumphalism of numerically powerful churches in the developing world. Recognition of this danger is not a reason to shun the Covenant, though it may remind us that communion must constantly be rediscovered in one place, and one place only: the cross of Christ, who is the source of our unity and our mission alike.

In the Revelation to John, the Seer sees "a great multitude that no one could number, from every nation, from all tribes and peoples and languages." They are called out of their previous ethnic and cultural identities, into a new unity in God. Such a unity might fittingly be called a *koinōnia*. But when John inquires who this white-robed army might be, he is told that they are those who have "washed their robes and made them white in the blood of the Lamb."[66] In short, they have become one body through their participation in the cross — and hence the mission — of Jesus Christ.

The amendment I have proposed to the ecclesiology of communion is really quite a modest one. The catholic theme of *koinōnia* needs to be supplemented, not by a "Protestant principle," but by the costly grace of God in Jesus Christ.[67] Keeping that grace constantly before us is one of the tasks of ecclesiology, nowhere better exemplified than in the work of Carl Braaten. His theological existence has been a blessing to the whole *ekklēsia*. May it long continue.

66. Rev. 7:9, 14b.
67. It may seem surprising that I have not cited Dietrich Bonhoeffer in this essay, but his influence should be everywhere apparent. One need only read the ecclesiological sections of *Discipleship* (Part IV).

Freedom, Authority, and the Priesthood of All Believers

Michael Root

I. The Johannine Polarity

The reader or addressee of First John encounters in the letter's first verses a vigorous claim of authority:

> That which was from the beginning, which we have heard, which we have seen with our eyes, which we have looked upon and touched with our hands, concerning the word of life — the life was made manifest, and we saw it, and testify to it, and proclaim to you the eternal life which was with the Father and was made manifest to us — that which we have seen and heard we proclaim also to you, so that you may have fellowship with us; and our fellowship is with the Father and with his Son Jesus Christ. (1 John 1:1-3)[1]

That which was from the beginning, that concerning the word of life, that *we* (and presumably not *you*) saw, and thus we can testify and proclaim this word of life to you, "the eternal life which was with the Father and was made manifest to *us*." The letter opens with an implicit claim that the writers are in a position to know and thus possess what we might later call a teaching authority. This claimed authority is not narrowly concerned with teaching. The speaking or writing *we* proclaims this word "so that you may have fellowship with us, and our fellowship is with the Father and with his Son Jesus Christ." The not too subtle point is that if you want fellowship with the Father and his Son,

1. Biblical quotations will come from the Revised Standard Version.

you ought to be in fellowship with us. Teaching authority and soteriological authority, so to speak, go together.

After this opening, the reader might expect a discourse on the word of life which is to be accepted because the writers have the authority claimed in the opening verse: they saw, they touched, they know. That is not, however, the uniform content of the rest of the letter. John tells his readers, not that they do not know and thus should listen to him, but that they already know the truth and, in truth, need no teacher.

> But you have been anointed by the Holy One, and you all know. I write to you, not because you do not know the truth, but because you know it, and know that no lie is of the truth. . . . I write this to you about those who would deceive you; but the anointing which you received from him abides in you, and you have no need that any one should teach you; as his anointing teaches you about everything, and is true, and is no lie, just as it has taught you, abide in him. (2:20-21, 26-27)

This is, one might say, a knotty passage. Most of the tradition and most contemporary interpreters believe that the anointing referred to is baptism, although that is not explicit. This anointing or baptism seems to have taught something — the truth, or even "everything." How does this anointing teach? Here we must return to the letter's opening, the appeal to "what was in the beginning." The semantic changes rung on the word "beginning" in this text are central to its meaning. Sometimes the beginning is THE beginning, the beginning of all things at creation, as it is in the opening of Genesis or of the Gospel of John. At other points in the letter, however, the reference is to the beginning which is Jesus' life, death, and resurrection, or the beginning of the Christian life, baptism, and what was taught and learned at the beginning of the Christian life, in baptismal catechesis. As one contemporary commentator puts it: "The anointing that the readers have received from Jesus ('from him') probably consisted of both baptism and its accompanying, or preceding, catechetical instruction. That anointing in deed and word is trustworthy and true, 'no lie.' . . . Stick with what you have been taught from the beginning, John is saying."[2]

2. D. Moody Smith, *First, Second, and Third John*, Interpretation: A Bible Commentary for Teaching and Preaching (Louisville: John Knox Press, 1991), p. 74.

That something is odd in First John's juxtaposition of authority and the seeming denial of authority in the face of an anointing possessed by every Christian is not a merely modern perception. When Augustine preached on First John, he came up short at this discussion of anointing removing the need for the teacher and he almost scolds John. Why is he, Augustine, preaching, if his congregation already knows? "Then to what purpose is it that 'we,' my brethren, teach you? If 'his anointing teaches you concerning all things,' then it seems we labor without a cause. Let us leave you to his anointing, and let his anointing teach you. . . . To what purpose have you written an epistle like this? What teaching did you give them? What instruction? What edification?"[3]

First John lays out the problem of freedom and authority in the church in a nutshell. In the church, there are those called to preach with authority. They proclaim so that others may know the Father and his Son. Communion with these teachers is a non-trivial matter; it seems to mediate communion with the Trinity and thus salvation. And yet, every Christian can say, I have been baptized. I too have the Spirit; I have been taught. I have the freedom to exercise that charism. The Christian replies to authority "So you say" and seems to say it in the power of the Holy Spirit.

These two elements are prominently present in the Lutheran tradition and help to account, I believe, for its oscillation between clerical authority and lay rebellion against that authority. On the one hand, when the Lutheran Confessions refer to the authority of the ordained ministry of Word and Sacrament, they regularly cite Luke 10:16, the culmination of Jesus' charge to the Seventy whom he sends out to proclaim the Kingdom: "Whoever hears you, hears me and whoever rejects you rejects me, and whoever rejects me rejects him who sent me." Not unimportantly, the sending of the Seventy was taken by much medieval theology as the institution of the office of presbyter. For the Confessions, this text means that the ordained proclaim the gospel with the authority of Christ as a matter of divine law, *iure divino*.[4]

And yet also prominent in the Lutheran tradition is John 10:4-5:

---

3. Augustine, "Homilies on the First Epistle of John," in *Nicene and Post-Nicene Fathers,* Vol. 7 (First Series) (Repr., Peabody, MA: Hendrickson, 1988), p. 481.

4. "In this regard, churches are bound by divine right to be obedient to the bishops, according to the saying, 'Whoever listens to you listens to me.'" Augsburg Confession, Art. 28:22, in Robert Kolb and Timothy J. Wengert, eds., *The Book of Concord: The Confessions of the Evangelical Lutheran Church* (Minneapolis: Fortress, 2000), p. 95.

"When he [the good shepherd] has brought out all his own, he goes before them, and the sheep follow him, for they know his voice. A stranger they will not follow, but they will flee from him, for they do not know the voice of strangers." The sheep, the people of God, know the shepherd and are authorized not to follow false shepherds. When their pastors teach something other than the gospel, they will (if they are true Christians) notice this and should refuse to hear and obey. They can do this because they have their own charism, their own anointing.

The Lutheran tradition thus embodies the problem set by the polarity of teaching and hearing authority in First John. My word choice here is deliberate: Lutheranism embodies the problem; it has not solved it (if solution is the sort of thing called for here). If there is a virtue of the Lutheran tradition on this issue (and the "if" here is real), it is the virtue of not shying away from a problem set for us by scripture itself.

This is not, of course, a merely Lutheran problem. In recent ecumenical discussion, this nexus of issues appears under the heading "reception." The point at which the ecumenical discussion of authoritative teaching seems to touch the nub of the matter, the nerve, the hinge, is when it discusses the role of reception in relation to authority. The most thorough work on this matter has been done by the Anglican-Roman Catholic International Commission (ARCIC). ARCIC defined reception in this way:

> By "reception" we mean the fact that the people of God acknowledge such a[n authoritative] decision or statement because they recognize in it the apostolic faith. They accept it because they discern a harmony between what is proposed to them and the sensus fidelium of the whole Church. . . . Reception does not create truth nor legitimize the decision: it is the final indication that such a decision has fulfilled the necessary conditions for it to be a true expression of the faith. In this acceptance the whole Church is involved in a continuous process of discernment and response. (Elucidation: Authority, §3)[5]

ARCIC did not claim to have spoken the last word on reception. It lays out the issues in a helpful way more than it sees a way through

---

5. Harding Meyer and Lukas Vischer, eds., *Growth in Agreement: Reports and Agreed Statements of Ecumenical Conversations on a World Level* (New York: Paulist Press, 1984), p. 102.

them. Unfortunately, the Vatican, rather than seeing both the promise and the remaining problems left by ARCIC's work, chose simply to emphasize the remaining problems. "For the Catholic church, the certain knowledge of any defined truth is not guaranteed by the reception of the faithful that such is in conformity with Scripture and Tradition, but by the authoritative definition itself on the part of the authentic teachers" (§15).[6]

ARCIC and the Vatican response state in the clearest contemporary manner where the problem of ecclesial authority stands today. Unlike some other issues, the issues involved are not matters of concern to scholars and ecumenical professionals alone. Many non-Catholics are resistant to the Catholic Church because they see in it what they perceive as authority without the participation of the people of God. I cannot imagine the Lutheran, Anglican, or Reformed churches agreeing to a pattern of governance and teaching in which bishops and bishops alone decide matters. Conversely, many Catholics perceive in the non-Catholic western churches an absence of the authority that God has given his church through the offices of presbyter and bishop. Discussions of reception sound like the thin edge of the wedge of an ecclesiastical democracy in which the truth and the will of God are matters of majority vote.

In this essay, I will certainly not solve the problem or mediate the polarity set by First John. I hope only to frame the problem in an ecumenically helpful way, a way that will both let us see how much we actually have in common and help us move toward better forms of authority in our own churches, even while they exist in the anomaly of division. Reconciliation on this matter will not be achieved in a single great leap, but only as we make a running start within our own churches.

II. The Universal Priesthood

We in fact are closer together than one might think (or, put in other words, the chasm is deep but narrow). I think the best way to get at both the common ground and the difference is in terms of the priesthood of all believers, or of the baptized, or the common priesthood (I

6. Christopher Hill and Edward Yarnold, eds., *Anglicans and Roman Catholics: The Search for Unity* (London: SPCK, 1994), pp. 160f.

will use these terms interchangeably; I think nothing is at stake in the varying terminology).

For most of us, the term "priesthood of all believers" (traditionally, the most common term in English) has quite Protestant overtones, in a literal sense — the content of the concept is that of a protest against what is seen as clerical dominance. In the Lutheran Reformation, the concept is most prominent in Luther's writings of the early 1520s — *The Address to the German Nobility* and *The Babylonian Captivity of the Church* — which were attacks on what Luther saw as a clericalism rooted in works righteousness. For good or bad reasons, the concept fades from Lutheran theology as time goes on. There is almost no trace of it in the Lutheran Confessions, although underlying principles remain important for Lutheran thought and practice.

Today, that every Christian shares in Christ's priesthood and that there is thus a priesthood of all the baptized, is not ecumenically controversial. (Catholic theology never, to my knowledge, denied a common priesthood, even if it did not at certain periods emphasize it much.) Central is the notion that salvation is a form of participation in Christ, in his death and resurrection. Participation in Christ, through the Holy Spirit, is communion with the Father, and thus communion with the Trinity.

This participation in Christ is not just participation in the results of his work. Rather, the Christian is taken into Christ's work. At least since the Reformation, the work of Christ has been identified with the threefold office of prophet, priest, and king. These are the three Old Testament offices that involved anointing, and Christ, as THE anointed one, sums up these three offices. As prophet, Christ proclaims the revelation of God; as priest, he offers himself to God; as king, he is the eschatological ruler of all things (and of the church). Christ, even during his pre-resurrection life, includes others in his ministry; I have already mentioned the sending out of the Seventy to proclaim and heal, and thus to do precisely what Jesus was doing. After the resurrection, he sends the disciples out with the words: "As the Father sends me, so send I you" (John 20:21). The disciples do not just profit from Jesus' ministry; they are called to participate in it.

This participation is not limited just to the Seventy, or the disciples, or the apostles. The entire people of God are to be a "royal priesthood, a holy nation" (I Pet 2:9). This idea was not lost in the tradition. Augustine, for example, picks up the notion that Christians, as the name implies, are also anointed and that anointing links them to Christ's anointed offices: "As we call all believers Christians on account of the mystical chrism, so we call all priests, because they are members of the one Priest."[7]

Lutheran theology picked up on this theme. In *On the Freedom of a Christian,* Luther states: "Christ has made it possible for us, provided we believe in him, to be not only his brethren, co-heirs and fellow-kings, but also his fellow-priests."[8] Note, the Christian is priest and king only as fellow-priest and fellow-king with Christ. In the context of the emphasis on the union of Christ and the Christian in this text, this "fellow" status is an expression of the Christian's participation in Christ.

Similar language is to be found in the documents of the Second Vatican Council: "For by the regeneration and anointing of the Holy Spirit the baptized are consecrated as a spiritual dwelling and a holy priesthood, so that through all those works that are those of the Christian they may offer spiritual sacrifices and declare the power of him who called them out of darkness into his marvelous light."[9]

Our participation in Christ is the heart of any adequate notion of Christian freedom, whether that freedom is conceived negatively, as freedom from something (from the condemnation of the law, from the elemental spirits of the age, from death and the devil), or whether that freedom is conceived positively, as freedom for something (for life in Christ and even more, freedom to live out the anointing, the participation in Christ that we have been given). Authority and freedom come together in participation in Christ.

There is an ecumenical consensus that every Christian shares in Christ's priesthood. There is further agreement that there is a distinction between this universal priesthood (and prophethood and kingship) and that exercised by the ordained ministry. Vatican II is, as one would expect, quite clear on this question: "Though they differ from one another in essence and not only in degree, the common priesthood of the faithful and the ministerial or hierarchical priesthood are nonetheless interrelated: each of them in its own special way is a participa-

---

7. Augustine, *The City of God,* trans. Marcus Dodds (New York: Modern Library, 1950), XX,10, p. 729.

8. Martin Luther, "The Freedom of a Christian," in *Career of the Reformer I,* vol. 31 of *Luther's Works,* ed. Harold J. Grimm (Philadelphia: Fortress, 1957), p. 355.

9. "*Lumen gentium:* Dogmatic Constitution on the Church," in *Decrees of the Ecumenical Councils,* ed. Norman P. Tanner (London: Sheed & Ward, 1990), para. 10, trans. altered.

tion in the one priesthood of Christ" (LG 10). There are two forms of participation in Christ's priesthood, different in kind. They are interdependent, but the common priesthood has its own integrity.

These Catholic statements seem to me at least analogous and perhaps equivalent to Luther on the specificity of the pastoral office. The priesthood of all the baptized does not place every Christian in the ordained office. To return to Luther in "The Freedom of the Christian," written during his most lay-oriented period: "Although we are all equally priests, we cannot all publicly minister and teach. We ought not do so even if we could. Paul writes accordingly in 1 Cor 4, 'This is how one should regard us, as servants of Christ and stewards of the mysteries of God'" (LW 31:356). Or, from a commentary on Psalm 82: "It is true that all Christians are priests, but not all are pastors [*Pfarrer*]" (LW 13:65; WA XXXI/1:211). If the pastoral office is to be understood as a form of participation in the offices of Christ as prophet, priest, and king (and the use of Luke 10 — "whoever hears you, hears me" — clearly implies such), then Luther, like Vatican II, is saying that there is a difference of kind, and not of degree, between the way the universal priesthood participates in these offices of Christ and the way the pastoral office participates in these roles. On this point, stated at this level of generality, there is no ecumenical argument.[10]

Let me add two clarifications here. First, the priesthood of all was not for the Lutheran Reformation an egalitarian principle. As far as I can tell, it was always assumed that clergy and laity would play different roles in the church. Martin Chemnitz, writing toward the end of the 16th century, emphasizes the differing roles of laity and clergy in such an event as the calling of a pastor:

> The election and calling of the ministers of the church must not be subject only to the ministers or only to the ruler or only to the inexperience or temerity of the common multitude, but must be and remain with the whole church, yet with the maintenance of proper

10. The interrelation of the universal priesthood and the specific pastoral office has again become a controversial matter in Lutheran theology, as can be seen in the contrasting work of Harald Goertz, *Allgemeines Priestertum und ordiniertes Amt bei Luther,* Marburger Theologische Studien (Marburg: N. G. Elwert Verlag, 1997), and Timothy J. Wengert, *Priesthood, Pastors, Bishops: Public Ministry for the Reformation and Today* (Minneapolis: Fortress, 2008). I would suspect that Goertz would not agree with what I have said in this paragraph; I do not know how Wengert would respond.

order. For because God is not a God of confusion but of order, . . . the business of electing and calling of ministers both in the time of the apostles and after their time, in the older and purer church, was always handled with a certain definite order by particular members of the church in the name and with the consent of the whole church.[11]

Second, there does seem to be a difference between Catholic and Lutheran forms of speech in the relative weight they place on the functions of prophet, priest, and king in relation to ordained ministry. The Lutheran Reformation certainly shifted the emphasis onto the pastor as proclaimer of the word, with less stress (if any) on pastor as priest and, within my limited research, even less on pastor as king, as governor of the congregation. Catholic theology, by speaking of the ministry's role as teaching, sanctifying, and governing lines up more evenly with the threefold office. The significance of this difference needs further exploration.

There is thus ecumenical agreement on the existence of the common priesthood and for a distinction in kind between the ways this common priesthood participates in Christ's office and the way the ordained ministry does. Third, there is also agreement that these two forms of participation require one another. Each bears within it an orientation to the other. Obviously, the ordained ministry is called to teach, sanctify, and govern someone, a people of God this ministry serves. As Cardinal Newman once famously responded to a complaint by Bishop Ullathorne about the laity, "the Church would look foolish without them."[12]

Perhaps more important for our consideration is the importance of the pastoral office for the priesthood of the baptized, for both the Catholic and Lutheran traditions. The Christian's union with Christ (and thus the Christian's priesthood) is not unmediated; it comes through word and sacrament. The consistent commitment of the Reformation was that, even apart from questions of validity, word and sacrament require the pastoral office. When Luther imagines the case of

11. Martin Chemnitz, *Loci Theologici,* trans. J. A. O. Preus (St. Louis: Concordia Publishing House, 1989), p. 702. This passage is in Locus 17, Ch. 4: "On Teachers and Hearers in the Church."

12. Quoted in the editor's introduction to John Henry Newman, *On Consulting the Faithful in Matters of Doctrine,* ed. John Coulson (London: Collins, 1986), p. 19.

groups of lay Christians separated from pastoral ministry for extended periods of time, he does not suggest that a lay person preach and preside at the sacraments. He suggests that the community select one of their number and lay hands on that person with prayer and thus institute that person into the pastoral office (LW 40: 34, 36). The office is so important that, *in extremis,* lay ordination is preferable to life without the office.

It is the teaching, preaching, and sacramental ministry of the office that calls forth and sustains the common priesthood. The Lutherans within the most recent international Catholic-Lutheran dialogue make this point well: "The ministry has the task of proclaiming the gospel in such a way that the believers become familiar with Christ's voice and thus become 'the lambs that hear the voice of their shepherd.' This process of education itself is the presupposition for the congregation's ability to evaluate doctrine and the proclamation of the office-holders."[13] The freedom of the Christian to exercise his or her priesthood in Christ and his or her duty to listen only to the voice of the true shepherd is dependent upon the authoritative proclamation of the gospel in word and sacrament by the office of ministry.

Fourth, and finally, there is also extensive ecumenical agreement on infallibility of the laity as a whole in its grasp of the faith. The sheep do know the voice of the shepherd and they will not follow a false shepherd. They are granted a sense of the faith, a *sensus fidei,* so that the comprehensive *consensus fidelium,* the consensus of the faithful across time and space, will not go astray. What it grasps as the truth of revelation is in fact the truth of revelation. Luther has no hesitancy in affirming that the universal church is infallible. What it hears as the gospel of salvation *is* the gospel of salvation. To give a typical example, in the *Disputation on Faith and Law* of 1535 he states: "After the apostles, no one should claim this reputation that he cannot err in the faith, except only the universal church," i.e. the total body of believers (LW 34:113; WA 39/I, 61).

Vatican II was also quite clear on the infallibility of the total people of God: "The entire body of the faithful, anointed as they are by the Holy One, cannot err in matters of belief. They manifest this special property by means of the whole peoples' supernatural discernment in

---

13. Lutheran-Roman Catholic Commission on Unity, *The Apostolicity of the Church: Study Document of the Lutheran-Roman Catholic Commission on Unity* (Minneapolis: Lutheran University Press, 2006), para. 257.

matters of faith when 'from the bishops down to the last of the lay faithful' they show universal agreement in matters of faith and morals" (LG 12). The striking phrase, "from the bishops down to the last lay faithful," is a quotation from Augustine.[14] For Catholic teaching, then, just as the church's teaching authority will not fail rightly to teach the truth, so also the universal body of the faithful will not fail rightly to learn the truth. There are two matching infallibilities, each deriving from its participation in Christ.

There is thus ecumenical agreement that, even if there is a distinction between a teaching church and a learning church, there is an infallibility of the learning church. In fact, there is more ecumenical agreement on the infallibility of the total body of the laity than there is on the infallibility of the teaching church. (Protestants who deny any sort of infallibility of the teaching church, even of the infallibility of that which is taught by the consensus of teachers across the ages, should ask how there then could exist an infallibility of the learning church, if office and laity, teaching and learning, proclamation and hearing are interrelated and interdependent, as noted above).

There is then quite extensive agreement on the priesthood of the baptized: that priesthood is always a participation in Christ; that all participate in Christ's anointed offices of prophet, priest, and king; that laity and clergy participate in different, but interrelated and interdependent ways; and that the laity as a whole possess an infallible *sensus fidei*.

III. The Ecumenical Dissensus

Against the background of this extensive agreement, I believe we can formulate the remaining issue with greater precision. I would put it this way: Although there is an agreement *that* there is a distinction between how the clergy and the laity participate in the office of Christ, there is disagreement about just *what* that difference is. Just how do the clergy and laity differ in their participation in the offices of prophet, priest, and king? Comprehensively, what is the difference between the

---

14. Augustine, "On the Predestination of the Saints," in *A Select Library of the Nicene and Ante-Nicene Fathers of the Christian Church*, Vol. 5, ed. Philip Schaff (Grand Rapids: Eerdmans, 1956), para. 27.

participation in the offices of Christ by a priest/pastor or bishop (or by varying bodies of priests and bishops) and the participation in these offices by a lay person (or by varying bodies of lay persons); what forms of authority flow from this difference; and how do these differing forms of authority interrelate?

An advantage of this way of putting the issue (besides being able to draw on the agreement I have outlined) is that it connects the questions about authority to the wider range of issues outstanding between Catholics and Protestants that hinder communion. I have argued elsewhere that I think these questions center on how the church participates in the saving mission of Christ and the Spirit in the world.[15] Does the church participate in the proclamation of God's truth in such a way that certain organs of the church can under specific conditions state what that truth is and do so without fear of fundamental error? Are the historical development of the church and the guidance of the Holy Spirit so intertwined that at least some features of the church that are post-biblical developments (such as episcopal structures) can be discerned to be of divine institution and irrevocable? Are the works of the Holy Spirit in the Christian also the works of the Christian in such a way that there will be a fittingness of merit between the Christian and the eternal life granted in the Kingdom? All of these questions are questions about the shape of the Christian's participation in the work of God for salvation.

Let me note in more detail where I think the issues come to a head in relation to questions of freedom and authority: in reception and decision making.

A. Reception

I have already noted reception as a point at which the Johannine tension between authoritative teaching and authoritative learning is sharply expressed. Let me again quote the Anglican-Roman Catholic International Commission, now in their more recent statement on "The Gift of Authority":

---

15. Michael Root, "The Indwelling Spirit and the Agency of the Church: A Lutheran Perspective on the Catholic-Methodist International Dialogue," *Ecclesiology* 2 (2006): 307-23.

The exercise of teaching authority in the Church, especially in situations of challenge, requires the participation, in their distinctive ways, of the whole body of believers, not only those charged with the ministry of memory. In this participation the *sensus fidelium* is at work. Since it is the faithfulness of the whole people of God which is at stake, reception of teaching is integral to the process. (§43)

At this level of generality, there is not disagreement, but just how does the whole body of believers participate in the teaching of the church in ways that do not compromise the legitimate authority of those with a specific ministry of teaching in the church, be they bishops, teachers more generally, or some particular teacher, most notably, the Pope? When that question is asked, consensus breaks down. And it is only when that question is asked that we reach the level of specificity at which actual organs of teaching authority operate. At what point does a failure of reception constitute a sign of a problem in teaching? After all, it took decades for the decisions of Nicea to be genuinely received. Is the widespread non-reception in the North Atlantic world of official Catholic teaching on birth control of any doctrinal significance? At what point would a broader non-reception become significant? My sense is that the movement in North American mainline Protestantism toward inclusive language in relation to God, officially sponsored by authorities in many such churches, is still resolutely not received (even if not actively rejected) by the bulk of the laity. At what point does that non-reception take on theological significance?

Let me suggest here that one of the problems we have with this topic is a Northern European or more generally Anglo-Saxon juridical and canonical mindset, a concern to have a process for dealing with every problem. Is the role of reception something that can be formulated in a rule or process (when 85% of the people of God fail to receive a teaching for 75 years, the "correction by reception" procedure kicks in), or is the role of reception something real, but informal? In light of the interrelation of clergy and laity, can we trust that, sooner or later, non-reception has its effect? After all, every church leader, every pastor, bishop, or pope, was first a layperson, coming out of that *sensus fidelium*. Despite what Luther said on one occasion, no one is born or baptized a bishop (something we can probably thank God for). But is a trust in informal processes of reception and non-reception adequate? Does such an attitude overlook or repress the Spirit-given role of the laity?

Let me add that the question of reception cuts in more than one direction. The question of the role of reception is generally posed, even in ecumenical discussions, as a challenge to Roman Catholic practices of teaching. But the church throughout the world for centuries received, with something that appears to be unanimity, beliefs and practices about the Blessed Virgin Mary that Protestants have dropped. Did the universal church receive as part of the faith something contrary to the gospel? If not, can the concept of reception be pressed without reconsidering this deviation from what would seem to be a matter accepted by the learning authority of the church long before the teaching authority declared it?

B. Decision Making

A question less addressed so far in ecumenical discussions is the role of the laity in the church's governance and decision making. Does the freedom of the laity in the church to realize and use the charism given them in their baptismal anointing extend to some participation in the church's governance? Over the past century or two, Anglican, Lutheran, and Reformed churches have all moved toward complex synodical structures in which laity and clergy together make decisions regarding the church's life and mission. To some degree, these developments can be seen as parallels to the increasing democratization of society and such forces have undoubtedly played an important causal role.

While such synodical structures are new, they are not complete innovations. For the established Lutheran and Anglican churches of Europe, the lay state authorities and parliaments had extensive authority in relation to certain aspects of the life of the church. (Think of the English Parliament's rejection of the 1928 Prayer Book revision and the act of the Swedish state to appoint Nathan Söderblom Archbishop of Uppsala over other candidates at the beginning of the 20th century.) These earlier state church arrangements can be seen, among other things, as ways in which the laity participated in the governance of the church.

The development of synods needs to be seen, however, not just historically but theologically. This development, if valid, should be seen as rooted in the participation by the laity not only in Christ's priestly and prophetical offices, but also in his kingly office. But the question then arises, just as it did for teaching, how are the clerical and lay forms of participation in Christ's kingly office distinct but interrelated? What forms of church governance flow from that interrelation? Here, Roman Catholic governance structures and the governance structures of Reformed, Anglican, and Lutheran churches are markedly different, reflecting markedly different understandings of the way laity and clergy interrelate in the decision making of the church.

How much of an ecumenical problem exists here is not clear. The Orthodox churches have had various kinds of synodical structures, within a clearly episcopal polity, which have not been seen as a problem in Catholic-Orthodox relations. If some model of "united, not absorbed" is the ecumenical goal, then the existence of distinct synodical structures in reconciled churches should not present a difficulty. The question of decision making has, to my knowledge, not been taken up in ecumenical dialogue.

Particularly in areas of decision making, however, ecumenical discussion should not just be about reconciliation between churches, but also about renewal of our own churches. Non-Catholic western churches (and many Catholics) do have arguments to press about decision making structures in the Catholic Church. To use the title of a famous piece by John Henry Newman, how are the laity being consulted when decisions are made? Are the laity being permitted to play the role that would seem to follow from Catholic doctrinal commitments in such texts as Vatican II's Decree on the Apostolate of the Laity? In what way does a non-doctrinal, sociological clericalism hinder the freedom of the laity to realize the role given them in baptism?

Conversely, the synodical structures of contemporary Protestantism are open to serious question. I will limit my comments to two points. First, have these structures adequately attended theologically to the specific roles of clergy and laity? Are the specific gifts of each brought to expression when, as occurs in many but not all such assemblies, clergy and laity form one body and neither pastors nor bishops play a specific, distinct role in decision making? Should matters of, say, doctrine and worship always be taken up first by the ministerium, those who have a God-given calling to proclaim the word publicly and preside at the sacraments, and then be considered by a larger lay assembly? How does the preaching and sacramental role of the clergy find expression in Protestant governance structures?

Second, how is lay participation in decision making supported? Can lay delegates to a national church assembly, the majority of whom have never served before, who meet for only a week to ten days, really exercise an informed participation? Or will they inevitably need to look to those who have more information and experience, the clergy and especially the bishops? The freedom to exercise and realize our charisms is blocked when not supported. As First John relates the knowledge that comes with baptism to the teaching then received, so if churches are serious about lay participation in governance and decision making, they need to see that adequate support is given to lay roles, which may mean not just greater education, but also a revision of structures that allows the development of expertise over time by laity who participate repeatedly in church assemblies.

I would add that from my limited experience, it appears that the German and Scandinavian Lutheran churches and the Church of England are better structured in both of the respects I mention than many American Protestant churches, and especially the church I know best, the Evangelical Lutheran Church in America (ELCA). The differentiated roles of the clergy and laity are built into their structures. While many German Lutherans look askance at the ELCA's entrance into episcopal succession, some of the German Lutheran churches allow some form of episcopal veto over at least some synodical actions (e.g., when they touch on teachings related to doctrine or morals). Similarly, their synods meet with enough regularity and continuity for lay members to develop sufficient expertise to participate effectively. These churches have the advantage of covering smaller geographical areas, so that more frequent meetings are easier to manage, but geography is not destiny and American Protestant churches need to reflect theologically on the way the structures they have created function.

IV. Conclusion

Questions of authority have proven among the most intractable in modern ecumenical discussion. Not only are they theologically complex, touching on a large range of doctrinal loci, they are also of direct relevance to the lives of the churches. How to understand justification by grace may seem an abstruse question best left to experts; how decisions are made in the church, who makes them, and what authority such decisions carry are matters of obvious relevance. It is difficult to imagine a resolution to these differences being achieved soon. Both theological exploration and concrete experience with differing modes of decision-making are needed. A fruitful approach might focus less on the authority of the clergy than on the authority of the laity, of the whole people of God as participants in God's saving mission.

The Ecclesial Meaning of the Eucharist

Susan K. Wood

Discussions of the eucharist in an ecumenical context have most often focused on the manner of Christ's presence, the relationship between the sacrifice of the cross and the eucharist, or the minister of the eucharist. Largely absent from these discussions has been the ecclesial meaning of the eucharist, probably because this aspect of the eucharist has also needed attention within various ecclesial traditions. The "ecclesial meaning of the eucharist" includes the role of the eucharist in the formation of the communion of saints, the making of the members which make up the body of Christ, and the constitution of the church. The source of this meaning has biblical roots in Pauline theology and Patristic roots in Augustine's mystagogical theology. It can be traced in the historical changes of the use of the term *corpus mysticum*. It lies embedded in the scholastic analysis of the relationship between sign and reality and comes to life in the liturgical invocation of the Holy Spirit to transform the assembly in the second *epiclesis*.

A retrieval of the ecclesial meaning of the eucharist corrects an overly individualistic and privatized eucharistic spirituality. It manifests the Christological and pneumatological foundations of the church. It expresses the connections between church and sacrament.

In the face of dissension within the Corinthian community, Paul makes the appeal: "The cup of blessing that we bless, is it not a sharing in the blood of Christ? The bread that we break, is it not a sharing in the body of Christ? Because there is one bread, we who are many are one body, for we all partake of the one bread" (I Cor. 10:16-17). Paul grounds the bond of charity that should exist within the Corinthian community in their participation in the eucharist. The meaning of the Christian community, which the liturgy mediates, establishes, and maintains, is that the church is in some way the body of Christ. The unity of the church is the unity of Christ.

In his mystagogical instruction to the neophytes who have just received the sacraments of initiation, Augustine exhorts: "Take then, and eat the body of Christ, for in the body of Christ you are already made the members of Christ."[1] In this same sermon he explains: "Because you have life through Him, you will be one body with Him, for this sacrament extends the body of Christ and by it you are made inseparable from Him." The unity of the body received at the altar is a sign and measure of the unity of the ecclesial body. The eucharistic sacrament both signifies and effects the unity of the church. The sacramental realism of the historical Christ leads to the sacramental realism of the ecclesial Christ so that Augustine can say to the neophytes he is instructing, "there you are on the altar, there you are in the chalice."[2]

Henri de Lubac's historical study, *Corpus Mysticum,* traces a fascinating change in eucharistic and ecclesial terminology.[3] Before the eucharistic controversies with Berengar of Tours in the eleventh century, the church was designated as the *corpus verum,* the true body. In contrast, the eucharist was the *corpus mysticum,* the mystical body, just the reverse of the use of these terms today. For example, in the familiar eucharistic hymn "Ave Verum," composed by Thomas Aquinas after this shift in usage occurred, the "true body" is the eucharist, not the church. The Church Fathers, however, "had seen his [Christ's] ecclesial body as the *veritas* of his mystical eucharistic body." The eucharist was "mystical" because it was received spiritually. Within this earlier view, there was an inherent unity among the historical body of Christ born of Mary, his eucharistic body, and his ecclesial body. In response to the threat posted by Berengar, who emphasized a symbolic rather than real presence of Christ in the eucharist, the church emphasized the real presence of Christ in the eucharist, calling it the *"corpus verum."* To prevent any misunderstanding concerning the reality of Christ in the eucharist, it emphasized the link between Christ's eucharistic body and the true body

---

1. Sermon 3. This translation is from *Selected Easter Sermons of Saint Augustine* by Philip T. Weller (St. Louis: B. Herder Book Co., 1959), p. 113.

2. Sermon 6, translated in Weller, p. 109.

3. Henri de Lubac, *Corpus Mysticum: L'Eucharistie et l'Église au Moyen Age* (Paris: Aubier-Montaigne, Coll, Théologie 3., 1944).

born of Mary, dead and risen. As vital as this link is, the other connection with the ecclesial body was lost in the process. In the emphasis on eucharistic realism, the ecclesial realism of the Augustinian view of the *totus Christus,* the whole body of Christ comprised of Christ the head and his members complete only in the eschaton, was lost.

The expression *corpus mysticum* lost its eucharistic connotation when the church was considered apart from its sacramental context. As a result of the influence of Aristotle's *Politics,* the church was thought of as a visible reality or as a human society. In such a context, the unity of the body with the head was no longer understood sacramentally, scripturally, or eschatologically, but was modeled on a society with its human leader. A concept of church as "mystical body" changed to that of "visible body." Later, under the "symbolist" influence of Wycliffe, Hus, Luther, and Calvin, the mystical body of Christ became completely dissociated from the visible church.[4]

The scholastic analysis of the sacraments also shows the relationship among the sign of the sacrament, the sacramental presence of Christ, and Christian unity. The scholastics spoke of the *sacramentum tantum,* the sign of the sacrament, the *res et sacramentum,* the reality of the sacrament, and the *res tantum,* the effect of the sacrament. According to this schema, with respect to the eucharist, the *sacramentum tantum* is the outward sign and appearance of bread and wine. The *res et sacramentum* is the reality of the eucharist, that is the body and blood of the risen Christ. The *res tantum* is the effect of the sacrament, that is, the unity or bond of love created by the sacrament. Too often in eucharistic piety people get "stuck" at the level of the *res et sacramentum,* thinking that the purpose of the liturgy of the eucharist is to make the body and blood of the Lord present so that they can receive him in communion. Although true, this interpretation does not go far enough. The Lord does not give us his body and blood just to be adored and worshipped in the eucharist or even that the faithful may individually receive him, but so that a greater unity, greater bond of love may be created in forming the *totus Christus,* the whole body of Christ comprised of Christ the head and his members, what we call the mystical body of Christ. The *res et sacramentum* does not exist for itself, but so that the *res tantum* may be effected. What the scholastics called the *res* or the fruit of the sacrament of the eucharist is the unity

4. de Lubac, *Corpus Mysticum,* p. 130.

of the church, which is to say the ecclesial body of Christ in union with its Head. Thus there is an intrinsic relationship between sacramental realism, belief in the real sacramental presence of Christ in the eucharist, and ecclesial sacramental realism, wherein the church is also sacramentally present in the eucharist.

Within the eucharistic prayer the sacramental body of Christ in the eucharist is inseparable from his ecclesial body. In Eucharist Prayer IV of the Catholic rite, the double nature of the epiclesis, the invocation of the Holy Spirit, is particularly evident. The first epiclesis invokes the Spirit to change the bread and wine into the body of Christ. The second epiclesis invokes the Spirit to transform the assembly into the ecclesial body of Christ, so that joined to the Christ, they may be gathered up in his return to the Father. Thus the structure of the eucharistic prayer is a great *exitus-reditus,* a coming forth and a return. We receive the gifts of creation from the Father to whom we give thanks. These gifts are transformed into the Body of his Son, who joins us to himself and gives himself to his Father.

Yet another piece of evidence for the ecclesial meaning of the eucharist is its place as the third sacrament of initiation within Catholic theology. As such, it not only unites us to Christ, but also incorporates us into the church. Even though a baptized person who has not communicated is not less a member of the church, something in that person's baptism has not been brought to visible, sacramental expression in the absence of the eucharist. Baptism constitutes the baptized as a "liturgical person" oriented to worship in the official prayer of the church, the eucharist. That person has been incorporated into a priestly community by baptism, but without the eucharist, the priestly liturgical exercise of that person within community is missing.

Just as the restoration of the catechumenate has shown us that baptism of adults within the Easter Vigil constitutes the norm of baptism, so too, we should look to the Vigil for a deeper understanding of the eucharist. The eucharist at the Easter Vigil is where the eucharist is most itself in public and the "standard that defines the meaning of everything else — cross and sacrifice, memorial and presence, ministry and priesthood, intercession and prayer, participation and communion."[5] The eucharist is the culmination of initiation because it is there

5. Nathan D. Mitchell, *Forum Essays: Eucharist as Sacrament of Initiation* (Chicago: Liturgy Training Publications, 1994), pp. 109-10.

that the communion of believers with one another and with Christ is sacramentally visible in the sacrament of God's presence with us. In its associations with a messianic banquet, the eucharist is a sign of the ultimate and final union to which we are called and which will be completed only in the eschatological end time.

Catholic Ecclesial Consciousness Then and Now

Despite its deep historical and theological roots, the ecclesial meaning of the eucharist has not been at the forefront of pastoral sensibilities for Catholics and other Christians. The heritage of eucharistic piety for Catholics provides a helpful illustration of the difference of eucharistic piety and sensibilities before and after the liturgical renewal. Similarly, other Christians have also experienced shifts in their understanding and practice.

Catholic history gives evidence of a tension between a private, devotional eucharistic piety and a more ecclesial, communal one. Joseph Chinnici identifies the Eucharistic movement as "the most vital spiritual movement of the first fifty years of twentieth-century American Catholicism."[6] The second half of the nineteenth century witnessed the growth of tabernacle societies and nocturnal adoration groups. The Confraternity of Perpetual Adoration had the stated purpose "to adore the divine Lord in the Sacrament of His love and to make reparation for the many indignities offered this Holy Sacrament by ungrateful mankind."[7] This group promoted frequent communion, attendance at benediction, visits to the Blessed Sacrament, and eucharistic processions. Chinnici notes that the practice of forty hours became a major social event in New York in the last quarter of the nineteenth century. The understanding of the Blessed Sacrament during this period of history served as the sign not only of Christ's presence, but also of the identity of the priest, the role of the laity, and the place of women.[8] It also served a sociological function of supporting Catholic identity in a predominantly Protestant environment.

6. Joseph P. Chinnici, OFM, *Living Stones: The History and Structure of Catholic Spiritual Life in the United States* (New York: Macmillan, 1989), p. 146. I am indebted to this source for the history summarized in this section.

7. Chinnici, *Living Stones*, p. 146.

8. Chinnici, *Living Stones*, p. 152.

Hymns and prayers for private devotion suggest that the connection between object of devotion and liturgical action was not always in popular consciousness despite rather consistent magisterial teaching to the contrary. For example, the Second Plenary Council of Baltimore (1866) pointed out that the eucharist is intended primarily not as an object of adoration, but as spiritual food to be eaten.[9]

Chinnici comments that the eucharistic movement in the United States concentrated almost exclusively on the relationship between Jesus and the believer.[10] With respect to the Forty Hours devotion, Nathan Mitchell concurs, citing evidence that in popular prayer books and manuals of devotion, the liturgical aspects of Forty Hours were ignored in favor of prayers with a strongly sentimental and individualistic orientation.[11] A negative effect of the eucharistic movement was to constrict the meaning of the eucharist to the real presence and individual devotion. According to the piety (as contrasted with the official teaching) of the period, the primary purpose of the Mass was the consecration of bread and wine into the body and blood of Christ. The purpose of this consecration was individual communion with Christ and the reservation of the host in the tabernacle for private prayer. The presence is so objectified that Christ at times was popularly referred to as "Prisoner of the Tabernacle," and the piety of the time urged that people visit the Blessed Sacrament lest this prisoner be lonely. One particularly sentimental hymn occasionally used at the close of benediction was entitled "Goodnight, Sweet Jesus." The focus was on the objective presence of Christ in the sacrament. Much eucharistic devotion took place outside of the liturgy: in visits, processions, benedictions, and holy hours.

The theology of the Constitution on the Liturgy, the first document promulgated by the Second Vatican Council (1962-1965),[12] sought to expand Catholic piety and understanding. According to this document, the nature of the liturgy is fundamentally ecclesial. The document clearly states: "liturgical services are not private functions but are

9. Nathan Mitchell, *Cult and Controversy: The Worship of the Eucharist Outside Mass* (Collegeville, MN: The Liturgical Press, 1990), p. 334.

10. Chinnici, *Living Stones*, p. 154.

11. Mitchell, *Cult and Controversy*, p. 333.

12. *Sacrosanctum Concilium*, translation from Austin Flannery, *Vatican II: The Basic Sixteen Documents: Constitutions, Decrees, Declarations* (Northport, New York: Costello Publishing Co., 1996). Hereafter SC.

celebrations of the church which is 'the sacrament of unity,'" namely, "the holy people united and arranged under their bishops" (SC 26). This is evident in the following principles of liturgical renewal:

1. The primary principle of renewal is the "full, conscious, and active participation in liturgical celebrations which is demanded by the very nature of the liturgy, and to which the Christian people, 'a chosen race, a royal priesthood, a holy nation, a redeemed people' (1 Pet. 2:9, 4-5) have a right and obligation" (SC 14).

2. Private devotions "should be so drawn up that they harmonize with the liturgical season, according with the sacred liturgy, are in some way derived from it, and lead the people to it, since in fact the liturgy by its very nature is far superior to any of them" (SC 13). The 1973 reforms of eucharistic worship outside Mass emphasize the source of public and private devotion in the liturgical activity of the Christian people.[13]

3. The primary purpose for reserving the sacrament is for the communion of the dying. Devotion towards and adoration of the sacred species remain a secondary purpose.[14]

4. "Rites which are meant to be celebrated in common, with the faithful present and actively participating, should as far as possible be celebrated in that way rather than by an individual and quasi-privately" (SC 27). This applies with special force to the celebration of Mass and to the administration of the sacraments.

5. Christ is present most of all in the eucharistic species, but also in the person of the minister, in the word, and in the assembly (SC 7). Even though the eucharistic species remains a privileged locus of Christ's presence, this broadening to include minister, word, and assembly emphasizes the entire liturgical action as the arena of Christ's presence and action at the same time that it evokes a theology of the word as Christ the Word and a theology of the community as the body of Christ.

6. "The principal manifestation of the church consists in the full, active participation of all God's holy people in the same liturgical

---

13. Sacred Congregation for Divine Worship, "On Holy Communion and the Worship of the Eucharistic Mystery Outside of Mass," *Eucharistiae sacramentum*, 21 June 1973, Chapter II.

14. Ibid., §5.

celebrations, especially in the same Eucharist, in one prayer, at one altar, at which the bishop presides surrounded by his college of priests and by his ministers" (SC 41). This text identifies the church liturgically and emphasizes its communal and collegial nature.

These principles of liturgical renewal exhibit a concern for the primacy of communal worship over private devotion and the nature of liturgical prayer as the prayer of the church rather than private prayer. The context of the eucharist is ecclesial and its theological meaning is also ecclesial. By our communion with Christ in the eucharist we also enter into communion with one another.

Several conclusions can be drawn from the ecclesial character of the eucharist. First, "communion" is never exclusively an action between an individual and Christ, but incorporation into Christ's ecclesial body. The emphasis is never exclusively on an individual's union with Christ in communion, but on the union among individuals in Christ. When we are joined with each other in Christ we comprise the *totus Christus,* that is, the whole Christ made up of head and members.

Since the *totus Christus,* the whole Christ, represents the church in its eschatological dimension, it is only in this sense that we can say that the church is a continuation of the Incarnation. We can only affirm this of the church as the body of Christ, not as an organization. The eucharist signs and makes sacramentally real this fullness of Christ, which will be definitively achieved only eschatologically. We anticipate a fullness and wholeness under sacramental sign even while our present experience of the body is one of brokenness and alienation through sin.

Eucharistic Ecclesial Consciousness in Protestant Traditions

Various faith traditions emphasize that communicants receive the body of Christ when they receive the eucharist, but how conscious are most communicants that they also sacramentalize their communion with one another within the church that is the mystical body of Christ? All traditions have largely lost the ecclesial meaning of the eucharist in an almost exclusive focus on an individual's communion with Christ. For instance, for Lutherans, this may arise from Luther's concentration on the word of promise "for you" and "for the forgiveness of sins." The Lutheran liturgical scholar Beverly Nitschke remarks, "It may be argued that in Lutheran consciousness the forgiveness of sins which is received is an intensely individual experience. It is the individual experience of forgiveness which is received." She cites the German Lutheran theologian Wolfhart Pannenberg as identifying the "Lutheran distortion of the meaning of the Eucharist" to consist in celebrating it "primarily as a visible and touchable assurance to the individual of the forgiveness of sins."[15]

As in Roman Catholicism, the emphasis on the individual benefits of eucharistic reception eclipsed the communal and ecclesial meaning of the Lord's Supper in Protestant circles. Even though some ecumenical documents are recognizing the ecclesial meaning of the eucharist, this recognition has probably not passed into popular consciousness. Recent Ecumenical convergence on the eucharist has roots in the historical work of all our traditions in the history of liturgical rites.[16]

Frank Senn, Lutheran liturgist, comments that the contemporary church is struggling to retrieve the reality that "the sacramental body forms the ecclesial body, which is kept in union with the historical body of Christ, the head of the ecclesial body, by receiving his body and blood in the sacrament."[17] He notes that 1 Corinthians 10-12 represents the earliest eucharistic theology and the earliest ecclesiology.[18] This "communion ecclesiology," which links the Eucharistic body and the ecclesial body, reflected standard teaching in the church for the first five centuries.[19]

Recent eucharistic sensibilities may not reflect the whole of a tradition. In addition to his emphasis on the individual benefits of the

15. Beverly A. Nitschke, "The Eucharist: For the Forgiveness of Sins: A Lutheran Response," *Ecumenical Trends* (June 1991): 92.

16. See Maxwell Johnson, *The Rites of Initiation: Their Evolution and Interpretation* (Collegeville: Liturgical Press, 2007), and Frank Senn, *Christian Liturgy: Catholic and Evangelical* (Minneapolis: Fortress, 1997).

17. Frank C. Senn, *The People's Work: A Social History of the Liturgy* (Minneapolis: Fortress, 2006), p. 168.

18. Senn, *The People's Work*, p. 168.

19. J.-M.-R. Tillard, in *Flesh of the Church, Flesh of Christ: At the Source of the Ecclesiology of Communion* (Collegeville: Liturgical Press, 2001), develops this theme throughout this study. See also his *Church of Churches: The Ecclesiology of Communion* (Collegeville: Liturgical Press, 1992).

Lord's Supper, Luther, in his 1519 "Sermon on the Sacrament of the Holy and True Body of Christ," speaks of communion as a sharing or participation in the life of Christ through his body the church: "Thus in the sacrament we too become united to Christ and are made one body with all the saints, so that Christ cares for us and acts on our behalf . . . likewise by the same love we are to be united with our neighbors, we in them and they in us."[20] This text clearly speaks of the eucharist's role in forming the communion of saints.

The contemporary document "Toward a Lutheran Understanding of Communion" identifies the unity of the church with communion in holy baptism and the eucharistic meal.[21] Recognizing the link among sacramental communion, incorporation in Christ, and ecclesial unity, it states: "The ecclesial communion is the body of Christ."[22]

It is difficult to view the church as sacramentally constituted if the Lord's Supper is rarely celebrated. A move to more frequent celebration characterizes a shift in eucharistic practice in many Protestant churches, although for some traditions this represents a return to earlier practices. These earlier practices by the Reformers were even more remarkable given the fact that four communions a year were considered to be very frequent for late medieval communicants. John Calvin promoted a frequent celebration of the Lord's Supper, but he could not persuade the civil authorities in Geneva to authorize more than four celebrations a year.[23] Although John Wesley communed on an average four or five times a week and was highly critical of the infrequency of Holy Communion in the Church of England of his day,[24] American Methodism inherits a practice of infrequent, usually quarterly, communion that originated with the scarcity of ministers. For

20. Noted by Simo Peura, "The Church as Spiritual Communion," in *The Church as Communion: Lutheran Contributions to Ecclesiology,* LWF Documentation 42, ed. Heinrich Holze (Geneva: Lutheran World Federation, 1997), pp. 104-121. Citing *Luther's Works: American Edition,* Volumes 35 and 59. I am grateful to Cheryl Peterson for the reference.

21. Lutheran World Federation, "Toward a Lutheran Understanding of Communion" in *LWF Documentation: The Church as Communion,* No. 42 (1997) (Geneva: The Lutheran World Federation, 1997), No. 221, but see also Nos. 8, 11.

22. "Toward a Lutheran Understanding of Communion," No. 25.

23. John Calvin, *Institutes of the Christian Religion,* trans. Henry Beveridge II (Grand Rapids: Eerdmans, 1957), pp. 600-601.

24. He advised the American Methodists to administer the Supper of the Lord on every Lord's Day in his 1784 letter to Dr. Coke, Mr. Asbury, and Our Brethren in North America cited in "This Holy Mystery," p. 18 (see n. 25).

decades after the establishment of the Methodist Episcopal Church, the number of elders was too small to offer the sacraments regularly to Methodist communities, often serviced by circuit riders who came to a community only quarterly, at best. The custom of quarterly communion persisted well into the nineteenth and twentieth centuries. During this period the eucharist came to be understood as only a memorial of the death of Christ. As with other traditions, Methodism began to reclaim their sacramental heritage in the mid-twentieth century, especially with the introduction of new liturgical texts for the Lord's Supper in 1972. Both *The United Methodist Hymnal* and *The United Methodist Book of Worship* encourage congregations of The United Methodist Church to move toward a weekly celebration of the Lord's Supper at services on the Lord's Day. The Methodist document, *This Holy Mystery: A United Methodist Understanding of Holy Communion*,[25] reflects this reclaimed heritage. It identifies the ecclesial meaning of the eucharist:

> Holy Communion is the communion of the church — the gathered community of the faithful, both local and universal. While deeply meaningful to the individuals participating, the sacrament is much more than a personal event. The first person pronouns throughout the ritual are consistently plural — we, us, our. First Corinthians 10:17 explains that "because there is one bread, we who are many are one body, for we all partake of the one bread." "A Service of Word and Table I" uses this text as an explicit statement of Christian unity in the body of Christ. . . . The sharing and bonding experienced at the Table exemplify the nature of the church and model the world as God would have it be.[26]

While this text stops short of saying that the "eucharist makes the church," it does strongly identify the unity of the church with the unity of the sacrament and develop the spirituality of eucharistic reception toward a more communal understanding while retaining the

---

25. http://www.kintera.org/atf/cf/{3482e846-598f-460a-b9a7-386734470eda}/THM-BYGC.PDF; accessed December 7, 2010. (See Resolution 8014 in The Book of Resolutions of The United Methodist Church 2008, which contains the text for "This Holy Mystery: A United Methodist Understanding of Holy Communion." This text was adopted at the 2004 General Conference.)

26. "This Holy Mystery," p. 7.

traditional emphasis on the sacramental benefits as including forgiveness, nourishment, healing, transformation, mission and ministry, and eternal life.[27] Today many Methodists experience a richer sacramental life, including weekly celebration of Holy Communion.

The Evangelical Lutheran Church in America has also experienced a sacramental revival that includes a greater frequency of celebration of the Lord's Supper on Sundays. The 1994 ELCA document "The Use of the Means of Grace" reaffirms weekly communion as a normative Lutheran practice: "According to the Apology of the Augsburg Confession, Lutheran congregations celebrate the Holy Communion every Sunday and festival. This confession remains the norm for our practice."[28] Currently, 46% of ELCA congregations celebrate the sacrament weekly compared to 16% in 1989. Approximately the same number celebrates it more frequently than once a month, while only 5% offer it monthly or less often.[29]

For many traditions, including Catholics, Orthodox, Anglicans, and many Lutherans, the sacraments of baptism and eucharist are constitutive of the church. Both incorporate an individual simultaneously into the body of Christ and into the church, the ecclesial body of Christ. One is a member of the church by virtue of being a member of Christ.

An agreed statement between the Orthodox and Roman Catholics expresses this understanding of the relationship among baptism, the eucharist, and the church. The Joint International Commission stated in 1982:

> Believers are baptized in the Spirit in the name of the Holy Trinity to form one body (cf. 1 Cor. 12:13). When the Church celebrates the eucharist, it realizes "what it is," the body of Christ (1 Cor. 10:17).[30]

---

27. "This Holy Mystery," p. 8.

28. "The Use of the Means of Grace, A Statement on the Practice of Word and Sacrament, Adopted for Guidance and Practice by the Fifth Biennial Assembly of the Evangelical Lutheran Church in America, August 19, 1997," Principle 35. See http://www.elca.org/Growing-In-Faith/Worship/Learning-Center/The-Use-of-the-Means-of-Grace.aspx; accessed July 23, 2010.

29. Ibid., 41.

30. Joint International Commission, "The Mystery of the Church and of the Eucharist in the Light of the Mystery of the Holy Trinity" (1982) in *The Quest for Unity: Orthodox and Catholics in Dialogue. Documents of the Joint International Commission and Official*

The Report of the Anglican-Reformed International Commission (1981-84), "God's Reign and Our Unity," affirms the eucharist as constitutive of the church: "Along with baptism, the Eucharist is fundamental to and constitutive of the life of the Church. It is the sacrament given to the Church by her Lord for the continual renewal of her life in him."[31] This statement affirms a liturgically based identification of the church.

A Eucharistic Ecclesiology as Essential for Understanding the Church as Communion

A failure to grasp the ecclesial meaning of the eucharist impoverishes our understanding of the church, for they are necessarily interrelated. The Catholic Church believes that "the principal manifestation of the church consists in the full, active participation of all God's holy people in the same liturgical celebration, especially in the same Eucharist, in one prayer, at one altar, at which the bishop presides, surrounded by his college of priests and by his ministers."[32] This unity of celebration both signs and effects the unity of the mystical body of Christ, for the eucharist is where the faithful are gathered together by the preaching of the gospel of Christ and the celebration of the Lord's Supper so "that by the whole fellowship is joined together through the flesh and blood of the Lord's body."[33] Thus the church is sacramental, mystical, Christological, and pneumatological before it is sociological or juridical. The unity of the church is not psychological, political, or a federation of the like-minded, but a sacramental and spiritual unity in Christ first established in baptism and then expressed, nourished, and brought to maturity in eucharistic communion.

A eucharistic ecclesiology perfectly expresses the creedal marks of the church as one, holy, catholic, and apostolic. The holiness of the church is communion in Christ by the power of the Spirit. The catho-

---

Dialogues in the United States 1965-1995, ed. John Borelli and John H. Erickson (Washington, D.C.: United States Catholic Conference, and Crestwood, NY: St. Vladimir's Seminary Press, 1996), pp. 54-55.

31. Anglican-Reformed International Commission (1981-84), "God's Reign and Our Unity," §71 (g).

32. *Sacrosanctum Concilium*, 41.

33. *Lumen Gentium*, 26.

licity of the church embraces communion with the church's apostolic past as it obediently celebrates the eucharist in memory of Christ. It communes with the saints in heaven. It constitutes the unity of the church as the unity of the mystical body of Christ.

Eucharistic ecclesiology also structures the church as a communion. In Catholic ecclesiology, the church is gathered by the preaching of the word, the celebration of the Lord's Supper under the sacred ministry of the bishop.[34] The bishop then represents this community in the communion of particular churches, the bishops collectively in the college of bishops representing in their persons the communion of churches in union with the Bishop of Rome.[35] The Bishop of Rome exercises the Petrine ministry, defined as the charge to safeguard the church in unity and communion.[36] Thus the sacramental communion initiated in baptism and the eucharist is lived out in institutional relationships as well as in personal relationships.

Conclusion

Some who try to restore a more ecclesial understanding may be accused of a certain horizontalism in their eucharistic piety, implying that the transcendent nature of the eucharist has been lost. Such criticisms, however, fail to acknowledge that the ecclesial meaning of the eucharist is rooted in the identity of the ecclesial community as the body of Christ within the Pauline theology of 1 Cor. 10:16-17. In the eucharist, affirmation of the Christological reality leads to the affirmation of the ecclesial reality. The presence of the latter is as real as the presence of the first. When we commune with the sacramental Body of Christ, we commune not only with the resurrected Christ but also with the church, which is also the body of Christ. The eucharist simultaneously effects communion with Christ and communion in the church. The ecclesial meaning of the eucharist restores the connection between the personal communing with Christ and the communion of all communicants with each other in Christ.

A retrieval of the ecclesial meaning of the eucharist corrects an

34. *Lumen Gentium*, 26.
35. *Lumen Gentium*, 23.
36. *Lumen Gentium*, 18.

overly individualistic and pietistic approach to the eucharist that tends to drive a wedge between the sacramental life of a Christian and the communal life of the church. It demonstrates why the eucharistic celebration is primary and indispensable to the communion of the church and cannot be replaced by scripture study groups or private devotions. As J. M. R. Tillard has remarked, ". . . the Eucharist is not just 'the fountain of graces from which one drinks when one is thirsty.' It is the sacramental event by which the church 'that is in such and such a place' expresses its nature: to be a gathering of human diversity in Christ."[37] It is also the sacramental event that expresses the essence of the Christian life: to be "in Christ" in the power of the Spirit is to be joined to all the other members of the body of Christ. A Christian cannot live a solitary life for no one who shares in the body and blood of the Lord can live for himself or herself. In this sense the ethics of the Christian life also arise from the fusion between the meaning of the eucharist and the meaning of the church.

Finally, a eucharistic ecclesiology shows the church to be that place where all is reconciled in Christ. Salvation will ultimately be restored communion with God. More than simply a judgment and proclamation of righteousness for an individual, salvation is the reconciliation of all in Christ through the power of the Spirit for the glory of the Father.

---

37. Tillard, *Flesh of the Church*, ix.

The Local Church: A Critical
Point of Departure for a World Ecclesiology

Alberto L. García

In *Mother Church,* Carl E. Braaten offers an important point of departure toward an ecumenical vision for the church:

> The future of the ecumenical movement cannot be separated from the future of the one holy catholic church of Christ on earth. The hope and promise of unity can be encouraged by the "ecclesiology of communion."[1]

Braaten insists that an ecumenical "communion ecclesiology" must give priority to the local church. The local congregations have ontological priority because it is there where the church of God is concretely actualized through the preaching of the Word of God and the administration of the sacraments.[2] Local congregations exist in Eucharistic fel-

---

1. Carl E. Braaten, *Mother Church: Ecclesiology and Ecumenism* (Minneapolis: Fortress Press, 1998), p. 5.
2. Braaten, *Mother Church,* p. 8.

This essay is directed to a global vision for ecclesiology. I am using in this essay the terminology preferred by Lamin Sanneh in *Whose Religion Is Christianity?* (Grand Rapids, Mich.: W. B. Eerdmans, 2003). Sanneh uses the term "world" to underscore a Christianity that is more spontaneous and rooted in the lives of the inhabitants. The term "global" sometimes has the connotation of an "imported" Christianity. Cf. also Bryan T. Froehle and Mary L. Gautier, *Global Catholicism: Portrait of a World Church* (Maryknoll, N.Y.: Orbis Books, 2003). This book also offers this distinction. Other world-known writers such as Philip Jenkins, *The New Faces of Christianity: Believing the Bible in the Global South* (New York: Oxford University Press, 2006) prefer the term "global" for indigenous communities of Christian faith.

lowship with each other. The church catholic lives and has its being in this "communion of communions" or "communion of churches."[3] Ecumenism is not limited to the institutional hierarchical level. It truly exists at the local level where, as Braaten observes, "the Spirit of God is at work in the hearts and minds of the people of God across ecclesiastical lines."[4] In fact, the institutional church should be a "sign and servant" of what the Spirit of God is working at the local level.[5]

This essay is directed toward this particular vision within Braaten's larger ecumenical vision. We will be exploring how the theological reflection, mission and ministry of local communities of faith constitute a critical point of departure for a world ecclesiology. It is only in the affirmation of the local communities of faith that a world ecclesiology can truly be ecumenical.

Understanding the Meaning of "catholic" in Light of World Ecumenism

Early Christian writers such as Justin Martyr (?-c. 165) used the term "catholic" to mean "universal" or "general." This is how Justin makes reference to Jesus' "catholic resurrection," meaning a "universal" resurrection.[6] Ignatius of Antioch (c. 35-c. 107) is the earliest extant Christian writer who uses the expression "catholic church."[7] Ignatius affirms that wherever Jesus Christ is there is the "catholic church."[8] Patristic scholars such as J. B. Lightfoot have argued that Ignatius used the term "catholic" in this context to mean "universal" or "general." Justo González enlightens us with another plausible interpretation in light of the context of Ignatius's arguments.

Ignatius is giving episcopal advice to some who care nothing about love and withdraw from the Eucharist celebration of the church.

3. Braaten, *Mother Church*, p. 8.

4. Braaten, *Mother Church*, pp. 8-9.

5. Braaten, *Mother Church*, p. 9.

6. Justo L. González, *Out of Every Tribe and Nation* (Nashville: Abingdon Press, 1992), p. 22. Chapter 2, "A Vision of Catholicity" traces the development of the word in Christian thought. Cf. *Dial.* 82).

7. González, *Out of Every Tribe*, p. 20. Cf. *Ad. Smyr.* 8:2.

8. González, *Out of Every Tribe*, p. 21, n. 3. Cf. J. B. Lightfoot, *The Apostolic Fathers* (Hildesheim: Georg Olms, 1973), Part II, 2:310, n. 2.

He is counseling the Smyrneans to flee from all *merismoi* (divisions), which are the root of all evil. Contrary to this way of thinking, the whole church should be where the bishop is, just as the "catholic church" is present where Jesus is.[9] Ignatius is using the phrase to distinguish between orthodoxy and heresy. It is in this context that he uses the term "catholic" which has the etymological meaning of "according to the whole." He uses this term in admonishing against the *merismoi,* the divisions and sectarianism present in the church. The difference between Ignatius and his critics is clear. Ignatius holds to a vision of the church that is "catholic," i.e. one that is holistic. This holistic vision is not generic. It is a catholicity that etymologically understood affirms the local witness of faith communities. Ignatius affirms as "catholic" doctrine the entire catholic "witness" of the "entire" catholic Church whereas his opponents hold to the partial opinion held by a particular group.[10] According to Bishop Ignatius, the doctrinal foundation of the Christian church cannot exist apart from the testimony of the church catholic. The apostolic faith is grounded on the incarnate witness of Christ among all people of the world. This understanding of catholicity is elucidated further by Irenaeus of Lyon (?–c. 202).

Irenaeus's understanding of catholicity is clearly expressed in his defense of the use of the four gospels:

> For, since there are four zones of the world and four principal winds, while the church is scattered throughout all the world, and the pillar and ground of the Church is the spirit of life; it is fitting that she should have four pillars, breathing out immortality on every side. . . . He who was manifested to me, has given us the Gospel under four aspects, but bound together by one Spirit. . . . For this reason were four principal covenants given to the human race: one prior to the deluge, under Adam, the second, that after the deluge,

9. González, *Out of Every Tribe,* p. 20.

10. González, *Out of Every Tribe,* pp. 20-21. Cf. Richard R. Gaillardetz, *Ecclesiology for a Global Church* (Maryknoll, N.Y.: Orbis, 2008), p. xx. Gaillardetz offers a similar interpretation of Ignatius. He writes: "St. Ignatius of Antioch would refer to the church as 'catholic' (a Greek compound of *kata* and *holos,* literally 'pertaining to the whole') as a means of describing the church as an inclusive and expansive reality. In the third and fourth centuries, the 'catholicity' of the church took on a somewhat different meaning; now it denoted the whole church over against various sectarian or dissident groups."

under Noah, the third, the giving of the law, under Moses, the fourth that which renovated man, and sums up all things under the Gospel.[11]

Modern scholars have misunderstood Irenaeus's use of the number four. He is not conjuring in this reflection some magical incantation. He is not saying that because there are four regions there should be four gospels. What he is saying is that the witness to the Gospel must represent the entire *oikoumenē*, the entire inhabited earth. His perception of this *oikoumenē* is not merely geographical. It is also chronological. The Western church understood this perspective to a certain extent.

Tertullian (c. 155-220) affirms the importance of the local witness of the church for her catholicity. This is how he affirms the "rule of faith" of the church catholic. He identified this rule of faith as the baptismal confession adopted by Christians everywhere, which distinguished them from unbelievers and heretics. He writes in *De Virginibus Velandis* that this "rule of faith is altogether one, alone *(sola)*, immovable, and irreformable."[12] In spite of his rigidity, Tertullian maintains that this early Christian Creed was not absolutely identical in all of the Christian congregations. In fact, during the course of time various changes and additions were made. "Tradition," observes Tertullian with respect to the baptismal confession, "has enlarged it, custom has confirmed it, faith observes and preserves it."[13]

If we were to take the theological journey of Tertullian as a case study of the phenomenon of catholicity, we will discover that he is the first theologian to write in Latin for the Western church. Certainly, he is the creator of a significant number of the theological Latin terms employed by the church to this day. He created and gave meaning to such terms as *persona, substantia,* and *satisfactio*.[14] Tertullian was aware that he had to use the language and context of his time to proclaim the

11. As quoted in González, *Out of Every Tribe and Nation*, p. 19. The quote is taken from *Adv. haer.* 3.11.8-9.

12. F. Bente, *Historical Introduction of the Symbolic Books of the Evangelical Lutheran Church*, vol. III (Milwaukee: Northwestern, 1921), p. 11.

13. Bente, *Historical Introduction*, 12.

14. Cf. *The Ante-Nicene Fathers*, vol. III: *Translations of the Writings of the Fathers down to A.D. 325*, ed. Alexander Roberts and James Donaldson (Grand Rapids: Eerdmans, 1980-85).

rule of faith. But he was not aware like Irenaeus concerning the importance of a world-local Christianity in enriching the witness of the catholic church. A true ecumenical vision of the church, a communion of communions, can only be maintained when the world community of local congregations plays an important role in enriching the catholic witness of the church. This is a key principle in twenty-first-century ecumenical ecclesiology. The witness and life of local communions of faith ensures what is envisioned as catholic by the early church fathers. This is also the vision of Vatican II.

In *Lumen Gentium* (13.3), the Dogmatic Constitution on the Church, Vatican II affirms that the church is truly the People of God when it lives in the following catholicity:

> In virtue of this catholicity each part contributes its own gifts to other parts and to the entire church so that the whole and each of the parts are strengthened by the common sharing of all things and by the common effort to achieve fullness in unity.[15]

In other words, it is not just that the church has to adopt a new language and customs in proclaiming the Apostolic faith. This vision of catholicity affirms that the Holy Spirit is outpouring his gifts in a special manner among all people to strengthen and bind the proclamation of the Apostolic church. This is the crucial issue. The important question now is: how does the witness of local communions of faith contribute toward building this kind of world ecclesiology?

There are three key ecclesiological dimensions that are impacted by the local communion of faiths in constructing a catholic world ecclesiology. These are the liturgical, redemptive, and sacramental dimensions. This essay will use these three dimensions to show how the local communions of faith enrich our ecumenical and catholic ecclesiology.

Lex orandi lex credendi

The worship life and prayers from the various communities of faith have been the major factor in the development of the confessions and

---

15. *Concilio Vaticano II; Constituciones, Decretos y Declaraciones* (Madrid: Biblioteca de Autores Cristianos, 1970), 62. My translation from the Spanish.

creeds of the Christian faith in Christendom. It is from this fountainhead that theological terminology unfolds and develops in Christian doctrine.[16] There are no creeds and theological formulations apart from the liturgical life within the local communities of faith. This is clearly evident within the Pauline corpus in the earliest confession of faith concerning Jesus Christ. Jesus is first confessed as Lord in the baptismal liturgy of the New Testament church (Romans 10:9; 1 Corinthians 12:3). Jesus is not merely identified with *Yahweh*, the *Kyrios* of the Greek Septuagint. His lordship is not a kingship as ruler or emperor in line with the Roman or Greek gods. He is the divine answer present to the community of faith because of his suffering and death in obedience to God.[17] Jesus Christ's lordship points to him as the first fruit of the resurrection for those who suffer and for those who have fallen asleep (1 Corinthians 15:12-28). "Jesus is Lord" is a baptismal prayer for the faithful in the context of the world and culture of the local community.[18] It is a word of hope and new life for those who live his presence among them. This was also the case for the early church.

It is the confession of Christians in liturgical adoration that gives credence to the rule of faith in the three major divisions of Christendom.[19] A case in point is the development of the Trinitarian dogma of the Creed of Nicea of 325. Long before there was an explicit explanation of the Holy Spirit in the Niceno-Constantinopolitan Creed of 381, the baptismal creed adopted at Nicea already confessed in the reality of the

---

16. Cf. Jaroslav Pelikan, *Credo: Historical and Theological Guide to Creeds and Confessions of Faith in the Christian Tradition* (New Haven: Yale University Press, 2003), pp. 166-85. Robert W. Jenson rightly defines *lex orandi lex credendi* as a Roman Catholic principle whereby there are distinguishing regularities in the church's life of prayer that govern the church's formulation of her beliefs. However, it is simply in Jenson's definition a law to guarantee the church's formulation of its belief. There is more to consider. The people pray as the community of believers affirming God's grace in their midst. The daily lives and experience of the people engage the tradition and teaching of the church. Therefore, their focus is also to be a living witness of the Gospel. Their prayer lives contribute, therefore, to the catholicity of the church. Cf. *Systematic Theology,* Volume 1: *The Triune God* (Oxford: Oxford University Press, 1997), p. 13.

17. Werner Foerster, *"kyrios,"* in *Theological Dictionary of the New Testament,* ed. Gerhard Kittel (Grand Rapids: Eerdmans, 1965), III:1088-91.

18. The Pauline benediction in 2 Corinthians 13:13 is also a living doxology for the faith of the people.

19. Pelikan, *Credo,* p. 166.

life of the people the place and function of the Holy Spirit in the community of faith.[20]

The language of prayer seemed also more intent on acknowledging Jesus as God in the midst of the lives of the people even before there existed a conceptual precision and terminological consistency.[21] This dynamic and principle is of crucial importance in the vision of a world ecclesiology. We must, therefore, affirm our church traditions in light of the faith of the people as it is expressed within their liturgical life. In the words of John Meyendorff:

> The Christian faith has never been a matter of simple individual convictions or propositional affirmations: It is a matter of reaching through baptismal death and resurrection to a new dimension of personal existence in the communion of the risen body of Christ.[22]

The communion of the risen body of Christ creates in hope a new language, a new beginning for those who celebrate Christ's presence in that place. The rule of faith is confessed with this new language created within the contextual horizon of the people of God. It is a confession that lives necessarily within the cultural and social realities of the risen body of Christ because it is a confession of the living Christ leading people from death into life.[23] This requires that we present a case study

20. Pelikan, *Credo,* p. 167.

21. Pelikan, *Credo,* pp. 168-69. A case in point is the early homily that came to be known as *The Second Epistle of Clement* (c. 150 A.D.). This is how the letter begins: "Brethren, we ought to think of Jesus as we do God — as the 'judge of the living dead.'" (2 Clement 1:1). This letter was written to be read within the liturgy and prayer life of the church.

22. John Meyendorff, "The Nicene Creed: Uniting or Dividing Confession?" in *Faith to Creed: Ecumenical Perspectives on the Affirmation of the Apostolic Faith in the Fourth Century,* ed. S. Mark Heim (New York: Commission of Faith and Order, 1991), p. 3. Meyendorff makes this statement in reference to what is characteristic of the pre-Nicene era before the "Constantinian" period.

23. Cf. George A. Lindbeck, *The Nature of Doctrine: Religion and Theology in a Postliberal Age* (Philadelphia: The Westminster Press, 1984). I believe that Dr. Lindbeck's cultural linguistic approach has something to offer. However, it has limitations in understanding the validity of the local communities of faith in world Christianity. He writes: "[R]eligious change or innovations must be understood not as proceeding from new experiences, but as resulting from the interaction of a cultural-linguistic system with changing situations" (p. 39). I concur with him that the cultural linguistic life of the community of faith is important in speaking of the "regula fidei," i.e. the rule of

on how the liturgical life of the local communities of faith is important for world Christianity. This case study will lead us to reflect on the second important dimension for a world ecclesiology, the redemptive dimension. The redemptive life and witness of the people of God is clearly born out of the prayer life and doxology of the local communities of faith. We must listen to these local witnesses of faith if we are to live a truly ecumenical world ecclesiology.

Returning from Exile: The Confession of a Catholic Evangelical Living within the Redemptive Witness of My People

Dr. Carl E. Braaten, my Doktorvater, in two separate instances uses the examples of Cubans in exile to speak of the state of ecumenical relationships between the Lutheran and Roman Catholic Churches.[24] Lutherans are Catholics in exile. Some exiles hope to go home again when all the conditions are favorable. Others do not care to go home. The point is, however, that many Roman Catholics and Lutheran exiles have gone home again to Cuba. This going back home has helped returning exiles in light of their local communities of faith to offer some constructive proposals in working toward a truly catholic world church as envisioned by Irenaeus and Vatican II.[25] This is my point of reference as a returning Cuban exile from the Diaspora.

In the year 2000, after exactly forty years, I returned to La Habana, Cuba for the first time. One of the first things I did upon my return was to visit the Iglesia San Agustín with several of my cousins. There I

---

faith, in a way relevant for today. However, the lived experiences of the people in new situations are important in the religiosity of the people. I will offer as a case study in this essay the Cuban Roman Catholic experience to provide some insights toward the contribution of the local communities of faith to world Christianity. This experience is offered as a case study that resonates with the faith of the people from other Latino/a communities.

24. Carl E. Braaten, *That All May Believe: A Theology of the Gospel and the Mission of the Church* (Grand Rapids: Wm. B. Eerdmans, 2008), p. 48; Braaten, *Mother Church*, p. 13.

25. The reflection that follows in light of this "going back" has been enriched by the "teología en conjunto," a theology carried out by Latino/a theologians from various nationalities and across denominational lines in communal conversations. The literature is prolific in this area. For a recent effort toward a Latino ecumenical theology cf. Orlando E. Espín, editor, *Building Bridges, Doing Justice: Constructing a Latino/a Ecumenical Theology* (Maryknoll, N.Y.: Orbis, 2009).

touched the baptismal font where I was baptized by the Augustinian Father William So Frank on June 8, 1947. On the wall behind the baptismal font there is a statue of the Lady of Charity, the patron saint of Cuba.[26] This encounter made me reflect on the Roman Catholicism that I left in Cuba vis-à-vis the Roman Catholicism that Luther attempted to reform in the sixteenth century. I hope that this point of departure will help illustrate from one corner of the world how important are the local communities of faith in providing a redemptive witness for a world Christianity.

In Cuba as well as in other Latin American countries the faith of the people is primarily grounded on popular Catholicism. What is meant by "popular" is not that which is simply widespread among the people. "Popular" is the adjectival correspondence to the noun "people." As Orlando Espín correctly argues, "this popular Catholicism is 'popular' because it is the people's own."[27] Most Latinos share in this tradition within Catholicism, and most of our Hispanic cultures are clearly grounded in it. This popular religiosity lives in the prayers and worship experience of the people. In fact, it lives in the daily faith experience of the people as they struggle with the many problems present in life. This popular religiosity presents many challenges as well as many opportunities for the official hierarchy of the Catholic church and the many evangelical and Protestant denominations doing mission among Latino communities. Some theologians would simply dismiss at first glance this religious experience as "superstitious." They do this by simply identifying popular Catholicism with the sum of Latino devotions. This a priori rejection would dismiss the catholic witness of redemption within the Latino Christian communities. It would limit the ecumenical unity of world Christianity by failing to understand how the incarnate Christ lives within the faith of the people. It would stifle the vision of a true ecumenical faith where the rule of faith is enriched by

26. Cf. Miguel H. Díaz, "Dime con quién andas y te dirés quién eres: We Walk with Our Lady of Charity" in *From the Heart of Our People: Latino/a Explorations in Catholic Systematic Theology,* ed. Orlando O. Espín and Miguel H. Díaz (Maryknoll, N.Y.: Orbis, 1999), pp. 153-72. He explains the place of "La Virgen del Cobre" within the popular religiosity (Catholicism) of the Cuban people.

27. Orlando O. Espín, *The Faith of the People: Theological Reflections on Popular Catholicism* (Maryknoll, N.Y.: Orbis, 1997), p. 3. This is an excellent introduction to the role and function of popular Catholicism among Latinos and Hispanics in Latin America, the Caribbean and the United States.

the testimony of the Latino church. Our first goal is to point out how popular religiosity takes on an important role in the prayer and liturgical life of Latino catholicity. The first step in this process is to understand how the Catholic tradition unfolded in the Caribbean and Latin America.

This is an important exercise for Protestants and Roman Catholics alike. The heirs of the Lutheran reformation and post-Tridentine Catholicism share in a similar tradition. In a sense, the Protestant Reformation had as an important focus to rid the church of its popular Catholicism. The reformers earnestly sought to reform the church in light of the Holy Scriptures. This is how they strove to preserve the truth of the faith handed down from the Apostles. John Eck was not an obscurantist as many Protestant theologians caricature him. He was a scholar of the Holy Scriptures pursuing his own translation of the Scriptures into German. He wished to reform the church also from its many errors. This was also the case with many Roman Catholic scholars and leaders such as Cardinal Ximenes de Cisneros, Ignacio Loyola and others. There was a great pursuit toward going back to the biblical sources and toward ending popular religious superstition. There was a great reform toward a more erudite clergy and church catechesis. In a sense, while there were differences in terms of authority in the church, there was a common vision to minimize and keep in check the popular religiosity of the people.[28] This post-Tridentine tradition, however, did not impact the catholic tradition being forged in Latin America during the sixteenth century. The control that the church hierarchy claimed and obtained in Europe was not generally present in Latin America, where the distances were great and communication difficult. Also, there was a scarcity of missionaries and clergy in a vast land where the native (and later African) populations to be Christianized were enormous. This set of affairs gave way to various forms of popular religiosity and piety. The reason that Christianity made an impact in Latin America was not due to post-Tridentine Catholicism. It was due to the prevalent Iberian Medieval Catholic popular spirituality in Spain and the wisdom of the missionaries to use this popular piety as a point of contact for an incarnational witness within the lives and popular piety of the people. There is no doubt that there were some major challenges

28. Espín, *The Faith of the People*, pp. 4-7; Justo L. González, "Reinventing Dogmatics," in *From the Heart of Our People*, pp. 218-22.

that still exist. Some of the adapted forms of popular religion were plainly syncretistic. The African or Amerindian worldviews prevailed as the necessary fundamental key in the conversion of many to Christianity. Their appropriation of Christianity was colored by this popular religiosity. There was an attempt in other communities to break away from their popular religiosity, but their popular religiosity resurrected in moments of crisis. Other communities have maintained (consciously or unconsciously) two faith systems in tension while negotiating a solution to their daily struggles. This panorama continues to exist in the landscape of the Latin American religious experience. In fact, it is difficult to understand what is meant by "conversion" to Christianity in light of this fluid or porous experience of popular religiosity within Christianity in Latin America.[29]

The primary purpose of this essay is not to provide a contextual witness for Latin American Christianity in light of the popular religiosity of the people. It is not to provide a specific experience of faith as truly valid for that specific community at the expense of a catholic evangelical faith. Although these are valuable themes to consider, the purpose of this essay is to underscore how particular witnesses of Christian communion of faiths are necessary for a truly catholic world ecclesiology. Otherwise our witness of the faith becomes sectarian and the rule of faith becomes unintelligible and meaningless to a vast number of God's people. Also, these particular witnesses of the faith enrich our catholicity by calling to the front line neglected elements of the Gospel within other communities of faith. It is in this light that I believe it is appropriate at this juncture to reflect on the faith of my people.

There is a consistent multiform experience of God in the Latin American popular Christian religiosity. God is generally found as Father and Creator caring for and remembering his children. Jesus Christ is present in his redemptive suffering and in the suffering of God's people. The crucifixion of our Lord Jesus Christ is a crucial key symbol. The Holy Spirit lives in the daily experience of God's people. This is how Pentecostalism has made an impact in appropriating Latin American religiosity. The Virgin Mary as mother of God and in her many ma-

29. Cf. Timothy J. Steigenga and Edmund L. Clearly, eds., *Conversion of a Continent: Contemporary Religious Change in Latin America* (New Brunswick, N.J.: Rutgers University Press, 2007). Christián Parker, *Popular Religion and Modernization in Latin America: A Different Logic* (Maryknoll, N.Y.: Orbis, 1996).

ternal "manifestations" occupies an integral part in walking with the suffering and helpless communion of faiths in Latin America. The affirmation of popular saints, such as San Lázaro, San Martín de Porres, and others who walk as instruments of God in accompanying the people in their struggles is also a common picture.[30] The point of departure in this catholic popular tradition is the experience of faith within the community of believers. This does not mean that Latin Americans or U.S. Latinos/as have abandoned a cognitive expression of the Christian faith. Dogma, and other doctrines, however, need to be affirmed within the popular catholic faith and witness of the local community.[31] The prayers and actions of the people within the context of their everyday experience are central to the local witness of the church. They are also crucial in the reading of Scriptures and in the forging of a truly catholic tradition for a global church. U.S. Latino/a Catholic theologians affirm a distinct Catholic popular Latino tradition that is a valid expression, a valid vision of the Christian tradition.

In the context of a Latino/Hispanic vision of the Christian tradition, we might find significant differences in the symbolic, cultural, and analogical use of language, in liturgical expressions or in doctrinal emphases. There has been a tendency to read the popular catholic religiosity as anti-institutional within many circles in the Roman Catholic church. Many Protestant denominations have also rejected without much thought Latino/a popular religiosity as anti-Scriptural. Roberto Goizueta has provided solid arguments for this opinion. It is mainly because of a Western intellectual bias rather than the reality itself.[32] The essential point is, however, that popular Catholicism has always been an important component in the worship experience and witness of world Christianity beyond Latin America and U.S. Latino Catholicism, e.g. in Spain and Poland. Popular Catholicism does not affect the essential elements of the faith but rather contributes to the ecumenical catholicity of the church.[33] This is also crucial for a world ecclesiology where mainstream European or American ecclesiologies do not play a protagonist role. Moreover, this is crucial to understand

30. Parker, *Popular Religion and Modernization in Latin America,* pp. 89-91.

31. Cf. Roberto S. Goizueta, *Caminemos con Jesús: Toward a Theology of Accompaniment* (Maryknoll, N.Y.: Orbis, 1995), pp. 18-46.

32. Goizueta, *Caminemos con Jesús,* pp. 47-76.

33. Goizueta, *Caminemos con Jesús,* p. 24. Goizueta reflects here on the work of Sixto García and Orlando Espín.

Alberto L. García

in the context of a North American ecclesiology where the impact of the Latino/Hispanic communities is undeniable. However, we find two different devotional traditions within the same church. The European and American devotionalism promoted by the Roman Catholic Church in the nineteenth century became a vehicle to evangelize the faithful and to encourage identification with the Catholic church in the midst of a hostile Protestant culture. While the popular Catholicism in Latin America (and continued in the U.S. Hispanic religiosity) was developed without the support or encouragement of the hierarchy, the people did not reject the official liturgy and clerical leadership but developed a religious identity and liturgy also grounded on their popular religiosity.[34]

The Liturgical Life of Nosotros, the People of God

What kind of contribution may the Latino Church make to the liturgical life of the People of God? I have found the liturgical life of American Catholicism and Protestantism to be more focused on the individual relationship to God. There is also a Gospel witness directed to the felt needs of the consumer. Several of the biblically grounded churches find their chief witness to be how the individual understands the right message and the right doctrine in order to be in the right communion with God.[35] The liturgical life and prayers of the people follow from this witness of God. There is certainly an individual dimension to worship. However, the Latino communities of faith live more within a communitarian doxology of the faith. This doxological expression of faith is not only expressed in a temple but also in the everyday life of the people. Let me offer some examples of the Latino worship life in light of popular religiosity.

1. The Holy Family, Joseph, Mary, and Jesus, occupy a central role. The life and struggle of the family is very real. The narrative of how this Holy Family struggles in finding a shelter for "el niño

34. Cf. Mark R. Francis, "Building Bridges Between Liturgy, Devotionalism, and Popular Religion," *Assembly* 20:2 (April, 1994): 636. Cf. Goizueta, *Caminemos con Jesús*, pp. 26-27.
35. Cf. Robert N. Bellah et al., *Habits of the Heart: Individualism and Commitment in American Life* (New York: Harper and Row, 1985).

Dios" (the baby God) to be born is an integral part of the celebration of the "Posadas." This is a celebration that occurs in many Hispanic neighborhoods to share the narrative of God coming to be among us and our families.[36] This is crucial for the undocumented immigrant who lives in the redemptive hope of God being present for a people in Diaspora.

2. Holy Week is also an important experience, where the people walk with the suffering Christ through many processions. The people find in the narratives a Christ that is with the people. Holy Week is not a hopeless remembrance. In spite of the suffering relived and evoked in the remembrance of his death in many Latino parishes, there is a sense of peace in that the incarnate Christ who died for us continues to accompany us, and we accompany him and our fellow believers in the midst of our lives' vicissitudes. There are many parish celebrations that involve our families in this communal sharing with Jesus during the Holy Week *triduum*. This is the celebration that occurs between Holy Thursday and the Easter Vigil.[37]

3. There are many religious celebrations of "patron saints," as well as Christian holydays such as Nochebuena (Christmas Eve), and el dia de los Reyes Magos (Epiphany) that are celebrated as "fiestas" in the community. This is a place that all are welcome. A sacred space is created were the individuals are not mere individuals but valuable members of the Christian community.

What can we learn from the worship experience of most Latin Americans or U.S. Latino Parishes?

1. God is a relational God. He does not exist in abstraction but exists in the history and lives of the people. There is here an intimate family relationship between the Father and Son that exists in the lives of the people.

2. There is no separation, therefore, between the Jesus of history and the Jesus of faith. In fact, Latinos pray to "Jesucristo" to empha-

36. Cf. C. Gilbert Romero, *Hispanic Devotional Piety: Tracing the Biblical Roots* (Maryknoll, N.Y.: Orbis, 1991); James Empereur and Eduardo Fernández, *La Vida Sacra: Contemporary Hispanic Sacramental Theology* (New York: Rowman & Littlefield, 2006).

37. Goizueta, *Caminemos con Jesús,* pp. 32-37.

size this. The incarnate Christ came to be with his people as "Jesús." The two cannot be separated.[38]

3. The church is a Christian community. It is not about me, but about *nosotros* (we). The church exists as a communion of believers, as the People of God in everyday life.

4. The individual has her/his identity because he/she is a welcomed member in the community of believers as the community celebrate God among them.

How may this perspective strengthen and recover important elements of our "catholicity"? I find some important contributions:

1. God may be better approached as the Holy Trinity because God exists and lives in a relational community with us.

2. It helps us to engage in a Christian theology that does not separate creation from redemption.

3. It helps us to return to a biblical narrative in which God is always involved in the history of his people. In this sense, it helps us recover the presence of God among us as we live in God's history and promise. In other words, it helps us to recover the historical eschatological element of our tradition. God is not a *Deus ex machina* but a God that is present and walks with the people toward a new creation. The history of the people of Israel may be recovered in this light as an important element of our tradition.

4. We are able to address a redemption that is holistic in light of the proclamation of God's kingdom among us and not just for the individual.

5. Our celebrations point to an incarnational witness of God among us. God is always celebrated and doxologically praised in the midst of his people.

Please understand that Latin American and U.S. Latino theology also needs the catholic witness of the world community. We have many blank spots. I wish, for example, that there was a more explicit rather

---

38. Cf. Ada María Isasi-Díaz, *La Lucha Continues: Mujerista Theology* (Maryknoll, N.Y.: Orbis, 2004), pp. 242-43. Professor Isasi-Díaz makes a valid point here in affirming that the Latino/a prayer and faith life is always directed to "Jesucristo." The incarnate Christ/Jesus is called upon in the daily lives of the people.

than implicit witness of Christ's resurrection for our eschatological hope. The witness of the resurrection is not absent. It is understood in the celebration of Christ's death but I believe that it should be emphasized more in our dialectics of cross and resurrection. Also, I realize that many who pursue Hispanic Latino spirituality place on equal footing the canonical revelation of Holy Scriptures with the popular religiosity of Amerindian and African religions. In spite of this problem, these natural religions make valid contributions in so far as they point to a creator that is relational and involved with his people. They have been able to focus on the communal broken conditions of sin in everyday existence. They have a place to play in reconsidering and opening our Christian tradition to the Kingdom of God. In the words of Carl Braaten:

> A Christian tradition wholly fixed on itself, closed to its own further transformation, and satisfied to be a religion of a particular era or region would forfeit its right to be a servant and sign of the still eschatological future of all the religions. The history of religions is under way. Their final meaning can be discovered neither in their past nor limited present, but only in the end to which they are historically moving through forces beyond their control. Our aim of the Christian mission is to create a space in the other religions, for a future that will not negate them but fulfill them in accordance with the revelation of the divine love and mercy revealed in the ministry of Jesus and the apostolic mission.[39]

Therefore, in reconsidering our popular religiosity, the church catholic is able to give once again priority to the Gospel narratives where Jesus is our companion, brother, representative in our personal and communal existence.[40] He is "Jesucristo," the incarnate God for us. Jesus Christ is our representative in our everyday existence, what U.S. Hispanics call "lo cotidiano."[41] There is no separation between the life and ministry of

39. Carl E. Braaten, *No Other Gospel: Christianity among the World's Religions* (Minneapolis: Fortress, 1992), p. 47.

40. Cf. Carl E. Braaten, "The Christocentric Principle" in his *Principles of Lutheran Theology,* second edition (Minneapolis: Fortress Press, 2007), pp. 102-7.

41. José D. Rodríguez, "Shaping Soteriology *a la latina*" in *Building Bridges, Doing Justice: Constructing a Latino/a Ecumenical Theology,* ed. Orlando E. Espín (Maryknoll, N.Y.: Orbis, 2009), pp. 112-40. Rodríguez take note of this principle and applies it to a Latino Protestant religiosity in the U.S. He also affirms how I use this principle in my book

Jesus and his death for us. In an implicit sense there is no separation between incarnation and redemption. His suffering for us begins in his living with us and for us. This is the most powerful image that permeates our communal lives grounded in our popular religion. Our cultural moorings are, in other words, a fertile ground for a theology of the cross where God is doing his work in the midst of his people. He represents us and lives with us and for us.

This point of departure brings also some important considerations to the ecumenical table as we come to grips with our "catholicity," where the specific traditions contribute to a more complete vision of our Lord. In the words of Gabriel Fackre, "[t]hose on an ecumenical path have a mandate to quest for a holistic understanding in the work of Christ." This is also Carl Braaten's insistence in the construction of a communion ecclesiology. As Braaten observes, "[a]ll these salvation events are essential in a complete christological narrative faithful to the church's Scripture, creeds and liturgy."[42] They are here not to cause divisions but to provide a complete, should we say "catholic" unity in the way that Irenaeus envisioned it. We consider now the redemptive dimension of our catholicity for U.S. Latino/a Christians in the Diaspora.

Living in the Redemptive Life of the Crucified On

I would like to begin this section with a personal narrative. This narrative portrays also what I have encountered as a parish pastor in Chicago and Fort Lauderdale during ten years of pastoral ministry. In essence, it is a case study of how important it is to consider the communion of faiths in constructing a world ecclesiology. I begin by making reference to the faith of my father Antonio García. He gave me the middle name Lázaro to honor the popular Cuban Saint Lázaro.

Cristología: Cristo Jesús: Centro y Praxis del Pueblo de Dios (Saint Louis: Concordia Publishing House, 2006), pp. 125-38.

42. Cf. Gabriel Fackre's contribution to this volume, "Ecumenism and Atonement: A Critical Issue in Ecclesiology." Fackre comments on Braaten's arguments in *That All May Believe: A Theology of the Gospel and the Mission of the Church*, p. 155. Braaten makes reference to a few more important components for a redemptive Christology such as the Ascension, work of the Holy Spirit, and Eastern Theology of the Resurrection. They are here to provide a more complete picture and not divisions in the church.

This saint is identified in the Cuban folklore with the beggar in Jesus' parable in Luke 16:19-31. My father was an evangelical catholic. There was on a small table next to his deathbed a copy of the Holy Scriptures. He had underlined well his Bible and understood the doctrine of justification by faith as expressed in Romans 3. However, he also had a small statue of his San Lázaro close by. He considered himself a faithful catholic and never left his mother church. However, his closeness to God was marked by his connection to San Lázaro. I could not understand as a young parish pastor in my early days of ministry why many of the new church members "converted" to a Lutheran evangelical faith still thought necessary to keep close tabs with their popular religiosity. They even kept hidden statues of their favorite popular saint. Other of our church members returned to their popular faith in a few months or years. This going back may be attributed by some to Vatican II. The reality, however, is that they returned to their popular catholic religious roots.[43] The question becomes then, why is it that the doctrine of justification by faith had to be mitigated by the popular religiosity of the people for my father and other U.S. Latinos ? What does this have to do with the Gospel and the message of grace? How did the popular religiosity of my father contribute to his catholic evangelical faith? What does the message of salvation have to do with our Latino/Hispanic popular religiosity?

In the case of my father and many of my former parishioners, they affirmed justification not in very precise theological terms.[44] This was not due to my negligence. It was due to the fact that, for them, the most important thing was that God forgave them, walked with them, and called them as the people of God to service. It was God acting and making of the people the new People of God. My father knew also that God was in Christ completely forgiving his sins because of his death

---

43. A case in point at a more sophisticated level is the trajectory of the late Cuban Jesuit professor Dr. Alejandro García-Rivera (d. 2011), who returned from Lutheranism to Roman Catholicism. See in particular his early work *St. Martin De Porres: The "Little Stories" and the Semiotics of Culture* (Maryknoll, N.Y.: Orbis, 1995).

44. There is no doubt that tensions exist even within Lutheranism as to what "being justified" means. There are points of differences among denominations even between Roman Catholics and Lutherans after the signing of the *Joint Declaration on the Doctrine of Justification by Faith* on December 31, 1999. Cf. The Lutheran World Federation and the Roman Catholic Church, *Joint Declaration on the Doctrine of Justification* (Grand Rapids: Wm. B. Eerdmans, 2000). Cf. Braaten, *That All May Believe*, pp. 53-60.

and resurrection. He knew that God accompanied him and his family because of this fact. However, this faith was very much understood within his popular religious following of San Lázaro. Why? This is the question. It is also the question of our U.S. Hispanic/Latino communities and many Latin American communities. Why is our popular religiosity important for our justification? It has to do with ecclesiology! It is important to look at this tension to understand how important are the communions of faith for our catholicity.

San Lázaro, the Virgen del Cobre, the Virgen de Guadalupe, all point in a significant sense to God walking with his people. The specific popular saints are a sign of grace to the specific people of God who gather in those specific communities. God is incarnationally present in the lives of the people. This is generally demonstrated by the popular saints accompanying on God's behalf his people as they move around in the desert of life in search of the land with milk and honey. This is why these saints occupy such significance to the Latinos who now live in the Diaspora. The same saints upon whom God had compassion, and who spoke of his presence among his people in their homelands, have also come to live and dwell among his people right now.

Harold Recinos underscores this active vision of the crucified Christ in the telling of the parable of Lazarus in Luke 16:19-31. Granting that this is a parable, still it is in Christ's word about this "San Lázaro," that the Cuban and Salvadoran have found an important identity. This narrative is a powerful popular religious sign of God's grace among exiled Salvadorans in the city. It expresses for them that the despised ones as a people are affirmed by God. They have a name and a future as God's people. The rich man is nameless, but Lazarus is loved by God in his human condition. God is active in this parable to transform the fate of the helpless and destitute community. In other words, Lazarus is a symbol of Christ's incarnate presence. He stands as an active disciple of the cross and God honors him for his stand of faith. The Christ that dies for our sins and rose for our justification is the incarnate Christ that never abandons his people.[45] This is how the presence of God's grace is understood in our communion of faith. This is powerfully understood by the Mexican commu-

---

45. Harold Recinos, "The Barrio as the Locus of a New Church," in *Hispanic/Latino Theology,* ed. Ada María Isasí-Díaz and Fernando F. Segovia (Minneapolis: Fortress Press, 1996), pp. 186-87.

nities in relationship to the Virgen of Guadalupe. Her presence is a sacramental presence. She is not the sacrament. But God's grace is present in her witness of the Gospel. She is there with the grace of her son to bind and heal the community of faith with her witness and presence of the incarnate and crucified Christ. Virgilio Elizondo has captured the essence of the problem. We are not here to canonize or reject the popular religiosity of the masses. However, we need to offer a continuous reinterpretation of it in light of the Gospel.[46] If we do not do this, we proclaim the redemptive message of the Gospel apart from the community of the people. We proclaim an austere Gospel, a sterile Gospel that trumps or defaults the communion of believers. We proclaim a redemptive Gospel that is not engaged in gathering or building the People of God. The witness of the faith is done without taking into consideration the communion of believers in that particular place. If we do not take those communities seriously, our proclamation of the Gospel creates a particularistic vision and does not take into account what our catholicity is all about. Scriptural, canonical redemption is offered in multiform expressions in Scripture. The specific communities of faith help us to resurrect a holistic witness of the Gospel. They help us to fill the vacuum created by insisting on one part of Scripture while neglecting others.

A Reading of the Augsburg Confession in Light of a Redemptive Communion Ecclesiology

Lutherans find in the Augsburg Confession (1530) the defining confessional document to express the confessional faith. We have, however, made more emphasis of Luther's insistence on justification by faith as the article upon which the church stands or falls. This is primarily expressed in his Smalcald Articles of 1537 (II, art. i. par. 4).[47] Luther, as well as the other confessors, builds a careful theological highway in the Augsburg Confession that emphasizes other essential elements to the witness of the Gospel. These are important to our understanding Arti-

46. Virgilio Elizondo, "Our Lady of Guadalupe as a Cultural Symbol" in *Beyond Borders: Writings of Virgilio Elizondo and Friends,* ed. Timothy Matovia (Maryknoll, N.Y.: Orbis, 2000), pp. 118-25.
47. Robert Kolb, Timothy Wengert, et al. *The Book of Concord: The Confessions of the Evangelical Lutheran Church* (Minneapolis: Fortress Press, 2000), p. 301.

cle VII, the teaching concerning how we achieve the unity of the church. We read from the translation of the Latin text:

> And it is enough for the true unity of the church to agree concerning the teaching of the gospel and the administration of the sacraments. It is not necessary that human traditions, rites, or ceremonies instituted by human beings be alike everywhere. As Paul says [Eph. 4:5-6]: "One faith, one baptism, one God and Father of all."[48]

The question that I always ask is, what is this "teaching of the Gospel"? We need to explore the Augsburg Confession further.

The Augsburg Confession (AC) underscores as important for the proclamation of this Gospel a Trinitarian faith and the understanding that original sin has entered our life in terms of a broken relationship, i.e. being born "without fear of God, without trust in God."[49] This broken relationship is referred to as the loss of our "original righteousness" by Melanchthon in the Apology to the Augsburg Confession (II). The loss of this "original righteousness" is understood by Melanchthon as a loss of community between God and humanity as well as a broken relationship within humanity.[50] Article III points to the Son of God, not only using the formulas of the Council of Chalcedon (451) but also concerning his work for us. There is also one important theological emphasis made in the original Latin text that is left out in the German translation made by Justus Jonas. While AC III in the German makes reference to a "sacrificial atonement," in that Christ died to "propitiate God's wrath" *(und Gottes Zorn versöhnte)*, the original Latin

---

48. Robert Kolb, Timothy Wengert, et al. *The Book of Concord: The Confessions of the Evangelical Lutheran Church* (Minneapolis: Fortress Press, 2000), p. 43.

49. *The Book of Concord,* p. 36.

50. "Original sin is the absence of original righteousness. But what is righteousness? Here the scholastics quibble over philosophical questions and do not explain what original righteousness is. Furthermore, in the Scriptures this righteousness includes not only the second table of the Decalogue, but also the first, which requires fear of God, faith, and love of God. Thus original righteousness was intended to include not only a balanced physical constitution, but these gifts as well: a more certain knowledge of God, fear of God, and confidence in God, or at least the uprightness and power needed to do these things. And Scripture affirms this when it says [Gen. 1:27] that humankind was formed in the image and likeness of God. What else does this mean except that a wisdom and righteousness that would grasp God and reflect God was implanted in humankind, that is, humankind received gifts like the knowledge of God, fear of God, trust in God, and the like?" (Kolb, *The Book of Concord,* pp. 114-15).

document underscores that Christ died in order that "he might reconcile the Father to us" *(ut reconciliaret nobis Patrem).*[51] In light of the AC III Latin manuscript, there cannot be salvation outside of the people of God being reconciled with the Father. The proclamation of the Gospel is not a mere individual act. It is the Father's act of grace in Jesus Christ that gathers by the power of the Spirit the communion of saints to live this act of reconciliation.

This leads us to ask the question, again, in light of AC IV "Concerning Justification," what do we mean by the Gospel? This is what is stated in light of Romans 3 and 4: "God reckons this faith as righteousness." It is important to explore the gospel of reconciliation in relationship to Melanchthon's explanation of the term "justification" in the Apology to the Augsburg Confession IV, 252. He explains this term using only juridical terms: "And 'to be justified' here does not mean for a righteous person to be made out of an ungodly one, but to be pronounced righteous in a forensic sense as also in this text [Rom. 2:13]."[52] In the Lutheran evangelical confessional tradition there is an emphasis to keep distinct the work of redemption from the act of justification. One has to do with what Christ has done; the other has to do with how God offers this gift of redemption to us. Here lies the problem that we need to address. If we give the emphasis to justification alone, we fail to understand what is truly Christ's work for us. This needs to be clearly spelled out in relationship to our justification. This is essential if we are to understand what is meant by God "restoring" our original righteousness. The lost of our original righteousness is understood in our biblical narrative as a loss of community with God and consequently within our community of faith (Genesis 3 and 4). God being in Christ reconciling the whole world to himself cannot be merely described in forensic terms (2 Cor. 5:18-19). It involves God calling to redemption the whole world, and it involves the communion of saints as bearers of this witness of reconciliation. It is not a mere return to an "upright" human judicial state with God. We are called to a new life. This new life cannot really exist apart from a new life within the community of faith. This is why the local communities

51. Quotes are taken from Augsburgische Konfession, Artikel III, *Bekenntnisschriften* (Göttingen: Vandenhoeck & Ruprecht, 1979), p. 44, and Augsburg Confession, Article III, 4, in Kolb, *The Book of Concord,* p. 54.

52. Kolb, *The Book of Concord,* p. 159.

of faith are important within our catholicity. The call to live within the hope of the Gospel is a call to live a "new" original righteousness with the People of God in witness to the world. God's yes, his precious grace, cannot be lived or spoken outside of this redemptive life with others. This is Luther's understanding in his *Lectures on Genesis* (1535-45) reflecting on Genesis 1:26:

> And indeed, we are reborn not only for life but also for righteousness, because faith acquires Christ's merit and knows that through Christ's death we have been set free. From this source our other righteousness has its origin, namely, that newness of life through which we are zealous to obey God as we are taught by the Word and aided by the Holy Spirit. But this righteousness has merely its beginning in this life, and it cannot attain perfection in this flesh. Nevertheless, it pleases God, not as though it were a perfect righteousness or a payment for sin but because it comes from the heart and depends on its trust in the mercy of God through Christ. Moreover, this also is brought about by the Gospel, that the Holy Spirit is given to us, who offers resistance in us to unbelief, envy, and other vices that we may earnestly strive to glorify the name of the Lord and His Word, etc. In this manner the image of the new creature begins to be restored in this life.[53]

Luther certainly understands that the redemptive life is more than the doctrine of justification. Being justified means that we are set free in Christ. But this setting free calls us to a new righteousness. This righteousness incorporates another righteousness, which is to live Christ's reconciliation within the communion of believers and the world. He elucidates this point in detail in his Treatise on "Two Kinds of Righteousness" (1519). We live a discipleship of the cross. We take on the form of God as servants in line with Philippians 2:7-8.[54] There is no redemptive life apart from serving the weak and the helpless within our

---

53. Martin Luther, *Luther's Works*, vol. 1: *Lectures on Genesis: Chapters 1-5*, ed. J. J. Pelikan, H. C. Oswald & H. T. Lehmann (Saint Louis: Concordia Publishing House, 1999, c. 1958), 1: 64-65.

54. Martin Luther *Luther's Works*, vol. 31: *Career of the Reformer I*, ed. J. J. Pelikan, H. C. Oswald, and H. T. Lehmann (Philadelphia: Fortress Press, 1999, c. 1957), 31:302. Luther writes: "Paul's meaning is that when each person has forgotten himself and emptied himself of God's gifts, he should conduct himself as if his neighbor's weakness, sin, and foolishness were his very own."

community. Therefore, the popular religious symbols, signs, and narratives expressed within the Latino communities cannot be cast aside if we are to proclaim the Gospel of reconciliation. It is there where the grace of God becomes incarnate and brings forth Christ's cruciform communion within the pains, brokenness and hopes of the Latino communities' everyday existence. This popular religiosity becomes an important partner in constructing our catholic witness of the Gospel. It is an important element in offering a "new" original righteous order to the People of God. This is the case because it offers important contact points to speak of salvation not merely in judicial terms within a world ecclesiology. A truly catholic world ecclesiology must take seriously the message of reconciliation within the communion of saints. Salvation is not a separate locus in systeatic theology from ecclesiology. It is an integral message within the communion of saints. We cannot speak of one without the other. The reason is evident: Christ lives in the midst of the people's everyday existence. His incarnate presence lives in communion with the *koinōnia*/communion of believers. We must always be attuned, therefore, to the signs, symbols, and presence of God's grace within the world communions of faith. This is clearly seen also as we consider the sacraments. Sacraments are empty of their meaning outside of the local communion of faith.

The Sacraments in Light of the Local Communions of Faith

There is no doubt that communion ecclesiology has become, as Professor Joseph L. Mangina suggests, a kind of ecumenical *lingua franca* in the pursuit of church unity.[55] "For Roman Catholics," Mangina affirms that "communion ecclesiology elevates the mystical and sacramental aspects of the church over its institutional expression."[56] Mangina explores how important it is to consider the cruciform existence of our Lord Jesus Christ in light of his *koinōnia*/communion with the people of God in the Eucharist (1 Cor. 10-12). In light of 2 Corinthians 4, this cruciform existence implies a sharing in the life, infirmities, shortcomings, afflictions of the People of God as Christ shared in their

---

55. Cf. Joseph L Mangina, "The Cross-Shaped Church: A Pauline Amendment to the Ecclesiology of *Koinōnia*" in this book.

56. Mangina, "The Cross-Shaped Church," p. 68 above.

sufferings. We share in Christ's sufferings with our brothers and sisters in the church and in the world. This participatory sharing is eschatological in that we live in Christ's suffering the hope of a new life for the People of God and the world. This is how we live our new life in Christ. Luther's theology of the cross follows within this vision.[57] The institutional church across denominational lines has falsely assumed that an "ecclesiology from below" or "Christology from below" negates a high ecclesiology, Christology, and doctrine of salvation.[58] This is not necessarily the case. In fact, the appropriation of specific sacramental offers of grace within our world communions is essential to a truly catholic sacramental theology. This is why the narratives concerning the faith of the people in their everyday experiences cannot be ignored. Let us briefly consider this in light of the sacrament of baptism.

Baptism and the "Catholicity" of the Church

The doctrine of Baptism is central for the unity of the church: "There is one body, and one Spirit — just as you were called to one hope when you were called — one Lord, one faith, one baptism, one God and Father of all, who is over all and through all and in all" (Ephesians 4:4-6). Baptism is the sine qua non for the people of God to be reconciled with one another: "You are sons of God through faith in Christ Jesus, for all of you who were baptized in Christ, have clothed yourselves with Christ. There is neither Jew nor Greek, slave nor free, male nor female, for you are all one in Christ Jesus" (Galatians 3:26-28). The texts cited point to

57. Cf. Alberto L. García, "Signposts for Global Witness in Luther's Theology of the Cross" in *The Theology of the Cross for the 21st Century,* ed. Alberto L. García and A. R. Victor Raj (Saint Louis: Concordia, 2002), pp. 15-36.

58. I find this to be the case in some of the pronouncements made by the Congregation of the Faith in recent years concerning liberation theology. A case in point is the notification of the congregation on the works of Jon Sobrino on November 23, 2005. We read: "The ecclesial foundation of Christology may not be identified with 'the Church of the poor', but is found rather in the apostolic faith transmitted through the Church for all generations." The "church of the poor" may be understood as an important aspect or foundation of the "catholicity" of the church. It may speak of the people's eschatological hope within a new creation without negating other important elements in Christology. An ecclesiology that gives credence to the cries of the local communities must incorporate their cries of oppression and inequality. It is not the only element but a very important element as God brings his word of Grace to the communion of faith.

two important elements in baptism. First, it is through baptism that we become the People of God. We become the church, the communion of saints. Secondly, it is because we are clothed with Christ that divisions disappear among various ethnic and economic groups, and between the genders. It is important to understand this unity in light of the Trinitarian, cruciform, and eschatological existence that undergirds our communion of faith.[59]

Unfortunately baptism has been relegated in many sacramental churches to an individual act of obtaining salvation. However, Christ's command is to baptize in the name of the Father, Son, and Holy Spirit (Matthew 28:19). Jesus' prayer to the Father is that his disciples and his church live within this Trinitarian communion as they give witness to the world (John 17:20-23). Christ's mission within the world is guided by this Trinitarian existence. We live the Trinitarian relationship of oneness and love within our community of faith. This life, however, is a cruciform way of life. We put on Christ's way of life by dying and rising daily in his death and resurrection. Notice how Romans 6:4-5 expresses this cruciform existence. The communion of believers live in Christ's death and resurrection the Trinitarian purpose that we "may live a new life." This eschatological way of existence for the communion of the baptized is described by Paul in several places as a "new creation" (2 Corinthians 5:17; Galatians 6:15). Please note that the adjective "new" *(kainē)* used in these texts implies a new order, a completely new creation. It implies something completely qualitatively new, fresh.[60] Baptism as a sacramental act calls the baptized to be an integral member of the community. But it is a call to live in Christ's cruciform way of life for the sake of the future of the community. Sr. Susan Wood has captured the essence of this eschatological redemptive life in her recent book on baptism:

> The eschatological meaning of baptism, like that of the Eucharist, points to salvation as a social reality. The second sentence in chapter 2 of *Lumen Gentium* [LG 9] makes the remarkable claim: "He (God) has willed to make women and men holy to save them, not

---

59. Susan K. Wood, *One Baptism: Ecumenical Dimensions of the Doctrine of Baptism* (Collegeville: Liturgical Press, 2009), pp. 1-19. Sister Wood has provided an excellent summary concerning the Trinitarian, eschatological, and cruciform components of a communion ecclesiology.

60. The specific term used here is the adjective καινὴ *(kainē)* from καινός *(kainos)*.

as individuals without any bond between them, but rather to make them into a people who might acknowledge and serve him in holiness."[61]

Baptism binds the community of believers, therefore, to live with one another the message of reconciliation in the power of the Spirit. The eschatological vision is that the community of believers renew their lives in light of God's new creation. They are called together to be and to become the new creation.

Baptism, as Professor Wood correctly points out, is not an individualistic act. It is a fundamentally ecclesial act. The individual is baptized within the public liturgical prayer of the church. This demonstrates the individual's (or family's) intentions "to live out faith in the context of the faith community that receives the baptized."[62] Wood's conclusions lead us to see why there is no catholicity outside the specific communion of believers:

> It is baptism in this local community that gives the baptized their ecclesial identity as Catholic, Lutheran, Presbyterian or Anglican. No rite says "I baptize you Catholic, Lutheran, or a Baptist." The faith of the community that baptizes and receives and nurtures the newly baptized in faith determines the ecclesial identity of the person baptized.[63]

Sr. Wood's conclusions help us to point out again how the specific communities of faith are essential to constructing a world ecclesiology that is truly "catholic." Catholicity necessitates that we listen to the faith of the people within each corner of the world as they give a living witness of the Gospel.

Baptism in the Context of the Faith of My People

I shared earlier about my return to the baptismal font where I was baptized in Cuba. I shared how my baptism in the name of the Father, Son, and Holy Spirit has always been accompanied by the popular religiosity

61. Wood, *One Baptism*, p. 16.
62. Wood, *One Baptism*, p. 175.
63. Wood, *One Baptism*, pp. 175-76.

of my parents and grandparents. In the case of the *Iglesia San Agustín* the image of the Lady of Charity *(Virgen del Cobre)* stands behind the baptismal font. How should we read this in terms of providing a constructive key toward a world ecclesiology? I was not baptized to be a Roman Catholic or Lutheran but in the name of the Triune God within my nurturing community of faith. What does this popular religiosity symbolize for my faith life? First of all, the message of reconciliation is an incarnate event that leads the community of believers to understand that God affirms them with his sacramental presence among them. The proclamation of the forgiveness of sins involves reconciliation in the specific places where the community is found desolate and broken. This hope of the people within this specific religiosity is to a certain extent countercultural. They are calling for a new life order where the strong do not destroy the weak. This hope is incarnational in that those religious symbols point to the continual walk of Christ with the broken communities and the helpless. Negating the religious symbols that point to the People of God's eschatological hope of a new creation is to negate the sacramental meaning of the Gospel. This walking together calls people to affirm one another and to welcome one another as they celebrate life and hope for the future in their religious festivities. The fact that these symbols have led some to fall into idolatry or syncretistic practices does not invalidate the fact that the people's expressions of faith may be signs of God's presence among them. This is why the various expressions of Christian faith are necessary to hear a truly catholic Gospel for all nations. It will help the church hierarchy become servants of the people as Christ lived as servant of all. As we take this principle to heart, we may engage other languages, symbols, and signs that will help us to rediscover and employ neglected elements of the biblical witness. The local church and communions of faith are essential, therefore, to a truly catholic and vibrant world ecclesiology.

Lutheran Principles for Ecclesiology

Cheryl M. Peterson

Lutherans have a long history of being suspicious about (or bored by!) ecclesiology as a theological topic.[1] When Lutheran theologians have ventured to broach the topic of ecclesiology, often their goal has been to articulate a "Lutheran concept of the church." Invariably this has led many of them to search for Luther's own concept of the church as the best way forward for Lutherans today.[2] The difficulties with this approach are several, not least of all the fact that Luther lived in the context of Christendom and we in North America do not.[3] At the same

1. Kent S. Knutson relays this anecdote from K. Skydsgaard: When Wilhelm Hermann came to visit Uppsala in 1910 and learned that a young Swedish scholar named Gustaf Aulén was writing a book on the topic of "the Lutheran concept of the church," he remarked, "I congratulate Swedish theology that it has so much time and peace that it can occupy itself with something so peripheral." Knutson, "The Community of Faith and the Word: An Inquiry into the Concept of the Church in Contemporary Lutheranism" (PhD diss., Union Theological Seminary, 1961), pp. 9-10.

2. See, for example, Knutson's dissertation, cited above, where he examines various Lutheran ecclesiologies and promotes the one that best exemplifies Luther's "dynamic community." Knutson published two articles that summarized the main ideas of his dissertation: "Community and the Church," in *The New Community in Christ: Essays on the Corporate Christian Life,* ed. James H. Burtness and John P. Kildahl (Minneapolis: Augsburg, 1963), pp. 37-61; and "Pluralism in Lutheran Ecclesiology," *dialog* 1 (1962): 59-66. I first learned of Knutson's work from Carl E. Braaten's *Mother Church* (Minneapolis: Fortress, 1998), pp. 83-86.

3. See my dissertation, "The Question of the Church in North American Lutheranism: Toward an Ecclesiology of the Third Article" (PhD diss., Marquette University, 2004), pp. 234-239, for a discussion of some of the methodological issues related to using Luther as a resource for ecclesiology.

time, I do believe there are uncovered treasures in Luther's theology that might contribute to the task of ecclesiology today.

The title of my chapter is a play on one of Braaten's most known and read books, *Principles of Lutheran Theology*. Originally I thought I might call the chapter "Principles in Lutheran Ecclesiology," but I changed the title to reflect my conviction — one I share with Carl E. Braaten — that the task is not to write a Lutheran (or any denominational) ecclesiology, but to offer a Lutheran contribution to a theological understanding of the one, holy, catholic and apostolic church that Christians profess in the Nicene Creed. In other words, ecclesiology by definition ought to be an ecumenical endeavor.[4]

My purpose then, is not to present a set of principles for a *Lutheran ecclesiology*, but to propose and explore key Lutheran principles toward an ecumenical understanding of the church. I begin with a brief discussion of the Lutheran principle par excellence, the christological principle and its corollary, the criterion of justification by grace through faith. Although this principle is central and primary for Lutherans, I argue that it is insufficient as a stand-alone principle for ecclesiology. Next I trace the shift in ecclesiology from a christological to a trinitarian framework in the larger ecumenical scene beginning in the mid-twentieth century. I explore this shift specifically in reference to the work of Lutheran ecumenist and theologian, Edmund Schlink. Finally, in light of the preceding, I propose and explore two complementary principles — the pneumatological and the sacramental — as authentically *Lutheran* principles to contribute to the task of ecclesiology today.

The Christological Principle and the Criterion of Justification

The Lutheran movement is not defined by a church concept or polity but by a confessional tradition. While ecclesiology (especially the ques-

---

4. A new ecumenical paradigm for ecclesiology has begun to emerge in the last half-century that is theologically grounded in the doctrine of the Trinity and centers on the concept of *koinōnia* or "communion." This paradigm has been engaged by Lutherans, most thoroughly in the 1997 LWF study "The Church as Communion," but also by individual theologians such as Robert W. Jenson. Others propose "mission" as a better organizing motif for ecclesiology which is also grounded in Trinitarian theology through the concept of the *missio dei*. Both paradigms have much to commend them and are in the background of what I propose.

tion of the church's authority) was an important issue in the Reformation, the defining theological issue was the doctrine of justification. As the Joint Declaration on the Doctrine of Justification states, "The doctrine of justification was of central importance for the Lutheran Reformation of the sixteenth century. It was held to be the 'first and chief article' and at the same time the 'ruler and judge over all other Christian doctrines'"[5] and therefore serves as an "indispensable criterion" for theology, including ecclesiology.[6] Thus, a Lutheran approach to ecclesiology rightly begins with the christological principle and its corollary criterion of justification.

This means that in the Lutheran understanding, as Ola Tjørhom notes, "The church is a sign of and a service to the gospel of justification, and not the other way around."[7] The gospel comes to us first and foremost through the proclamation of the Word of Promise, the living Word who is Christ. Whatever else Lutherans say about ecclesiology, the church exists to serve the free proclamation of the gospel of justification. Lutherans furthermore understand that the church receives its very being, authority, and purpose from this same gospel.[8] As the International Lutheran-Catholic Dialogue (1994), *Church and Justification*, states, "Consequently, the main ecclesiological concern of the Reformation was perpetual dependence on the gospel and subordination to it. This was concentrated in the formula that the church is *creatura Evangelii*."[9]

The christological principle and its corollary criterion of justification remain primary for any Lutheran approach to ecclesiology. However, when Lutherans take this principle and criterion as com-

---

5. The Joint Declaration on the Doctrine of Justification, §1.

6. JDDJ, §18.

7. Ola Tjørhom, "The Church as the Place of Salvation: On the Interrelation between Justification and Ecclesiology," *Pro Ecclesia*, Vol. IX, No. 3 (2000): 292.

8. How this plays out in structures is beyond the scope of this essay, but this very principle has allowed Lutherans to be flexible with regard to the question of polity and has enabled Lutheran church bodies, such as the Evangelical Lutheran Church in America, to be in full communion relationships with denominations of varying polities, including Episcopal, Presbyterian, and Congregationalist.

9. The Lutheran-Catholic Joint Commission, *Church and Justification: Understanding the Church in Light of the Doctrine of Justification* (Geneva: Lutheran World Federation, 1994), 2.4.1 §36. Citing Luther (WA 7, 721), the document goes on to say: "One of the key principles of Lutheran ecclesiology takes this up: 'The entire life and nature of the church is in the Word of God.'"

pletely sufficient for ecclesiology, it too easily can lead to the idea that "the ecclesiological significance of the doctrine of justification is that there is no ecclesiology."[10] This tendency can be seen in certain "Radical Lutherans," such as Steven Paulson. For these theologians, the church is almost epiphenomenal, defined in functional terms by which the proclamation which is necessary for faith occurs, most radically, in the preaching office itself.[11] In this way of thinking, the church is a "happening," or an "event," rather than a communion or a people. This protects the theological priority of justification but it leads to a thin (and I might add unbiblical) concept of the church.

The church is more than the Word-event that creates faith in individual believers through the Word and Sacraments; it is the community that is created simultaneously by this same Word. In their understanding of justification, Lutherans emphasize the gift of the forgiveness of sins which is personally appropriated by the believer ("pro me") through faith; however, this does not "mean individualism, but birth into a communion of believers, the body of Christ which is the church."[12] For Paul, the justification event also includes "acceptance into communion with God: already now, but then fully in God's coming kingdom (Rom 5:1f). It unites with Christ and with his death and resurrection (Rom 6:5). It occurs in the reception of the Holy Spirit in baptism and incorporation into the one body (Rom 8:1f, 9f; I Cor

10. Tjørhom, "The Church as the Place of Salvation," p. 292.

11. Paulson suggests this minimalistic definition in his critique of the Evangelical Catholic position, "Do Lutherans Need a New Ecclesiology?" *Lutheran Quarterly* 15 (2001): 217-234. The term "Radical Lutheran" comes from Gerhard Forde, "Radical Lutheranism: Lutheran Identity in America." *Lutheran Quarterly* 1, no. 1 (1987): 5-17.

12. "Common Statement: The One Mediator, the Saints, and Mary," Section II.A.50, in Lutherans and Catholics in Dialogue VIII, *The One Mediator, the Saints, and Mary,* ed. H. George Anderson, J. Francis Stafford, and Joseph A. Burgess (Minneapolis: Augsburg Fortress, 1992), p. 41. The communal aspect of justification is also addressed in the Joint Declaration on the Doctrine of Justification. JDDJ states that although justification and the renewal that follows must be distinguished, they cannot be separated. They are joined together in Christ, who is present to the believer in faith. Methodist theologian Lyle Dabney suggests that rather than speaking of "a forensic act of 'gracious exclusion,' as one Reformed theologian has termed it, *Christus extra nos* and *Christus pro nobis*," we need to speak, rather, of "God's acts of gracious inclusion in the life of the resurrecting Spirit of God who incorporates us into the life and death and resurrection of Jesus Christ our Lord." Dabney, "Justification of the Spirit: Soteriological Reflections on the Resurrection," in *Starting with the Spirit: Task of Theology Today II,* ed. Stephen Pickard and Gordon Preece (Adelaide: Australian Theological Forum, 2001), p. 75.

12:12f)."[13] While these ecclesial aspects of the doctrine of justification often have been neglected by Lutherans, the christological basis of both justification and ecclesiology has led some Lutherans such as Scott Hendrix to acknowledge this lacuna in Lutheran theology and to suggest that "justification and ecclesiology articulate the same reality from different angles and explore complementary dimensions of the one new life in Christ."[14] In this sense, the christological principle may be expanded beyond the traditional Lutheran emphasis on the event of justification to refer to "Jesus Christ [as] the chief link between justification and the church, salvation and ecclesiology."[15]

This linkage of Christ, salvation, and the church was a prominent topic of theological discussion in the mid-twentieth century. Many important Protestant theologians were exploring the application of this more broadly interpreted christological principle to ecclesiology while avoiding a strict identification between Christ and the church. They especially were concerned to steer clear of any notion of the pre–Vatican II Catholic understanding of the church as Christ's mystical body and in particular the concept of the church as the "extension of the incarnation" or "ongoing incarnation." The potential dangers of this view are addressed by several Protestant authors writing on the doctrine of the church at mid-century.[16] First of all, they fear that by too closely identifying ecclesiology with christology, such a concept of the church seemed to challenge the unique and complete nature of Christ's incarnation. As Lesslie Newbigin states, "What is absolutely clear from this evidence is that Christ's presence with His Church since

13. JDDJ §11.

14. Scott Hendrix, "Open Community: The Ecclesial Reality of Justification," in *By Faith Alone: Essays on Justification in Honor of Gerhard O. Forde,* ed. Joseph A. Burgess and Marc Kolden (Grand Rapids: Eerdmans, 2004), p. 237.

15. Tjorhom, "The Church as the Place of Salvation," p. 293.

16. For the following, see J. Robert Nelson, *The Realm of Redemption: Studies in the Doctrine of the Nature of the Church in Contemporary Protestant Theology* (Greenwich, CT: Seabury Press, 1951), pp. 97-104. Other key texts are Claude Welch, *The Reality of the Church* (New York: Charles Scribner's Sons, 1958); Lesslie Newbigin, *The Household of God: Lectures on the Nature of the Church* (New York: Friendship Press, 1954) and *The Reunion of the Church: A Defense of the South India Scheme,* revised edition (London: SCM Press, 1960); and Emil Brunner, *The Misunderstanding of the Church,* translated by Harold Knight (Philadelphia: Westminster Press, 1953). The Second Vatican Council also acknowledged the difficulties in speaking of the church as "extension of the incarnation," shifting to language of the church as "sacrament."

Pentecost is in a different manner from His presence on earth 'in the days of flesh.'"[17] It also implies that Christ loses his identity in and is somehow contained by the church. Citing Newbigin, J. Robert Nelson also argues that if the church is truly the continuation of Christ's incarnation, "there is no need for it to point beyond itself to Christ — as true preaching must do."[18]

During the same period, ecumenists were appealing to the christological principle as the theological basis for the unity of the church. This was a shift from the previous comparative method in ecumenism whereby "instead of beginning with one's own church and viewing Christ's activity in the other churches as 'elements' of one's own church," one rather begins with "Christ's activity and views one's own church as part of Christ's total sphere of activity."[19] This new method gained traction at the Third World of Faith and Order Conference held in Lund (1952). The Lund Conference reported: "We have seen clearly that we can make no real advance toward unity if we only compare our several conceptions of the Church and the traditions in which they are embodied." This new christological method was viewed as a means to penetrate behind ecclesial divisions. It affirmed "the conviction of the conference participants that 'As we come closer to Christ we come closer to one another."[20] The Conference concluded with the recommendation that future studies of Faith and Order treat the doctrine of the Church in close relation to the doctrine of Christ and the doctrine of the Holy Spirit.[21]

Indeed, both on the ecumenical stage and in the academic theological community, this christological focus turned out to be the first step toward a fully trinitarian emphasis. This was made clear in a recommendation of the next World Council in Montreal (1963), "The Church and the Purpose of God": "It would appear in retrospect that

17. Newbigin, *The Household of God*, p. 60.
18. Newbigin, *The Household of God*, p. 61.
19. Edmund Schlink, *After the Council* (Philadelphia: Fortress, 1968), p. 248. Schlink calls this shift nothing less than a "Copernican revolution."
20. *The Lund Report, The Report as Submitted for the Consideration of the Participating Churches,* Oliver S. Tomkins, ed., The Third World Conference on Faith and Order, Lund, 15-28 August 1952 (London: SCM Press, 1953), 15-65; the quotation is from "I. A Word to the Churches," p. 15.
21. Cited in *A History of the Ecumenical Movement*, Vol. 2 *(1948-1968),* ed. Harold E. Fey (Geneva: WCC, 1970), p. 151.

the study of the doctrine of the Church over the past twenty years has in fact been carried out at least implicitly with reference to a trinitarian understanding of God."[22]

The Trinitarian Principle

In the last several decades, this shift has been made much more explicit in ecumenical documents, dialogues, as well as by an increasing number of theologians writing on the church.[23] In his own work on ecclesiology, Braaten proposes that Lutherans follow the ecumenical pattern of framing our ecclesiology in trinitarian, rather than only christological terms. There are at least two ways (which are not mutually exclusive) that this pattern is followed in ecumenical and systematic treatments of the church. One is to draw on the three-fold designation for the church as drawn from scripture: the church is the people of God, the body of Christ, and the temple of the Holy Spirit.[24] Another is to follow the new ecumenical paradigm that has emerged that is rooted in the Trinity and focused on the concept of "communion," whereby the church's "being" is understood in terms of God's own Triune being, which is communion.[25] I propose a third way, which is to "start with the Spirit" within a trinitarian framework because in the economy of salvation, that is how God "starts" with us. This pattern can be discerned in Luther's treatment of the Apostles' Creed. Even though Luther follows the traditional order in beginning with the first article, his

---

22. Harold E. Fey, ed., *The Ecumenical Advance: A History of the Ecumenical Movement,* Vol. 2, *1948-1968,* 2nd ed. (Geneva: World Council of Churches, 1970), p. 151. Konrad Raiser, general secretary of the World Council of Churches, speaks of this as a "paradigm shift" whereby the earlier "Christocentric universalism" of the early WCC is replaced by a trinitarianism that is shaping a new model of unity as the participatory fellowship of the entire human race. See Raiser, *Ecumenism in Transition: A Paradigm Shift in the Ecumenical Movement* (Geneva: World Council of Churches, 1991). For a critique of Raiser on this point from a missional perspective, see Lesslie Newbigin, "The Trinity as Public Truth," in *The Trinity in a Pluralistic Age: Theological Essays on Culture and Religion,* ed. Kevin J. Vanhoozer (Grand Rapids: Eerdmans, 1997), pp. 7-8.

23. The Orthodox and Catholics are very much ahead of Protestants on this shift; in fact, this has been a major contribution of the Orthodox to the ecumenical movement and to ecclesiology.

24. See for example, *Church and Justification* (1994).

25. See note 4 above.

narrative of salvation starts with the work of the Holy Spirit, in what
Wengert calls Luther's "reversed Trinity." The Spirit makes known the
Son who in turn shows us the Father's heart.[26]

Within a trinitarian framework, Braaten further proposes that
Lutherans need to consider two additional principles — the pneumatological and sacramental principle — to balance out the Christological
principle which has been central to our ecclesiology. Some Lutherans
may protest that these principles do not sound very "Lutheran." To
speak of the "sacramentality" of the church sounds "too Catholic" to
some Lutheran ears and to speak of the church as a creature of the
Spirit sounds "too Pentecostal." In what follows, I explore these in Luther's writing, showing both how they can be embraced as *Lutheran
principles* for ecclesiology and, especially when taken together, they can
help to flesh out the christological principle toward a fully trinitarian
ecumenical ecclesiology that Lutherans can authentically embrace.

26. Timothy J. Wengert, *Martin Luther's Catechisms: Forming the Faith* (Minneapolis:
Fortress, 2009), pp. 43-44. In a recent article, Stephen Bevans argues for the concept of
"God inside out." Following Johannes Hoekendijk's insight that we can only know the
essential nature of the church (its *ad intra* nature) by discovering its mission (its *ad extra*
nature), Bevans proposes that this same logic applies to the Triune God. He writes,
"Echoing Rahner's now-famous dictum about the immanent and economic Trinity
(Rahner 1970: 22), I propose that *God's* 'inside,' i.e. God's mystery, can only be known
from God's 'outside,' i.e. God's movement to creation in Mission. Furthermore . . . this
movement is accomplished in the first place through the action of the Holy Spirit.
God's deepest nature, in other words, is discerned not by focusing on God's inner Trinitarian, communal life, but on God's 'ec-centric,' 'centrifugal' reaching out to the world
in love." Bevans rightly identifies the activity of the Holy Spirit as the first way that God
reaches out to the world. "The Spirit is divine mystery sent from 'inside' to be that mystery fully present and active 'outside' — in the world, in human history, in human experience: the Spirit is God Inside Out." What I would add to (or perhaps simply make
more explicit in) Bevans is that the church is created by and as a part of this movement
of the Spirit outward. See Stephen Bevans, "God Inside Out: Notes toward a Missionary
Theology of the Spirit," *International Bulletin of Missionary Research* 22, no. 3 (July 1998):
102-5. Neil Ormerod makes the same point in his assertion that while the attempt to
link ecclesiology to the Trinity by means of *communio* and *perichoresis* is admirable, in the
end it is problematic because "the divine unity is where God is most different from
God's creatures, even the creation that we call church. What is first in our knowledge of
the triune nature are the divine missions of Word and Spirit, which in turn ground our
knowledge of the processions and persons of the Trinity." Ormerod, "The Structure of a
Systematic Ecclesiology," *Theological Studies* 63 (2002): 3-28, 29.

Cheryl M. Peterson

"Starting with the Spirit" in a Trinitarian Ecclesiology

Edmund Schlink is a helpful dialogue partner in this endeavor for two reasons. First, as Braaten himself notes, Schlink had credentials both as a Confessional Lutheran and an ecumenical theologian. Braaten states, "I know of no Lutheran theologian more faithful to the Lutheran confessional tradition and at the same time more committed to the ecumenical goal of church unity."[27] More specifically for the purposes of this essay, Edmund Schlink not only makes the shift from a christological to a trinitarian framework in the development of his ecclesiology, but does so in a way that highlights the role and work of the Holy Spirit.

Schlink's early theology was shaped as much by Karl Barth's idea of the church as Word-event as it was by the Lutheran symbols.[28] He pointed to Article VII of the Augsburg Confession as providing a full, sufficient and accurate definition of the church which states two things: First, the church is a community of believers; and secondly, this community is "defined by what is done in its midst."[29] That is, the

27. Eugene Skibbe, *A Quiet Reformer: An Introduction to Edmund Schlink's Life and Ecumenical Theology — From a Gospel Voice in Nazi Germany to a New Vision of Christian Unity* (Minneapolis: Kirkhouse Publishers, 1999), quoted on the back cover. Schlink remains better known in this country for his textbook on the Lutheran Confessions than for his later ecumenical theology. It seems that Schlink is able to combine the two in a way that has not had the same success on American soil, where there is a more clear-cut split between Lutherans who follow a "confessional" method and those who follow an "ecumenical" method for doing theology. Schlink was able to see in the Lutheran confessions an ecumenical openness and freedom. The basis for his combined approach lies in his understanding of the Lutheran Confessions as a prolegomenon to theology, and not as theology proper.

28. An early articulation of the church as "event" by Barth is found in "The Church — the Living Congregation of the Living Word Jesus Christ," in *Man's Disorder and God's Design: The Amsterdam Assembly Series,* Vol. I, *The Church's Witness to God's Design,* ed. W. A. Visser 't Hooft (New York: Harper & Brothers, 1948), pp. 67-76. Barth's most thorough treatment of the church appeared in "The Holy Spirit and the Gathering of the Christian Community," in *Church Dogmatics* IV, Part 1, ed. G. W. Bromiley and T. F. Torrance (Edinburgh: T&T Clark, 1956), pp. 643-739, and "The Holy Spirit and the Sending of the Christian Community," in *Church Dogmatics* IV, Part 3, ed. G. W. Bromiley and T. F. Torrance (Edinburgh: T&T Clark, 1962), 681-901. The emphasis on church as "event" remains in this later work: "The Church *is* when it takes place, and it takes place in the form of a sequence and nexus of definite human activities" (Barth, *CD* IV:1:652, italics are his).

29. Schlink, *Theology of the Lutheran Confessions,* translated by Paul F. Koehneke and Herbert J. A. Bouman (Philadelphia: Fortress Press, 1961), p. 198.

proclamation of the Gospel and the administration of the sacraments in accord with this Gospel.[30] This happening or event is both the means by which the assembly of believers is created and the means which the community performs to carry out its service. And yet even the early Schlink recognized that as the assembly of believers, the church is also properly understood as "the communion of saints," which pushed him beyond the word-event concept. Citing Luther, Schlink states that the community created by God's acting is defined in terms of faith and love:

> The Holy Spirit through the Word and sacrament gives faith and a new obedience in love. . . . Therefore *"communio sanctorum"* is not only the assembly of the saints, but also "the sharing of the members with one another, each becoming a partner with all the others, each active for the other"; the brothers are in a fellowship of grace and of burden — and their fellowship is a sharing in each other's grace and burden.[31]

This communion is both the work of the Holy Spirit and the living body of Christ, since all action of the Holy Spirit is at the same time the action of Jesus Christ the Son.

In the essay "Twelve Theses for an Ecumenical Discussion between Theologians of the Evangelical and Roman Catholic Church,"[32] Schlink explicitly develops his thinking in a more Trinitarian direction. This essay is important because it provides the framework for Schlink's more developed understanding of the church[33] and also be-

---

30. Schlink notes that the Augsburg Confession names the Gospel, and not the Word in general, or the law, in connection with this proclamation.

31. Schlink, *Theology of the Lutheran Confessions,* p. 204, citing Paul Althaus.

32. Schlink, *The Coming Christ and the Coming Church* (Philadelphia: Fortress, 1968), pp. 96-118. This essay was first published in 1953.

33. Schlink, *Ökumenische Dogmatik: Grundzüge* (Göttingen: Vandenhoeck & Ruprecht, 1983). The titles of several sections listed under "The Church" in *Ökumenische Dogmatik* come directly from these Twelve Theses. For example, the first three theses — "The People of God Called Out of the Word," "The Prophetic, Priestly and Kingly People of God Sent into the World," and "The Worshipping Assembly" — are found in *Ökumenische Dogmatik,* pp. 566-578. Other sections reflect Schlink's more fully developed trinitarian framework. For example, in place of the original theses 4-7, which define the church more Christologically, is a section entitled "The Called Out *(Ekklēsia)* of God, the Body of Christ, the Temple of the Holy Spirit: The Increasing New Creation," pp. 578-585.

cause it offers an interesting contrast to perspectives that appear nearly to identify ecclesiology with christology.[34] First, Schlink notes that the New Testament contains a variety of terms for the church, not all of which are christological. In particular, there are many pneumatological designations, such as the temple of the Holy Spirit. This suggests, first of all, that the question of the origin of the church demands a Trinitarian answer, in order to account for the variety of answers that are customarily given (Jesus' death and resurrection, the Pentecost event, the election of the Israelites as God's covenant people).[35] Second, this means that

> ecclesiology must be taken as a whole and expounded and developed in a Trinitarian way; and in this we should not forget that in the primitive Confessions the articles concerning the Church are directly connected with the articles on the Holy Ghost. This suggests that, within a Trinitarian context, one should expound the doctrine of the church as the *opus proprium* of the Holy Ghost.[36]

In his magnum opus, *Ecumenical Dogmatics* (1984), Schlink develops a much more robust concept of the church from the third article. The church is treated in Part III, "The Doctrine of New Creation," in four different chapters: "The Church," "Charisma and Office," "The Preservation of the Church," and "the Unity of the Church and Divided Christendom." Schlink presents the nature and mission of the church in Chapter 19, "The Church," which follows a chapter on "The Pouring out of the Holy Spirit" (thus, Schlink here follows the suggestion he made in the Twelve Theses). Schlink speaks of the "double movement" of the church in pneumatological, communal, and missional terms, following the New Testament narrative: The church

---

34. Schlink, *The Coming Christ*, p. 96. In addition to his argument for a Trinitarian basis for ecclesiology, Schlink offers another reason to avoid the equation of ecclesiology with Christology, one that reflects his experience in the Confessing Church. Such an equation — especially as related to the image "body of Christ" — expresses only one connection between Christ and the church. Christ is also the head of the church, and the church is described elsewhere as Christ's bride. Each of these designations suggests distinction, rather than identification. Schlink also notes, "Then one has to take into consideration all the places where Christ confronts the Church as Lord, and even as Judge." Schlink, *The Coming Christ*, p. 97.

35. Schlink develops this point more fully in *Ökumenische Dogmatik*, pp. 561-566.

36. Schlink, *The Coming Christ*, p. 96.

is both the people of God called *out* of the world and the prophetic, priestly and kingly people *sent into* the world. "In this double movement of those being called and those being sent by God, the church exists."[37] In between these movements the church has its life in the worshipping assembly. This assembly is further defined by the tri-fold designation: the *ecclesia* of God, the body of Christ, the temple of the Holy Spirit.

One may still affirm that the church is created by the "event" of the Word through which the Spirit calls, gathers, enlightens, sanctifies and holds in truth the people of God. But the later Schlink no longer describes the church itself solely in Christological terms as a Word-event, but now as a people who are created in and live by this double-movement of the Spirit. The same Spirit that calls the people of God out of the world and into the worshipping assembly sends them into the world to bear the gospel in word and deed.

The Pneumatological Principle

Traditionally, the work of the Spirit has been interpreted by Lutherans (as well as by other Reformation traditions) as an application of the event of justification to individual believers, making the objective work of the cross and resurrection of Christ into a subjective experience of the believer through faith. Eilert Herms is an extreme example of this, describing the work of the Holy Spirit in individual terms using the category of revelation.[38] Without the work of the Spirit, the redeeming work of the Incarnate Son of God on the cross would remain hidden and unknown, and therefore lost. The Holy Spirit works externally through the preaching of the Word, and internally in the human heart, to reveal the meaning and truth of the gospel into each believer's heart.

---

37. Schlink, *Ökumenische Dogmatik*, p. 566. The translation is mine. The original German reads, "In dieser doppelten Bewegung des von Gott Berufen- und Gesandtseins existiert die Kirche."

38. Eilert Herms, *Luthers Auslegung des Dritten Artikels* (Tübingen: J. C. B. Mohr [Paul Siebeck], 1987). Jared Wicks points out that the concept of "revelation" only became theologically important after Luther's time, suggesting this category may not be the most appropriate to Luther's own context and concerns. See Wicks, "Holy Spirit–Church–Sanctification: Insights from Luther's Instructions on the Faith," *Pro Ecclesia* 2, no. 2 (1993): 156, n. 29.

Thus, the Holy Spirit brings an existential transformation to the believer and a new eschatological standing before God.[39] The work of the Holy Spirit, then, is sanctifying in that it endows each human person with new existential knowledge about their redemption.[40] Forgiveness of sins for Herms is also understood as a revelatory experience, as "nothing other than recreated existence in light of the appearance of the truth of the gospel."[41]

In spite of his focus on the individual, Herms does recognize the necessity of the church for the proclamation of the gospel through which the Holy Spirit reveals the truth of the cross. In this sense, Herms can state unequivocally, "Outside of this community of his body, there is no access to Christ."[42] As believers are brought to the "lap of the Church" by the Holy Spirit to receive Christ, they are simultaneously made members of his body. Or to put it another way, the incorporation into the assembly of the saints is simultaneous with the believer's transfer into his or her new eschatological existence before God.[43]

Although Luther does speak of the transformative power of the Holy Spirit, of a process of growth and holiness, many Lutheran theologians such as Herms have interpreted this in existential terms, in

39. Herms, *Luthers Auslegung*, pp. 65 and 100.

40. Herms, *Luthers Auslegung*, p. 74.

41. Herms, *Luthers Auslegung*, p. 96. The original German reads: ". . . nach nichts anderes als eben die durch das Heiligungswirken des Geistes geschaffene Existenz im Lichte der erschienenen Wahrheit des Evangeliums." Jared Wicks notes that his approach to Luther's concept of sanctification differs from that of Herms, who in Wicks' words, "presents it primarily as a process of developing certainty and knowledge." Instead, Wicks emphasizes a more transformative work of the Holy Spirit in the behavior of the believer, not just the believer's existential standing before God. Although the Holy Spirit works in the church through the Word and the sacraments, "anthropologically the proper locus of the Spirit is the human heart, where his work hits home and brings about a transformation." Wicks recognizes the paradox of this in light of the traditional Lutheran emphasis on God acting *extra nos*. See Wicks, "Holy Spirit–Church–Sanctification," pp. 164-168.

42. Herms, *Luthers Auslegung*, p. 52. The original German reads: "Außerhalb dieser Gemeinschaft seines Leibes gibt es keinen Zugang zu Christus."

43. Herms, *Luthers Auslegung*, p. 110. Wicks also understands Luther to hold an instrumental use of the church by the Holy Spirit in the *Large Catechism*. According to Wicks, as early as his 1520 catechetical writings, Luther calls for pastors and believers to "envisage the church as a *communio* — necessary to salvation — of shared spiritual gifts. Wicks, p. 152.

order to avoid the potential dangers of works righteousness and moralism. Whereas Herms speaks of sanctification and communal incorporation as two simultaneous events, Luther describes a more mutual relationship between these in his description of "making holy" in the Large Catechism. Sanctification is more than a new existential awareness for the believer and includes a communal element. For it is in community that God's "holy people" corporately lives out and experiences the new existence given through Christ and the Spirit, until the day of resurrection.

A close reading of the text may be helpful here. Following Luther's introduction to his explanation of the Third Article, where he calls the Holy Spirit the Sanctifier, the one who makes us holy, and states that the point of this article is sanctification (§34-37), his explication may be split into three sections. Luther discusses sanctification in relation to (1) the community of saints or the Christian church and (2) the forgiveness of sins, which together comprise the two means by which the Holy Spirit effects our holiness; and (3) the resurrection of the body and life everlasting.

(1) *The Holy Spirit effects our being made holy through the community of saints* (§37-53). In this section, Luther emphasizes the instrumental role of the church, as the means by which believers are drawn to Christ (as noted above in the discussion of Herms). Simon Peura points out that the word Luther uses is not *Gemeinschaft* (community) but *Gemeine* (*Gemeinde* in contemporary usage), which is perhaps closer to the English "fellowship" or "sharing or participative community."[44] Even though individual believers are "called through the gospel," it is through the spiritual community of the church that this gospel first is proclaimed. Luther writes, "The Spirit first leads us into his holy community, placing us in the church's lap, where he preaches to us *and brings us to Christ*."[45] And again, "Being made holy is nothing else than bringing us to the Lord Jesus Christ to receive this blessing [the redemption won for us by Christ on the cross], to which we could not have come by our-

---

44. See his discussion of Luther's third article of the creed in "The Church as Spiritual Communion," in *The Church as Communion: Lutheran Contributions to Ecclesiology*, LWF Documentation 42, ed. Heinrich Holze (Geneva: Lutheran World Federation, 1997), pp. 104-21. I will refer to his study in more detail below.

45. Martin Luther, "The Large Catechism," ed. Robert Kolb, Timothy Wengert, et al., in *The Book of Concord: The Confessions of the Evangelical Lutheran Church* (Minneapolis: Fortress Press, 2000), pp. 435-436, hereafter cited as the *BC*.

selves."[46] The church is described by Luther as the "mother" who begets and bears each Christian through the Word, i.e., a community of new birth. There is no direct illumination apart from the holy community. The church serves as an instrument through which individual believers are brought to faith by the proclamation of the gospel.

Luther describes holiness first in personal terms as the gift of faith, i.e., a knowledge and understanding in believers' hearts of the benefits won by Christ for his people on the cross. The Holy Spirit reveals and proclaims the Word of God, "through which [the Spirit] illuminates and inflames hearts so that they grasp and accept it, cling to it and persevere in it."[47] However, in the second part of this first section (§47-53), Luther goes on to emphasize the communal aspect of this new life that Christians receive through Christ through the sanctifying work of the Holy Spirit. Believers are "incorporated" into this community by the Holy Spirit and the Word. The proclamation that brings the good news to each individual believer is therefore not only an individual existential experience. Believers are incorporated into the holy community as "a part and member, a participant and co-partner in all the blessings it possesses."[48] They receive not only blessings, but membership in a community in which to experience these blessings. Luther calls this community a "holy little flock" that the Spirit gathers in one faith, mind, and understanding, under the headship of Christ. Being a member in this "holy little flock" means, therefore, to be ruled together by the one head, Christ.[49] Further, Luther states that this community

---

46. *BC*, p. 436. This discussion clearly assumes and I would even say overlaps with justification (especially the first sub-section when Luther speaks about the gift of faith). In his discussion of the Second Article (on the Son of God), it is interesting to note that Luther does not use the word justification once. He refers to it in other ways: being redeemed and released, being brought back from the devil to God, from death to life, from sin to righteousness; and "being restored to the Father's favor and grace," and being Christ's own possession.

47. *BC*, p. 436. This is the only section (§37-46) in which Luther uses "heart" language (three times).

48. *BC*, p. 438. Wilhelm Pauck agrees that Luther's view is personalist without being individualistic, because of Luther's emphasis on the church as a fellowship of mutual self-giving love. Indeed, for Luther, "to be a Christian and to be in the church, the community of believers, is one and the same." Pauck, *The Heritage of the Reformation*, revised and enlarged edition (Glencoe, Ill.: The Free Press, 1961), p. 33.

49. This is the closest Luther comes to describing the holy community as the "body of Christ" in his explanation of the third article.

"possesses a variety of gifts, and yet is united in love without sect or schism."[50] In addition to the gift of faith, Luther also speaks of "its fruits," which the Spirit produces.[51] By these means, faith and the fruits of the Spirit, the holy community grows in holiness and becomes strong. The new life is also experienced in community.

(2) *The Holy Spirit effects our being made holy through the forgiveness of sins* (§54-56). The primary blessing believers receive in the holy community is the daily forgiveness of sins, which believers obtain through "the holy sacraments and absolution as well as all the comforting words of the entire gospel."[52] Forgiveness is needed continually, because believers are never without sin in this life. However, this blessing is experienced not only existentially, but communally, that is, in relationship to other members of the community. The Christian experiences new life as "full forgiveness of sins, both in that God forgives us and that we forgive, bear with, and aid one another."[53] Because we have been incorporated into this holy community, we can experience this forgiveness and not be harmed by our sin. Luther defines holiness — the process of sanctification — in terms of the gospel and the forgiveness of sins; indeed, holiness is dependent upon the daily experience of the forgiveness of sins. "All who would seek to merit holiness through their works rather than the gospel and the forgiveness of sins" separate themselves from the holy community.[54] Holiness is the experience of new life given through the gospel and the Spirit, received in faith, which originates from outside of the believing community through the Word, but nonetheless is experienced daily within the community and its members through the power of the Holy Spirit.

(3) *The Holy Spirit effects our being made holy through the resurrection and the life everlasting* (§57-62). Here Luther speaks of the growth of the holy community in eschatological terms. Holiness has begun and is growing daily, but "now we remain only halfway pure and holy."[55] The

---

50. *BC,* p. 438. Here I must take issue with Wicks, who interprets "gifts" as means of grace, that is, the Word and sacraments. In this context, it is more likely that what Luther has in mind in this specific instance is the variety of spiritual gifts listed by Paul, in 1 Corinthians 12, who begs the church in Corinth to exercise their gifts in a unity of love.

51. *BC,* p. 438.

52. *BC,* p. 438.

53. *BC,* p. 438.

54. *BC,* p. 438.

55. *BC,* p. 438.

Holy Spirit will continue to work in us, increasing holiness on the earth through the church and the forgiveness of sins, until the last day, when there are only perfectly pure and holy people. In its earthly pilgrimage as God's "holy flock," the Christian community is to bear the blessings it has received, for the sake of the world. As Luther states, "The Holy Spirit continues his work without ceasing until the last day, and *for this purpose he has appointed a community on earth, through which he speaks and does all of his work.* For he has not yet gathered together all of this Christian community, nor has he completed the granting of forgiveness."[56] The Holy Spirit not only speaks the Word of Promise to the holy community, but also through the holy community extends the blessings and benefits of Christ to others.

In his explanation of the third article of the Apostles' Creed, Luther uses the locus of sanctification to draw together a picture of salvation that is ecclesial as well as personal. As Christoph Schwöbel notes, by reorganizing the Apostles' Creed into three rather than twelve articles, Luther purports the integration of a series of formerly independent articles of belief in the church, so that "the Spirit's work of sanctification is now not only related to a particular aspect of the doctrine of grace; it now comprises the whole dynamic of God's Trinitarian action. The Spirit thus becomes the common denominator of ecclesiology, soteriology, and eschatology."[57] Grace is experienced personally by individuals but not in solely individualistic terms. Individuals experience the blessings of Christ as members of a community (body) of which Christ is the head and into which they are incorporated by the Holy Spirit. This community grows and increases in holiness until the eschaton, a reality promised and given through Christ's resurrection.

The Sacramental Principle

Braaten also proposes that Lutherans should also draw on the "sacramental principle" in their ecclesiological reflections. For some Lutherans, this principle raises more concerns than the pneumatological principle.[58] As Günther Gassman has noted, "The designation of

---

56. *BC,* p. 438.
57. Schwöbel, "Quest for Communion," in *The Church as Communion,* p. 273.
58. As an example, see Eberhard Jüngel, "The Church as Sacrament?" in *Theological*

church as 'sacrament' is ambiguous and conceals a wide range of different ecclesiologies."[59] For Roman Catholics, the mediating category of "sacrament" was adopted to show how Christ is related to the church in a way that avoids an understanding of the church as an elongation of the incarnation. However, this designation has been a point of controversy in the ecumenical movement. For many it has served to confuse rather than clarify.[60]

It is important to be clear on what we mean by "sacramental" as applied to the church. While the church is a "sacrament" only in relationship to Christ, who is the foundational sacrament of salvation, this designation still raises concerns for many Protestants for fear that it still too closely identifies the church with Christ. Gassman proposes that the concept "sacrament" must be further interpreted by "'sign' and 'instrument' as a means of communion with God and the unity of all humankind."[61] As a visible sign and instrument of God's saving grace, the church is the means through which the Holy Spirit works to reconcile humanity to God and human beings one to another. Because Lutherans and other Protestants can affirm that Christ is known in the church and Christ's presence is made available in the church through the sacraments themselves,[62] they can agree with Catholics that the church is instrument and sign of salvation, and in this sense, a "sacrament" of salvation.[63] However, Lutherans can affirm the application of the term to the church only in a derivative way, if you will, as a "means of grace." This

Essays, translated with an introduction by J. B. Webster (Edinburgh: T&T Clark, 1989), pp. 189-213.

59. Gassman, "The Church as Sacrament, Sign and Instrument," in *Church — Kingdom — World: The Church as Mystery and Prophetic Sign,* ed. Gennadios Limouris, Faith and Order Paper No. 130 (Geneva: World Council of Churches, 1986), p. 1.

60. See the essays in Section 1, "Does the Church Have a Sacramental Nature?" in *One, Holy, Catholic and Apostolic: Ecumenical Reflections on the Church,* ed. Tamara Grdzeilidze, Faith and Order Paper No. 197 (Geneva: World Council of Churches Publications, 2005), pp. 17-87.

61. Gassman, "The Church as Sacrament," p. 2.

62. Tjørhom makes this point regarding Article 5 of the Augsburg Confession: "Already in the intial words of CA V, the interrelation between justification and ecclesiology is established. In order to obtain the faith that is a prerequisite of our justification in Christ, God has instituted the office of the ministry as a service with Word and Sacraments in the church." He adds, "These means do not float around freely, but are only available in the space of the church mediated by the ordained ministry within the frame of liturgical worship." Tjørhom, "The Church as the Place of Salvation," p. 290.

63. *Church and Justification,* no. 134, 19.

designation not only describes the relationship of the church to the world; it may also be used to describe the community that is created by the gospel (Word and Sacrament) and the relationship of members to another (in addition to their relationship to the world).

The sacramental principle may be appropriated by Lutherans as complementary to the christological principle *if* it is also interpreted in conjunction with the pneumatological principle. The community created by the Holy Spirit working through Word and Sacrament is also a sacramental community for Luther. This community "bears Christ to one another" primarily, but not exclusively through the gift of the forgiveness of sins. In embodying and living out the gospel in their life together, this community also bears Christ to the world. For the remainder of this essay, I explore the sacramental principle in light of the pneumatological by way of Luther's writings.

As we have seen in our discussion of Luther's explanation of the Third Article of the Creed, Luther treats the church primarily in pneumatological rather than sacramental terms. However, his earlier sacramental understanding of the *communio sanctorum* (the communion of saints) can be discerned as well, especially when read in light of other sections of his Large Catechism. In his 1519 treatise, "Sermon on the Blessed Sacrament of the Holy and True Body and Blood of Christ and the Brotherhoods (1519),"[64] Luther offers an understanding of the church in terms of the sacramental union with Christ.[65] As in much contemporary communion ecclesiology, "Luther found that the sacrament of the Lord's Supper both expresses and guarantees the reality of the church as the community of saints."[66] For a Christian to take part

---

64. Luther, "Sermon on the Blessed Sacrament of the Holy and True Body and Blood of Christ and the Brotherhoods (1519)," in *Luther's Works,* American Edition, Vol. 35, ed. E. Theodore Bachman (Philadelphia: Fortress, 1960), pp. 45-73. The background for his concept of *communio sanctorum* is his critique of the practices of the religious brotherhoods, civic associations, and craft guilds which, in contrast, offered a self-serving model of "communion."

65. Simon Peura, "The Church as Spiritual Communion in Luther," in *The Church as Communion,* 93-131. See also Vilmos Vajta, "The Church as Spiritual-Sacramental Communio with Christ and His Saints in the Theology of Luther," trans. Carter Lindberg, in *Luther's Ecumenical Significance: An Interconfessional Consultation,* ed. Peter Manns and Harding Meyer, in collaboration with Carter Lindberg and Harry McSorley (Philadelphia: Fortress, 1984), pp. 111-22.

66. Paul Althaus makes this point based on an evaluation of several of Luther's sermons and treatises written between 1519 and 1524. Althaus, *The Theology of Martin Lu-*

in the Eucharist means to be incorporated into Christ's spiritual body, analogous for Luther to the incorporation of a citizen into a city: "And whoever is taken into this city is said to be received into the community of saints and to be incorporated into Christ's spiritual body and made a member of him."[67]

However, unlike most contemporary communion ecclesiology, Luther describes this communion not in perichoretic terms, but in language that closely resembles that of the "happy exchange" in Luther's well-known 1520 treatise, "On the Freedom of a Christian." Luther speaks of an "interchange of blessings" by which Christ takes upon himself our form; i.e., our sin and infirmity, and we take on his form, i.e., his righteousness. This has implications for the communion among members of the body of Christ. Luther goes on to state,

> Again, through this same love, we are to be changed and to make the infirmities of all other Christians our own; we are to take upon ourselves their form and their necessity, and all the good that is within our power we are to make theirs, that they may profit from it . . . in this way we are to be changed into one another and are made into a community by love."[68]

Simon Peura explores whether or not Luther's early sacramental understanding of communion is reflected in his later Catechisms. In his 1519 treatise, Luther makes a direct link between the personal and sacramental meanings of *communio sanctorum* (as the communion or community of saints on the one hand, and communion in holy things, i.e., Bap-

---

ther, translated by Robert C. Schultz (Philadelphia: Fortress, 1966), p. 318. Althaus regards the later Lutheran emphasis on "real presence" (including in Luther's own works) as an impoverishment to what he understood as Luther's earlier, broader interpretation of the Lord's Supper as the sacrament of the *communio sanctorum*. See Peura, 93-131, for a discussion of scholarly views on Althaus' thesis, as well as Peura's own position.

67. *LW* 35:51.

68. *LW* 35:58. Christians are called to live out this horizontal aspect of communion in both spiritual and physical ways, from bearing one another's burdens and afflictions to sharing material goods with those in need. Luther recognizes how difficult this calling is: "Now if one will make the afflictions of Christ and all Christians his own, defend the truth, oppose unrighteousness, and help bear the needs of the innocent and the sufferings of all Christians, then he will find affliction and adversity enough, over and above that which his evil nature, the world, the devil and sin daily inflict on him." *LW* 35:56-57.

tism and Eucharist, on the other). However, a decade later when Luther discusses the "communion of saints" in his catechisms, the sacramental sense seems to be absent. There he interprets the expression as a gloss on the "holy catholic church,"[69] recognizing it as a later (fourth century) addition to the western baptismal creed.[70] In spite of this, Peura argues that Luther's early view of the church as a sacramental community is reflected in the Catechisms, albeit in a more indirect way. Peura draws attention to the motif of God's self-giving that he (along with Albrecht Peters in his magisterial commentary on Luther's Catechism) sees as dominating Luther's exposition of the Creed throughout. Luther writes,

> For in all three articles God himself has revealed and opened to us the most profound depths of his fatherly heart and his pure, unutterable life. For this very purpose he created us, so that he might redeem us and make us holy, and, moreover, having granted and bestowed upon us everything in heaven and on earth, he has also given us his Son and his Holy Spirit, through whom he brings us to himself.[71]

69. *BC*, p. 246. Paul Althaus offers a helpful explanation as to why Luther prefers "community" (*Gemeine* in the German) over "communion." Althaus, *The Theology of Luther,* pp. 294-297. For Luther, the idea of a transfer of merits from the treasury of Christ and the saints is replaced by serving one another (especially the living saints); we can help the faith and life of those through prayer, but Luther rejects the idea of a treasury of merits that can be drawn on (in Thesis 58, he states "no saint has adequately fulfilled God's commandments in this life"). Thus their good works cannot be meritorious for anyone — including oneself.

70. Scholarly opinion today favors the sacramental meaning, that is, as participation in Eucharist and Holy Baptism. In his historical study, Stephen Benko makes the argument that insertion of *communio sanctorum* into the Apostles' Creed resulted from a long process to find a connecting link between the holy catholic church and the forgiveness of sins in the western church: that is, the forgiveness of sins is granted through participation *(koinōnia)* in the Eucharist as well as baptism (holy things). The final step in the development of this connection came with Augustine, in the wake of the Donatist controversy. Previously, baptism alone had conferred participation in the body of Christ. Because baptism could not be repeated and because the question of readmission to ecclesial fellowship became critical during the Donatist controversy, restoration was effected through admission to the Eucharist. "*Communio sanctorum* is, therefore, a participation in the sacraments, within the church where, through the blood of Christ (this is the content of baptism and Eucharist) the forgiveness of sins is imparted." Benko, *The Meaning of Sanctorum Communio,* Studies in Historical Theology 3 (Naperville: Alec R. Allenson, Inc., 1964), p. 53.

71. *BC,* p. 439, §64-65.

If it were not for Christ our Lord, we could never come to recognize the Father's love and grace toward us, but neither could we know anything of Christ except that which the Holy Spirit reveals. According to Peura, the explication of the Third Article shows that Luther does emphasize the need for the *communio sanctorum,* but he links it with the Holy Spirit whose task it is to reveal the Son through the Word.[72] As noted above, the first task of the Holy Spirit is "to lead us into his holy community, placing us in the church's lap, where he preaches to us and brings us to Christ."

Although Luther does not explicitly mention Baptism and Eucharist in this connection, Peura rightly points out that "there is absolutely no justification for seeing a contrast between the preaching of Christ and the sacraments as means of grace,"[73] especially in light of Luther's "Confession Concerning Christ's Supper (1528)," another treatment of the Creed, and the fourth part of the Large Catechism itself, where Luther treats the sacraments separately. For Luther, what makes a sacrament is the Word of God (the gospel) joined to an element. By virtue of the Word of God, the water is truly "a saving, divine water" and the elements are truly the body and blood of Christ. It is through our baptism that "we are initially received into the Christian community" and it is through Christian community that we participate in the blessings that baptism promises and brings: deliverance from death and the devil, forgiveness of sin, grace, "the entire Christ," and the gifts of the Holy Spirit.[74]

However, even though we have been born anew through baptism, we still face the struggle against sin and evil until the last day. Luther writes, "Therefore the Lord's Supper is given as a daily food and sustenance so that our faith may be refreshed and strengthened and that it may not succumb in the struggle but become stronger and stronger. For the new life should be one that continually develops and progresses."[75] Just as in his explication of the Third Article, Luther here also affirms that the Christian life is a communal participation in the blessings of Christ and a process that involves both struggle and growth of the "holy community" called to be a blessing to the world.

---

72. Peura, "The Church as Spiritual Communion in Luther," 109.
73. Peura, "The Church as Spiritual Communion in Luther," 111.
74. *BC,* p. 461, §42.
75. *BC,* p. 469, §23-25.

He makes a direct connection between the Third Article of the Creed and the Lord's Supper when he writes, "Now the whole gospel and the article of the Creed, 'I believe in one holy Christian church . . . the forgiveness of sins,' are embodied in this sacrament and offered to us through the Word."[76]

Implications and Questions for Further Thought

Lutherans need not abandon the christological principle and its corollary criterion of justification in order to have a more robust ecclesiology. I have shown that both the pneumatological and sacramental principles can be embraced as complementary principles by Lutherans in their ecclesiological investigations; indeed, they are deeply rooted within Luther's own thought and offer Lutherans resources beyond the "word-event ecclesiology" that has come to dominate some Lutheran circles. Lutherans need not be suspicious of or bored by ecclesiology any longer.

However, some issues remain that require further attention, especially in regard to the emerging paradigm of "communion." While Lutherans have adopted this language for their ecclesial self-understanding,[77] the question of God's perichoretic communion as a pattern for ecclesial communion warrants more attention. For Lutherans, a concept of the church as "communion" that does not take into account the reality of sin is in danger of becoming an idealized concept, centered in the liturgical act of Eucharist but not in the real life of the community, experienced in relationships that are broken and always in need of healing through forgiveness.[78] Is *perichoresis* the appropriate model for understanding a communion that includes reconcilia-

---

76. *BC,* p. 470, §32.

77. Compilation of Resolutions and Statements Adopted by the Tenth Assembly of the Lutheran World Federation, Winnipeg, Manitoba, July 21-31, 2003, p. 10; available at http://www.lwf-assembly.org/PDFs/LWF_Assembly_Resolutions-EN.pdf

78. Indeed, in spite of its current dominance in ecumenical theology, Ormerod argues that the idealizing tendencies of "communion" do not make it the best candidate for an organizing principle for ecclesiology today and that a better candidate is mission, which through the symbol of the "kingdom of God" gives the church its proper orientation and thereby a norm for evaluating its life and structure. Neil Ormerod, "The Structure of a Systematic Ecclesiology," *Theological Studies* 63 (2002): 3-28. See also n. 26 above.

tion of relationships broken by sin as well as reconcilation of diversity and difference?[79]

A fuller examination of the linkage between the doctrine of justification and ecclesiology from a Lutheran perspective also would be welcome and warranted. If, as Hendrix states, justification and ecclesiology "are best understood not as separate theological loci, but as different facets of the one new reality that embraces Christians because they believe that Jesus of Nazareth inaugurated the kingdom of God," how might Lutherans more fully explore the complementary ways that they articulate the "one new life in Christ"?[80] An exploration of Hendrix's thesis from a more fully trinitarian perspective, rooted in the third (rather than the second) article, as suggested by this study, offers a promising venue for further research, one that I expect Braaten would heartily welcome.

79. This, of course, raises the difficult ecumenical question of "sin" in the church which is beyond the scope of this essay. For my reflections on this issue, see "Response to Michael Kinnamon and Peter Bouteneff," *Journal of Ecumenical Studies* 44, no. 3 (Summer 2009): 361-366.

80. Scott Hendrix, "Open Community: The Ecclesial Reality of Justification," in *By Faith Alone*, 237.

The Imperative for Unity
and the Question of Division

James M. Childs

Although unity is a mark that the Creed assigns to the church, the church on earth has divided and subdivided throughout its history, perhaps most notably since the time of the Reformation. In recent history, mergers of church bodies within a common heritage and ecumenical efforts to establish full communion across denominational lines have served to mitigate somewhat the scandal of those divisions and have advanced the witness of unity. At the same time, divisions and the threat of division, as well as resistance to seeking new expressions of unity, continue to arise.

When the rhetoric of division heats up in the face of a controversial issue or issues, to what do we appeal for unity in the face of pressures? Is there an overriding theological and missional imperative to seek and to maintain visible unity? By contrast, do some versions of the requirement for unity in fact conduce toward division or frustrate the advance of ecumenism? As an evangelical catholic who has brought a biblically and theologically well-grounded eschatological perspective to his confessional Lutheran theology, Carl Braaten has given us rich resources for addressing these questions.

Starting with Augsburg

Braaten has noted what the Lutheran reformers claimed themselves. They had no intention of creating a new church; their goal was the reform of the Roman Catholic Church to which they belonged and the only church they knew. "At the center of the Reformation movement was the proposition that the church and all its attributes of unity, holiness, catholicity, and apostolicity derived radically from the gospel of Jesus Christ as Lord and Savior as the foundation of the church and its reason for being."[1] This conviction finds its corollary in Article VII of the *Augsburg Confession,* which states that,

> Likewise they teach that one holy church will remain forever. The church is the assembly of saints in which the gospel is taught purely and the sacraments are administered rightly. And it is enough for the true unity of the church to agree concerning the teaching of the gospel and the administration of the sacraments. It is not necessary that human traditions, rites, or ceremonies instituted by human beings be alike everywhere.[2]

For Lutherans of the *Augsburg Confession* this would seem to settle the matter: the unity of the church is founded on the gospel in Word and Sacrament. Only that which compromises or violates the integrity of that foundation would be church-dividing. Nonetheless, unpacking what that agreement in the gospel entails has been the source of additional doctrinal requirements that have proven to be church-dividing.

A recent episode in Lutheranism illustrates this phenomenon and opens a window to my broader concern. The case is that of the Lutheran Church–Missouri Synod (LC-MS) and the doctrinal controversies that came to a head in the 1970's and ended in division. While this episode is hardly monumental in the grand scale of church history and global Christianity, it is a case study, if not a kind of parable, which is peculiarly illustrative of the questions we are addressing. The Missouri Synod controversy was at heart about competing versions of the authority of Scripture. As such, it is representative of any number of divisive controversies involving the doctrine of Scripture. Moreover, the implications of Augsburg VII and the question of scriptural interpretation and authority have been woven into Braaten's work as it relates to church unity and ecumenical commitment.[3] Thus, although this is a

---

1. Carl E. Braaten, *Principles of Lutheran Theology,* 2nd edition (Minneapolis: Fortress, 2007), p. 53.

2. The Augsburg Confession, VII, *The Book of Concord.* ed. Robert Kolb and Timothy J. Wengert (Minneapolis: Fortress Press, 2000), p. 43.

3. This was a moment in the history of American Lutheranism in which I was per-

particular Lutheran story, it also raises questions of church unity beyond the boundaries of the Lutheran tradition, as Braaten's own work will show.

The Lutheran Church–Missouri Synod:
The Bible and "Pure Doctrine"

While efforts at unity among Lutheran church bodies in America have always involved concern for doctrinal unity, the Lutheran Church–Missouri Synod has arguably been the most comprehensive and unbending of all the major Lutheran bodies in what doctrinal unity entails. Purity of doctrine was a foundational commitment of the LC-MS at its inception. It has been and remains the decisive factor in discussions of fellowship and union with other Lutheran bodies.

A key document for understanding what "pure doctrine" involves is *A Brief Statement,* formulated and adopted by the LC-MS in 1932 in the midst of what were considered unsatisfactory discussions of doctrinal unity with several other Lutheran synods.[4] In effect this document is a new confessional statement added to the Lutheran Confessions in order to make clear what true confessional subscription requires.[5] Historically, it has served as a test of doctrinal integrity within the LC-MS and a standard to be met before doctrinal unity could be proclaimed as a basis for fellowship or union with other Lutheran bodies.

Jaroslav Pelikan locates *A Brief Statement* among other new confessional statements developed by churches of the Reformation in response to the threat of historical-critical study of the Bible to traditional views of biblical authority. The confessions of the sixteenth century proclaimed biblical authority as the sole authority in matters of doctrine. However, they did not treat specifically the doctrines of

---

sonally very much involved. As a young theologian going through the trauma of that sad episode in the LC-MS, I was at the same time completing my doctoral studies under my mentor, Carl Braaten. It is not too much to say that the theological vistas he opened up for me made a significant contribution to my ability to work through the issues and move on with a sense of freedom in the gospel and the vision of a much larger gospel.

4. John H. Tietjen, *Which Way to Lutheran Unity?* (St. Louis: Clayton Publishing House, 1966), pp. 112-17.

5. Tietjen, *Which Way to Lutheran Unity?,* p. 150.

biblical inspiration and inerrancy thought to be essential to grounding biblical authority and thereby to maintaining pure doctrine. New confessional standards were therefore deemed to be necessary.[6]

A Brief Statement speaks to a number of doctrinal issues, but historically and theologically its doctrine of scripture has been and remains its most critical component. Moreover, its teaching on the inspiration and inerrancy of the Bible was at the theological center of the controversy that is the focus of our case study. This brief excerpt should serve to capture its concern and conviction:

> We teach also that the verbal inspiration of the Scriptures is not a so-called "theological deduction," but that it is taught by direct statements of the Scriptures, 2 Tim. 3:16, John 10:35, Rom. 3:2; 1 Cor. 2:13. Since the Holy Scriptures are the Word of God, it goes without saying that they contain no errors or contradictions, but that they are in all their parts and words the infallible truth, also in those parts which treat of historical, geographical, and other secular matters, John 10:35. [Failure to stand by this conviction] . . . overthrows the foundation of the Christian Church and its faith.[7]

The key point is in that final statement. The truth of the faith is a function of this view of inerrancy. One cannot argue then that differences in the doctrine of scripture can be tolerated as long as all agree on the confession of Augsburg VII.

As the products of critical scholarship began to surface in the life of the LC-MS — and, specifically within the faculty of Concordia Seminary, St. Louis — Synodical Conventions from 1950 through 1969 passed resolutions reaffirming the doctrine of scripture laid out in *A Brief Statement.* Though the resolutions did not name *A Brief Statement* as such, they clearly reiterated its stance on plenary verbal inspiration and inerrancy and punctuated that with specific concerns and affirmations regarding such matters as the historicity of Jonah, the historicity of Adam and Eve and the Fall, and the authorship of various books of the Bible, etc. They further indicate implicitly and explicitly that meth-

---

6. Jaroslav Pelikan, *Credo: Historical and Theological Guide to Creeds and Confessions of Faith in the Christian Tradition* (New Haven and London: Yale University Press, 2003), pp. 148-50.

7. http://www.lms.org. See "doctrine" under Beliefs and Practice.

ods of interpretation that undermine the literal truth of all biblical statements are unacceptable.[8]

In addition to these resolutions, President Jacob Preus later authored *A Statement of Scriptural and Confessional Principles* that subsequently became an authorized doctrinal standard of the LC-MS. *A Statement* makes clear what are the full implications of *A Brief Statement* with regard to the nature and authority of scripture. Affirming as it does that the Holy Spirit is the author of every word of Scripture, *A Statement* delineates a host of views on the authority and interpretation of the Bible deemed inimical to this basic conviction. Of particular concern in this regard was the need to counter the idea that the centrality of the gospel in scripture and confessions was also the locus of scriptural authority, rather than its infallibility as totally inspired.[9] Thus, *A Statement* stood in stark contrast to the position of the majority of St. Louis seminary faculty who contended that different interpretations are possible in matters such as the historicity of certain biblical events as long as the theological conclusions fit within the law-gospel correlation at the heart of the Bible. Moreover, the faculty stated that "Any tendency to make the doctrine of the inspiration and inerrancy of the Scriptures a prior truth which guarantees the truth of the Gospel or gives support to our faith is sectarian."[10]

The ensuing controversy finally led the majority of the St. Louis seminary faculty and most of their students to leave the campus and form Concordia Seminary-in-Exile on the campuses of Eden Seminary and St. Louis University, beginning on February 20, 1974. Later in 1976, 250 congregations initially left the LC-MS to form the Association of Evangelical Lutheran Churches (AELC).[11]

Before the division was consolidated with the constituting con-

---

8. For the text of these resolutions see the section "Concern for Pure Doctrine" in *Report of the Synodical President to the Lutheran Church–Missouri Synod in Compliance with Resolution 2-28 of the 49th Regular Convention of the Synod held at Milwaukee, Wisconsin, July 9-16, 1971* (St. Louis: The Lutheran Church–Missouri Synod, 1972), pp. 4-7. Hereafter referred to as *Report.*

9. Ibid., pp. 4-7.

10. *Faithful to Our Calling, Faithful to Our Lord,* Part One (St. Louis: Concordia Seminary, 1973), p. 21. This document was published by the faculty of the St. Louis seminary at the request of the LC-MS District Presidents. Part One is a joint faculty statement on some of the issues.

11. James E. Wilson, Jr., *The Association of Evangelical Lutheran Churches' Rhetoric of Unity, 1970-1987,* PhD Thesis (Indiana University, 1993), pp. 69-95.

vention of AELC, a theological convocation on the nature and function of scripture was held at Concordia Seminary, St. Louis, April 14-18, 1975, at the request of the Council of Presidents and under their sponsorship, together with the Board of Directors of the LC-MS and the Synodical president. The purpose was a public discussion of the issues dividing the church. The essays delivered on that occasion served not only to delineate the disparate positions on the nature and function of scripture represented there but also to focus more clearly two very disparate views of what constitutes a church-dividing issue.

The essay delivered by Dr. Ralph Bohlmann on that occasion is of special interest because he raises our question at the very outset: "In a church body under the Scriptures, how much disagreement, diversity and division can properly be tolerated without disrupting fellowship?"[12] Having raised that question, Bohlmann's paper goes on to argue that agreement on "all articles of faith," including the verbal inspiration and inerrancy of scripture, is entailed by Article VII of the *Augsburg Confession* and essential to true unity. A few key points in the development of this argument should suffice to demonstrate how this conclusion is reached.

Bohlmann begins by distinguishing between the church in the narrow sense and the church in the broad sense. The former is the "assembly of believers" brought to faith and sustained in faith by the Gospel and the sacraments. Wherever the Gospel is purely taught and the sacraments administered according to Christ's command, the church in this narrow sense is present. This reality is not coextensive with any particular church body. The church in the broader sense is that visible, institutional reality of the church on earth. It includes members of the church in the narrower sense, true believers, but it also includes hypocrites and unbelievers. Here too the Gospel and the sacraments are present for faith, but not all receive them in faith even though they belong to the church in the broad sense.[13]

The distinction between "narrow" and "broad" in Bohlmann's usage is readily translated as "invisible" and "visible." This time-honored distinction simply acknowledges that "church" in the proper sense as the "body of Christ" throughout time and space is invisible and transcends

---

12. Ralph A. Bohlmann, "The Church under the Scriptures," *The Nature and Function of Holy Scripture* (St. Louis: Concordia, 1975), p. 24.

13. Bohlmann, "The Church under the Scriptures," pp. 24-26.

the flawed reality of the visible, earthly, institutional church. The unity in Christ that marks the invisible church is a creation of divine grace through the Gospel and the sacraments. It follows that the ground for unity in the visible church is, as Augsburg VII puts it, faithfulness in the proclamation of the Gospel and the administration of the sacraments. This is the church's calling here on earth. Faithfulness to that calling testifies to the corollary conviction that the existence and unity of the assembly of believers is God's doing by the work of the Spirit through the Gospel of Jesus Christ. The church on earth confesses its sinfulness and places its hope in God's grace, and in its ecumenical endeavors seeks a unity in that hope, which in turn bears witness to the power of the gospel to unite people in Christ. Bohlmann's essay agrees with these points, and all parties in that dispute would have agreed as well.

Here, however, Bohlmann advances an additional requirement for unity that has roots in C. F. W. Walther's 1866 publication, *The Evangelical Lutheran Church, the True Visible Church of God on Earth.* In his theses Walther claims that the Lutheran church is the true visible church on earth because it preaches the pure Gospel and rightly administers the sacraments. Yet, despite this echo of Augsburg VII, most of the theses that follow deal with adherence to the infallibility of scripture as apparent evidence of faithfulness to the pure Gospel.[14] Without using the language of true visible church, Bohlmann nonetheless argues in much the same fashion as Walther did.

The unity of the church in the broad sense (the visible church) is to be based on agreement on what is the purely taught Gospel and rightly administered sacraments, and this criterion, in turn, entails agreement in all articles of faith. The Gospel is related directly to all articles of faith and all articles of faith are directly related to the Gospel.[15] Once again, all parties could agree that this is consistent with the Lutheran Confessions. However, the next move consolidates the tradition of Walther, the *Brief Statement,* and *A Statement.* Purity of doctrine in Gospel and sacraments is guaranteed by a totally inspired and inerrant Bible. For this reason, upholding the truth of every statement of Scripture is essential to the pure proclamation of the Gospel, even if every

14. C. F. W. Walther, "The Evangelical Lutheran Church, the True Visible Church of God on Earth," in *Walther on the Church,* trans. John M. Drickamer (St. Louis: Concordia, 1981).

15. Bohlmann, "The Church under the Scriptures," pp. 26-27.

statement is not an article of faith. This would include a host of issues not named by Bohlmann but evident in the LC-MS positions on matters such as women's role in the church, the institution of marriage, issues of human sexuality, and the historicity of all events reported in the Bible. "Therefore, the church consciously stands *under* the Scriptures and rejects all false approaches to the Scripture as jeopardizing the proclamation of the Gospel. For that reason, the church should accept *all* doctrine taught in the Scripture and avoid any association or action which would weaken or falsify 'pure doctrine'."[16] Adherence to the doctrine of the plenary inspiration and inerrancy of the Bible and its implications for all doctrine is the *sine qua non* for the pure teaching of the Gospel and therefore for unity in the church. It is a standard that brooks no compromise. This is the answer to his opening question as to how much diversity of theological opinion can be tolerated without disrupting fellowship. Bohlmann concludes, then, "When a choice must be made between external unity and the truth of the Gospel, unity must yield to truth. For it is better to be divided for the sake of the truth than to be united in error."[17]

The Source of Division

Carl Braaten has contrasted the heritage of Luther's and Melanchthon's view of scripture with that developed in post-Reformation Protestant orthodoxy in a way that easily serves as a succinct description of the conflict we have been reviewing.

> For Luther and Melanchthon and their closest pupils, the authority of Scripture is grounded in the testimony which the law and gospel imprint in the hearts of believers. The Scripture is to be believed on account of Christ, its essential content. The other doctrine holds that Scripture is trustworthy because of the testimonies that prove its divine origin by means of inspiration.[18]

The difference between the parties in the Missouri Synod dispute echoes this historical contrast.

16. Bohlmann, "The Church under the Scriptures," p. 35.
17. Bohlmann, "The Church under the Scriptures," p. 38.
18. Braaten, *Principles*, p. 15.

However, having briefly mapped these divergent positions on the authority of Scripture and its relation to the Gospel and church unity, we need to remind ourselves that both sides, each in their own way, contended that faithfulness to the Gospel is the foundation of church unity. In this contention they were both consistent in their allegiance to the Gospel center of the Lutheran Confessions in justification by grace for Christ's sake through faith. Consequently, both parties also contended that the other was divisive in their compromise of that Gospel foundation. Where then do we locate the source of the division that occurred and what does it tell us, albeit in a limited way, about what constitutes a church-dividing issue?

For those who finally felt compelled to leave the LC-MS and form the AELC, the insistence that subscription to a rigid doctrine of biblical inerrancy was essential to the pure teaching of the Gospel was a form of biblicism. Such claims of biblical inerrancy are for many impossible to sustain in the face of modern scholarship. However, that is not the real point in the end. Rather, I would argue that claims about pure doctrine and ecclesiology set forth in Professor Bohlmann's paper were essentially divisive and remain so to this day not simply because they advocate a particular doctrine of scripture, however vulnerable such may be to the critique of modern scholarship. Instead, they are essentially divisive because they claim a measure of certitude concerning the doctrine of scripture and the nature of scriptural truth and authority that belies the law-Gospel correlation they propose to defend. This sort of triumphalism is inimical to the Gospel foundation of the church's existence, which foundation is an ecclesiological hallmark of Lutheran witness in the church catholic.

The LC-MS conflict may be but a blip on the screen of church history. Some may consider its continued insistence on the doctrine of an infallible scripture as a condition of fellowship with others to be an odd and irrelevant vestige of Protestant Orthodoxy. However, questions of biblical authority continue to haunt efforts at unity and threats of division, especially in matters of ecclesiology and sexuality. How is the church to manage these problems without division and with an ongoing commitment to ecumenical advancement? It is at this juncture that I think Carl Braaten's contributions are very helpful.

The Imperative for Unity — Carl Braaten's Contributions

As I noted at the outset, Carl Braaten is both evangelical and catholic in his theology. As an evangelical he is a true son of the *Augsburg Confession* in theology and ecclesiology. As a catholic he is committed to visible unity of the church as a witness to its ultimate unity in Christ. Reflecting on his mentor Paul Tillich's insistence on the conjoining of "Protestant Principle" and "Catholic Substance," Braaten states the following conviction:

> Theology that is faithful to the evangelical — I prefer the term "evangelical" over "Protestant" — principle and Catholic substance of the Reformation will work toward an ecclesial synthesis in which Christians and churches will be reconciled around the Table of the Lord, eating and drinking as they did in the early church. Those who belong to Peter, or those who belong to Luther, or Calvin, or Wesley, or whomever will come to recognize at last that Christ has not been divided (1 Cor. 1:13).[19]

This evangelical catholic stance shapes his contributions in our area of discussion. They should help to move us toward a deeper understanding of the imperative for unity and, with that, a better understanding of what our case study reveals about that which is truly divisive. In the process we get an expanded sense of the key features of Braaten's theology.

Biblical Authority and Church Unity

For Carl Braaten the future of church unity lies beyond the ecumenical agreements of historically Protestant churches:

> I believe strongly . . . that our best hope is to move toward rapprochement with Roman Catholics and the Eastern Orthodox, leading eventually to Eucharistic fellowship in a communion of churches.[20]

---

19. Carl E. Braaten, *That All May Believe: A Theology of the Gospel and the Mission of the Church* (Grand Rapids, MI: Eerdmans, 2008), p. 6.

20. Carl E. Braaten, "Confessional Lutheranism in an Ecumenical World," *Concordia Theological Quarterly*, 71, nos. 3 and 4 (July/October 2007): 230.

James M. Childs

It is this conviction that lies behind his involvement in the founding of *Pro Ecclesia*.[21]

Of course, despite the breakthrough of the *Joint Declaration on the Doctrine of Justification* by the Lutheran World Federation and the Roman Catholic Church, Braaten recognizes that there are still serious issues that must be faced for this desired rapprochement to go forward. At the same time, he believes that Catholics and Lutherans share some common problems that may unite them in what would be, for many, unexpected ways. In the Winter 2001 issue of *Pro Ecclesia* he wrote an intriguing article that connects nicely with our case study in particular and our main concern in general: "A Shared Dilemma: Catholics and Lutherans on the Authority and Interpretation of Scripture."[22]

Braaten begins the discussion by reviewing the seven points of agreement that emerged from the ninth official dialogue of Lutherans and Catholics in the USA (1995). The focus of the dialogue was to deal with the historical divide over authority in the church between the Lutheran "Scripture alone" and the Catholic "Scripture *and* tradition." The seven points of agreement in the report raise the question of whether or not this degree of agreement overshadows the remaining difference so that it is no longer a church-dividing issue. The report states the remaining difference this way: "Lutherans hold that Scripture alone is the ultimate norm by which traditions must be judged. Catholics hold that the decisive norm by which doctrines or traditions are judged is Scripture together with living apostolic tradition, which is perpetuated in the church through the influence of the Holy Spirit."[23] Rather than answer the question of whether the seven points of agreement, if true, trump the remaining difference as stated, Braaten argues

---

21. From the website of *Pro Ecclesia*: "*Pro Ecclesia* is a journal of theology published by the Center for Catholic and Evangelical Theology. It seeks to give contemporary expression to the one apostolic faith and its classic traditions, working for and manifesting the church's unity by research, theological construction, and free exchange of opinion. Members of its advisory council represent communities committed to the authority of Holy Scripture, ecumenical dogmatic teaching and the structural continuity of the church, and are themselves dedicated to maintaining and invigorating these commitments." www.e-ccet.org/pe.htm.

22. Carl E. Braaten, "A Shared Dilemma: Catholics and Lutherans on the Authority and Interpretation of Scripture," *Pro Ecclesia*, 10, no. 1 (Winter 2001): 63-75.

23. Braaten, "A Shared Dilemma," p. 64.

that the statement of difference is not entirely accurate. If forced to choose, he would prefer the Catholic statement: "The affirmation that Scripture is the ultimate norm does not mean it is the only norm, exclusive of the apostolic tradition of beliefs and practices kept alive by the power of the Holy Spirit."[24] Common sense and the history of Christian thought make this clear.

Historically, however, the lines of difference on the matter of authority hardened between the churches of the Reformation and Rome so that a fundamentalism of scripture versus a fundamentalism of tradition developed from the time of Trent and was sustained until Vatican II. Lutherans for their part joined Protestant scholasticism, emphasizing the inspiration and inerrancy of scripture as the seat of authority for the church's teaching and preaching. Theologians like Calov and Quenstedt created what Braaten calls a docetic view of scripture, which appealed not to the content of the Bible as a witness to the Gospel of Jesus Christ but to the manner in which it was inspired in its every word by the Holy Spirit. Luther, Braaten maintains, would have dubbed this approach to scriptural authority as a false theology of glory. "Luther believed the Bible on account of Christ; Protestant scholasticism believed in Christ on account of the Bible."[25] This connection with Luther's theology of the cross versus a theology of glory is an important theme to which I will return a bit later.

The ground has shifted in the current situation, however. Braaten observes that the challenge to the Protestant doctrine of scripture as the authority for all doctrine in the church is no longer coming from the Catholic elevation of tradition. Rather, both Catholics and Protestants are being challenged by the products of Enlightenment criticism and the relativism of postmodernism. And neither can meet this challenge by repristinating the old systems of authority: the verbally inspired inerrant Bible of the Protestants or the hierarchical structure of Rome.[26]

Instead, Braaten believes there are promising developments among both Lutheran and Catholic scholars that are helpful in dealing with the contemporary problem of authority and that can also

24. Braaten, "A Shared Dilemma," p. 64.
25. Braaten, "A Shared Dilemma," pp. 66-67.
26. "The inerrant Bible collapsed amidst a host of absurdities identified by the techniques of historical criticism. And there is no turning back the clock." Braaten, "A Shared Dilemma," p. 68.

lead to a greater convergence on the relationship of scripture and tradition. Scholarly reconsideration of both Aquinas and Luther suggests that they were much closer on the relation of scripture and tradition than has been thought. For both there was always a lively interaction between scripture and tradition, with scripture providing the ground. The reformers, Luther and Calvin and their immediate followers, were not biblicists. Braaten believes that this apparent heritage of agreement opens a common path for both churches to steer a course between fundamentalism and modernism by placing the interpretation of the Bible in the community of the faithful.[27] Thus, Braaten applauds the statement from the Pontifical Biblical Commission: "Interpretation of Scripture takes places in the heart of the church: in its plurality and unity, and within its tradition of faith . . . the same Holy Spirit, who moved the authors of the New Testament to put in writing the message of salvation, likewise provides the church with continual assistance for the interpretation of its inspired writings."[28]

Trust in the Spirit's working through the Word among the faithful to build and to sustain the church is for Braaten the theonomous way of authority. This Tillichian term stands in contrast to heteronomy, an authoritarian approach embodied in the old Catholic hierarchical paradigm and in Protestant Orthodoxy's paradigm of an infallible scripture that we have seen repristinated in the tradition of Walther's "true visible church." For Tillich heteronomy makes unconditional that which is only conditional and is, therefore, "demonic," a source of division. The theonomous way of authority also rejects what Braaten has termed the sort of unbridled autonomy of contemporary relativism that undermines authority. The theonomous way is, then, a way toward unity, in this instance by enhancing the prospects of greater agreement on the relation of scripture, tradition, and authority in the church.[29] In general it is the way toward unity because it is the Spirit through the word of grace who "calls, gathers, and enlightens."

27. Braaten, "A Shared Dilemma," pp. 68-74.
28. Braaten, "A Shared Dilemma," p. 75.
29. Braaten, "A Shared Dilemma," p. 69. Braaten employs Tillich's categories here. The explanation of their meaning is mine, as is the application of heteronomy to Walther's tradition.

Gospel Mission and Church Unity — An Eschatological Perspective

As we have noted, the *Augsburg Confession* VII tells us that the church is the assembly of believers sustained by the Gospel in Word and sacrament. While Lutherans have often accepted this as a sufficient definition of the church, Braaten maintains that it is not. The statement contains no reference to the eschatological horizon of the church's existence or to its missionary nature. "Without linkage to the coming of God's kingdom and to the world for which Christ died, the church becomes turned in on itself — ecclesiocentric."[30] When the Gospel at the heart of the church's life is framed eschatologically, as it is in the Bible, the church's life becomes inherently missional. This is clearly so because the Gospel of Jesus the Christ is the manifestation of God's future for the whole world. The people of God, the assembly of believers, are those who have seen that future made present in the resurrection victory. They are called to be, as I have often styled it, a "people of anticipation," anticipating God's future by proclaiming its promise in Christ through word and deed.

Carl Braaten has also captured this truth in his understanding of the church's apostolicity, an understanding in which the church's ecumenical vocation and its missional vocation are wedded. The apostolate of the early Christian church was driven by an eschatological consciousness of having experienced in the Christ event the future toward which God is drawing all things. He comments: "The apostolic mission is not only a reflection of the light of God's eschatological action in Jesus Christ but also an instrument bearing God's universal promises to the nations. The eschatological meaning of Jesus is carried forward in the universal mission of the apostles. . . . The eschatological message and the apostolic mission define the being and meaning of the church in history."[31]

Braaten would have us consider our ecumenical strivings in this eschatological perspective. The eschatological message of the apostolic mission has clear implications for the unity and catholicity of the church. The fact that the gospel is an eschatological promise made present in Christ places the church in an already–not yet tension:

---

30. Carl E. Braaten, *That All May Believe: A Theology of the Gospel and the Mission of the Church* (Grand Rapids, MI: Eerdmans, 2008), pp. 146-47.

31. Braaten, *Principles,* pp. 62-63.

If the church catholic takes seriously its eschatological relativity, it will not turn in upon itself triumphalistically, absolutizing a sacred sphere, a sacred style, a sacred theology, a sacred language, a sacred liturgy — measuring proximity to the kingdom of God by the degree to which it cherishes the consecrated forms of its own tradition. In the realm of doctrine we no longer can expect a tightly defined *consensus doctrinae* that allows denominations to live as separate ghettos.[32]

The eschatological relativity of the church in its historical forms opens it up to the unity of its ultimate future in Christ.

The outward unity of the church on earth is an integral part of the church's gospel witness for it anticipates the unity of all things with God in the future of God's reign, revealed and assured in the Christ. The embodiment of unity in the church on earth, albeit penultimate, bears witness to God's grace in its power to forgive, reconcile, heal, and make all things new. The distinctions we have met between the church in the narrow and broad sense or the invisible and visible church are useful to a point, but when the existence of the invisible church as a transcendent spiritual reality becomes an excuse for tolerating divisions in the visible church — not to mention the temptation to claim status as the true visible church — we are in danger of what Braaten has called "ecclesiastical docetism."[33] The divided church detracts from the power of God's reconciling work in Jesus Christ. Doctrinal, moral, or spiritual standards other than that which is integral to the gospel witness of the church actually become divisive when rigidly imposed as the basis for the unity of the church body.

The Theology of the Cross: A Relevant Spirituality

At a number of points in the foregoing discussion of Carl Braaten's contributions, we have seen that he is no friend of triumphalism. In fact, the eschatological horizon within which the church finds itself certainly counsels humility in the pursuit of unity. This has been a consistent theme in Braaten's theology. Over thirty-five years ago he wrote,

32. Braaten, *Principles,* p. 66.
33. Braaten, *Principles,* p. 69.

"Only eschatological consciousness in the church can relativize its own haughty triumphalism, and all its arrogant talk about having an absolute authority, an inerrant book, or an infallible office. The church is always weakest when it claims too much."[34]

Braaten's compelling attack on triumphalism places him squarely within the tradition of Luther's theology of the cross. For the Christian community the theology of the cross leads us into truth, first of all by showing us the truth about ourselves and disabusing us of any and all religious pretensions. Luther was clear about the need for truth in the face of a pretentious theology of glory. His familiar words from *The Heidelberg Disputation* state the matter succinctly: "A theologian of glory calls evil good and good evil. A theologian of the cross calls the thing what it actually is."[35] One simply cannot look upon the crucified without seeing reflected back upon oneself the truth of one's brokenness and the utter need for the unfathomable mercy of God that is also manifest in that passion. Having one's self-awareness schooled in the truth of the cross leads to a theology and discipleship of humility. In his theology of the cross we find in Luther an echo of what Douglas John Hall names as his ". . . deep sympathy with human weakness and wretchedness — a sympathy, alas, that is nearly unique in the history of Christian scholarship, including the scholarship of the Reformation."[36]

The theology of glory Luther had in his crosshairs at the time of the Heidelberg Disputation was of course that of an authoritarian and presumptuous church brokering its demands for works needed in the process of salvation. He was pastorally concerned about the burdens that such demands placed upon the consciences of the people. However, the problem presents itself in every age. Douglas John Hall once again remarks,

> The *theologia gloriae* confuses and distorts because it presents divine revelation in a straightforward, undialectical, and authoritarian manner that silences argument, silences doubt — silences, therefore, real humanity. It overwhelms the human with its brilliance, its

34. Carl E. Braaten, *Christ and Counter-Christ: Apocalyptic Themes in Theology and Culture* (Philadelphia: Fortress, 1972), p. 147.

35. "Heidelberg Disputation," *Luther's Works,* vol. 31, ed. and trans. Harold J. Grimm (Philadelphia: Muhlenberg Press, 1957), p. 40.

36. Douglas John Hall, *The Cross in Our Context: Jesus and the Suffering World* (Minneapolis: Augsburg Fortress, 2003), p. 21.

incontestability, its certitude. Yet just in this it confuses and distorts, because God's object in the divine self-manifestation is precisely not to overwhelm but to befriend.[37]

The theology of the cross as a dimension of justification by grace through faith figures also in Paul Tillich's well-known "Protestant Principle." "The central principle of Protestantism," Tillich wrote, "is the doctrine of justification by grace alone, which means that no individual and no human group can claim a divine dignity for its moral achievements, for its sacramental power, for its sanctity, or for its doctrine."[38] Protestantism's self-critical principle continually confronts the idolatry of making the finite into the absolute.

However we come at the critique of triumphalism after the fashion of the theology of the cross versus the theology of glory, it is important to note before moving to a conclusion that the critique is first and foremost a *theological* critique, concerned in this case with matters of unity and mission. It is not an indictment of the individuals involved. There is no room here for questioning personal piety and faith, whether we are speaking of the players in the drama of Missouri or any similar conflict in the long history of divisions in the church on earth.

The eschatological tension in which the church exists, a reality that Braaten has so effectively developed in his theology, is a corollary of law-Gospel tension in which we exist, the tension of *simul justus et peccator*. All these themes which describe the pulse beat of Christian life, individually and as the church, are directly related to the spirituality that characterizes the theology of the cross. It is a spirituality that recognizes the penetrating truth of *sola gratia* and *sola fide*. It is a fit spirituality to accompany the quest for unity because it finally trusts God who in Christ and by the ministry of the Spirit has given us the unity for which we long.

Carl Braaten has blended themes of biblical eschatology, evangelical theology, and catholic vision in the service of his own passion for the church's unity and its Gospel mission. In so doing, he provides us all with important theological resources, both in his own thought and in his appreciation of the diversity of voices that mark the church's tradition and help to keep our vision clear.

37. Hall, *The Cross in Our Context*, p. 20.
38. Paul Tillich, *The Protestant Era*, trans. James Luther Adams (Chicago: University of Chicago Press, 1957), p. 226.

More Promise Than Ambiguity: Pneumatological Christology as a Model for Ecumenical Engagement

Leopoldo A. Sánchez M.

The presence and activity of *pneuma* or "Spirit" in Jesus has been interpreted in various ways throughout the history of dogma. In the last half of the twentieth century, and as the twenty-first century begins, a revival of Spirit Christology (known also as pneumatological Christology) as a systematic model for reflection on theological topics and issues has taken place.[1]

The term "Spirit Christology" encompasses a variety of meanings. In the history of dogma, ideas regarding "Spirit" *(pneuma, spiritus)* have informed and supported both orthodox and heterodox understandings of Jesus' identity. There is an early patristic type that identifies "Spirit" (and even "Holy Spirit" in a passage such as Luke 1:35) as the divine principle in Christ, or, more specifically, as the name of the

---

1. A few contemporary examples of pneumatological Christology include Walter Kasper, *Jesus the Christ*, trans. V. Green (New York: Paulist, 1976), esp. pp. 230-74; Yves Congar, "Pour une Christologie Pneumatologique," *Revue des Sciences Philosophiques et Théologiques* 63 (1979): 435-42, and *The Word and the Spirit*, trans. David Smith (San Francisco: Harper & Row, 1986), ch. 6; Luis F. Ladaria, "Cristología del Logos y cristología del Espíritu," *Gregorianum* 61 (1980): 353-60, and "La unción de Jesús y el don del Espíritu," *Gregorianum* 71/3 (1990): 547-71; John J. O'Donnell, "In Him and Over Him: The Holy Spirit in the Life of Jesus," *Gregorianum* 70/1 (1989): 25-45; Joseph H. P. Wong, "The Holy Spirit in the Life of Jesus and of the Christian," *Gregorianum* 73/1 (1992): esp. pp. 59-72; Jürgen Moltmann, *The Spirit of Life: A Universal Affirmation*, trans. Margaret Kohl (Minneapolis: Fortress, 1992), pp. 60-71; Michael Welker, *God the Spirit*, trans. John F. Hoffmeyer (Minneapolis: Fortress, 1994), ch. 4; and Clark H. Pinnock, *Flame of Love: A Theology of the Holy Spirit* (Downers Grove, Ill.: InterVarsity, 1996), ch. 3.

Leopoldo A. Sánchez M.

preexistent Logos.[2] There are also early Ebionite and adoptionist types that affirm the presence of God's Spirit in Jesus to the detriment of Jesus' preexistence and divinity.[3] Contemporary post-Chalcedonian proposals substitute a Spirit Christology for the church's classical Logos Christology by arguing for Jesus' divinity solely on the basis of his unique possession of Spirit, but leaving aside the question of his personal identity as the Logos.[4] In such post-Chalcedonian systems, the term "Spirit" (much like the terms "Logos" and "Wisdom") functions only as one of many viable biblical metaphors or symbols for describing in a general way God's simultaneously immanent and transcendent presence in humans.[5]

Our approach to Spirit Christology assumes a commitment to Nicene Trinitarian theology and Chalcedonian Christology and, therefore, adopts a biblical and theological understanding of Spirit as a personal agent in its own right. Otherwise stated, and to use Johannine language, the Holy Spirit is distinct from and related to the Father from whom it proceeds, as well as distinct from and related to the Son upon whom it remains and who breathes it upon the disciples. Within this Trinitarian-Christological framework, we can speak of a twofold differentiation in God the Father's self-giving to assumed (created) humanity, namely, in the incarnation of his Son *and* in the sending of his Holy Spirit. The former yields a Logos Christology, and the latter a Spirit-oriented one. In this essay, we will argue that a Spirit Christology, in spite of its potential ambiguity due to its common association with adoptionist views of Christ, need not be seen as a model opposed

2. A classic study is M. Simonetti, "Note di cristologia pneumatica," *Augustinianum* 12 (1972): 201-32.

3. Philip J. Rosato, "Spirit-Christology: Ambiguity and Promise," *Theological Studies* 38, no. 3 (1997): esp. pp. 429-38; see also Wolfhart Pannenberg, *Jesus — God and Man,* trans. Lewis L. Wilkins and Duane A. Priebe, 2d ed. (Philadelphia: Westminster, 1977), pp. 116-23.

4. See G. W. H. Lampe, "The Holy Spirit and the Person of Christ," in *Christ, Faith and History,* ed. S. W. Sykes and J. P. Clayton (London: Cambridge, 1972), pp. 111-30, later expanded in *God as Spirit* (Oxford: Clarendon, 1977); see also Roger Haight, "The Case for Spirit Christology," *Theological Studies* 53, no. 2 (1992): 257-87, and his subsequent treatment in *Jesus — Symbol of God* (Maryknoll, N.Y.: Orbis, 1999).

5. See Lampe, *God as Spirit,* pp. 37, 115-16; and Haight, "The Case for Spirit Christology," pp. 257, 267-68. Piet Schoonenberg's approach is similar, but allows for more differentiation between these modes of presence after Pentecost. See "Spirit Christology and Logos Christology," *Bijdragen* 38 (1977): 360-75.

to the classic Logos-oriented Christology of the church councils and, therefore, shows promise as a model for ecumenical engagement.

We will make our case by demonstrating the productivity of the Spirit-oriented model for bringing together, or closer to each other, ecclesial traditions on divisive issues in Trinitarian theology, Christology, and ecclesiology, namely, 1) the *filioque* controversy, a matter of contention between Eastern and Western churches since the eleventh century; 2) the problem of adoptionism, a historic Christological problem that resurfaced in sixteenth-century polemics via the Lutheran critique of Nestorianizing elements in Reformed views of Christ's person and the Lord's Supper; and 3) the locus of authority in the church, a question that Lutherans, Roman Catholics, and the Reformed have answered differently in their respective traditions.

Our goal here is not to review the controversies in all their historical and doctrinal accents, but rather to test the degree to which a pneumatological Christology in Nicene-Chalcedonian key has the capacity to provide churches a complementary theological paradigm for examining the issues. We hope to show the usefulness of Spirit Christology for ecumenical engagement in the spirit of what Carl Braaten calls a "collaborative model" of doing theology *pro ecclesia*.[6] Such an ecumenically responsible theology is grounded not in "the subjective idiosyncrasies of each theologian," but in the joint effort of Christians from various confessions to do theology in service to the church's witness to God's revelation in Christ as attested in the Scriptures and ecumenical creeds.[7] Our presupposition is that progress in ecumenism must face doctrinal differences seriously, even as we celebrate important theological insights from various churches and seek constructive theological contributions that can advance dialogue in service of a more unified witness to Christ.

I.

Although much has been written on the *filioque* controversy, Yves Congar's reading of Western (Latin) and Eastern (Greek) approaches to

---

6. Carl E. Braaten, *Mother Church: Ecclesiology and Ecumenism* (Minneapolis: Augsburg, 1998), p. 118. In terms of Braaten's "two ways of doing theology" (pp. 120-23), a Spirit Christology may be said to begin or function "from below," with the experiences and works of Jesus in the Spirit.

7. Braaten, *Mother Church*, p. 118. See also pp. 124-32.

the Trinity remains particularly insightful. Congar dedicated the third volume of *I Believe in the Holy Spirit* to an ecumenical endeavor and appropriately entitled it *The River of Life Flows in the East and the West*.[8] He asserts that the East tends to approach the person as a relatively independent reality in Trinitarian discourse, making hypostasis in general its privileged ontological category, and the hypostasis of the Father in particular its *sine qua non* point of departure. To use Eastern-Cappadocian language, there is no access to the unknowable divine *ousia* apart from the divine *hypostases*. Orthodox theologian John Zizioulas has traced such ontological ultimacy of the hypostasis in the East to the church's grounding of the divine substance in the concrete *person* of the Father and thus in his will to create the world not out of ontological necessity but freely and out of love.[9] The West, on the other hand, tends to view the three persons as strictly identical to the divine essence, and therefore gives an ontological ultimacy to the unity or simplicity of God in its Trinitarian logic.[10]

After dealing with the controversy with historical and theological responsibility as well as with pastoral sensitivity, Congar proposes that the West drop the *filioque* clause, unilaterally added to the Latin text of the original Niceno-Constantinopolitan Creed, as a gesture of ecumenical humility and goodwill towards the churches in the East. For its part, the East should agree to recognize not only the historical circumstances (namely, Arianizing elements in the West that undermined the essential unity of the Father and the Son), but also the theological rationale in the West (inspired by Augustine's *De Trinitate*) that made room for the introduction of the *filioque* in the Creed.[11]

In the Western-Augustinian tradition, the *filioque* arises out of a particular anti-Arian commitment to the simplicity of God, which allows for the divine persons to be defined as neither accidental nor sub-

8. For the complete three-volume set, see Yves Congar, *I Believe in the Holy Spirit*, trans. David Smith (New York: Crossroad, 1997).

9. John Zizioulas, *Being as Communion: Studies in Personhood and the Church* (Crestwood, N.Y.: St. Vladimir's Seminary, 1985), pp. 29-46.

10. For the differences between the East and the West, see Congar, *I Believe in the Holy Spirit*, vol. 3, pp. 72, 200, 202.

11. What follows is a summary of St. Augustine's classic anti-Arian theological rationale for his Trinitarian approach as developed in Book V of his *On the Holy Trinity*, in *Nicene and Post-Nicene Fathers*, 1st series (hereafter *NPNF1*), vol. 3, ed. Philip Schaff (reprint, Peabody, Mass.: Hendrickson, 1994).

stantial realities. The former definition would make the persons less than God, for in the one God there can be no accidents, parts, or divisions. The latter definition would logically lead to Arian subordinationism by making the Father's personal property of being unbegotten into an attribute of the divine essence. Such subordinationism would make only the Father "God," but not the Son who is begotten of the Father or the Holy Spirit who proceeds from the Father and the Son.

To distinguish the persons in God without compromising the unity or simplicity of the divine essence, Augustine speaks of the divine persons in "relative" terms (as opposed to accidental or substantial categories), that is to say, in terms of an "opposition in relation" *(oppositio relationis)* to one another. In the one divine essence, the Father is not the Son and vice versa. Moreover, since the Holy Spirit is neither the Father of the Son nor the Son of the Father, the Holy Spirit stands in another logical opposition in relation to both as the Spirit of the Father "and the Son" *(filioque)*. The Holy Spirit's existence from the Father *and* the Son fits quite well in the context of the *oppositio relationis* Augustinian framework, which arises out of an anti-Arian commitment to speaking of the persons without doing harm to the unity of the one God and thus affirms in the strongest possible way the consubstantiality of the divine persons.[12]

Congar also highlighted the importance of *kairos* in an account of the incarnation.[13] A *kairos*-oriented narrative shows that, in the hypostatic or personal union, the divine Logos does not simply assume a human *nature* conceived of somewhat abstractly, but also a human *history* with its new and special stages or *kairoi* along the way. These events do not merely reveal, confirm, or proclaim something that the Logos has always been (for example, the preexistent Logos), but are constitutive of his identity in salvation history.

Two events in Jesus' life, his baptism and resurrection, qualify as *kairoi* that do not simply reveal something prior to these events them-

---

12. Congar writes: "In the West . . . we have always been conscious of the principle that, in God, everything is common, apart from what is distinguished by an opposition in relationship. . . . [T]his principle is not a defined article of faith. It does, however, express a very acute sense of consubstantiality within the Trinity." *I Believe in the Holy Spirit*, vol. 3, p. 202. Although the roots of this principle are Augustinian, Congar ultimately traces the axiom *in Deo omnia sunt unum, ubi non obviat relationis oppositio* to Anselm (p. 98).

13. Congar, *I Believe in the Holy Spirit*, vol. 3, pp. 165-173.

selves (say, that Jesus is God) but actually affect the Logos in his human life and history in new ways.[14] At the Jordan, and not before, the Son is anointed with the Spirit to become our suffering Christ-Servant. He is "made" our Christ-Servant there, as it were. At the resurrection, and not before, the Son is "made" our Lord, opening the way for our resurrection. The Son's eternal sonship, his identity as the *unigenitus,* the only begotten, is not at stake in these assertions. Rather, the statements are meant to speak of the incarnate, anointed, and risen Son as our *primogenitus,* the firstborn among many brethren. One might say that a Spirit Christology gives a Logos Christology a more dynamic salvation-history orientation or trajectory.[15] Congar, for instance, is critical of Thomas's claim that, from the moment of the personal union and because of it, Christ's assumed human nature already shared in the beatific vision from the moment of conception — a conclusion which he sees as "non-historical theology" and thus unsuitable for a Christology that wants to give full weight to the *kairoi* of Christ's life and mission in the biblical narratives.[16]

Congar does not link his discussion of the *filioque* to his reflections on Spirit Christology. Only briefly does Congar warn against Orthodox theologian Paul Evdokimov's use of the *spirituque* (i.e., that the Son is begotten from the Father "and the Spirit") on the grounds that such language might read too quickly the conception of the Son by the Holy Spirit in the economy of salvation into the intradivine life (immanent Trinity).[17] Since the *filioque* is a confession about the immanent Trinity per se, Congar sees economic events such as Christ's conception, anointing, and resurrection as constitutive of his humanity and thus not transferable to the immanent *filioque* question. This hesitancy towards some strict equivalence of economic and immanent aspects of

---

14. Congar, *I Believe in the Holy Spirit,* vol. 3, pp. 167-69.

15. "In the case of Jesus, it is important to avoid Adoptionism. He is ontologically the Son of God because of the hypostatic union from the moment of his conception. . . . We have, however, as believers, to respect the successive moments or stages in the history of salvation and to accord the New Testament texts their full realism. Thus I suggest that there were two moments when the *virtus* or effectiveness of the Spirit in Jesus was actualized in a new way: the first at his baptism, when he was constituted (and not simply proclaimed as) Messiah and Servant by God and the second at the time of his resurrection and exaltation, when he was made Lord." Congar, *I Believe in the Holy Spirit,* vol. 3, p. 171.

16. Congar, *I Believe in the Holy Spirit,* vol. 3, p. 166. See also *The Word and the Spirit,* p. 85. Here Congar cites *ST* 3a, q. 34, a. 4 (see 97, n. 2).

17. Congar, *I Believe in the Holy Spirit,* vol. 3, p. 75.

the Trinity might be part of the reason for the separate treatment of Spirit Christology and the Trinitarian issues behind the *filioque* in Congar's third volume.

Yet later, in *The Word and the Spirit,* Congar argues for a closer correspondence between events in the Son's incarnate life and his being eternally begotten of the Father. Not a strict equivalence, but a correspondence. Here the Spirit has a role to play. With less hesitancy, Congar speaks of an eternal existence of the Son in view of or as destined to be the incarnate Son of God conceived by the Holy Spirit.[18] In light of the Son's economy, where the Holy Spirit is actively present as his companion, one can posit a corresponding immanent reality which Congar, now positively recalling Evdokimov's language, calls a begetting of the Son by the Father "and the Spirit" *(spirituque).*[19] We see a deployment of Spirit Christology for reflection on the Trinity.

If Congar's ambiguity and promise in the use of Spirit Christology as an ecumenically fruitful model has taught us anything, it is that any proposals related to the *filioque* have to deal with the theological basis for — or against, in the case of the East — the use of the clause as well as the question of the degree of correspondence one is willing to allow between events in the economy of salvation and the immanent Trinity. Our contention is that a Spirit Christology in Nicene-Chalcedonian key contributes to both types of concerns and thus fosters ecumenical dialogue.[20] Because a Spirit Christology focuses on the identity of the Son *of* God as the bearer and giver of the Spirit *of* God, it is sensitive to the Eastern concern for maintaining the ontological priority of the *hypostasis* of the Father as the one *from whom* the other two

18. Congar writes: ". . . the Word was conceived *incarnandum* and even *crucifigendum, glorificandum, caput multorum Dei filiorum* . . . in such a way that the Word proceeds *a Patre Spirituque,* from the Father and the Spirit, since the latter intervenes in all the acts or moments in the history of the Word *incarnate.* If all the *acta* and *passa* of the divine economy are traced back to the eternal begetting of the Word, then the Spirit has to be situated at that point." *The Word and the Spirit,* p. 93.

19. Paul Evdokimov, *L'Esprit Saint dans la tradition orthodoxe* (Paris: Cerf, 1969), pp. 71-72; see also Serge Boulgakof, *Le Paraclet,* trans. Constantin Andronikof (Paris: Aubier/Montaigne, 1946), esp. pp. 140-43.

20. See Leopoldo A. Sánchez M., "Receiver, Bearer, and Giver of God's Spirit: Jesus' Life and Mission in the Spirit as a Ground for Understanding Christology, Trinity, and Proclamation" (Ph.D. diss., Concordia Seminary, 2003), pp. 103-213, and *Pneumatología: El Espíritu Santo y la espiritualidad de la iglesia* (St. Louis: Editorial Concordia, 2005), pp. 91-120.

persons exist in the economic and immanent Trinity. The hypostatic uniqueness of the Father as cause *(aitia)*, source *(pēgē)*, or fountain *(fons)* of the Son and the Holy Spirit, which the East believes the Western *filioque* undermines by making the Holy Spirit proceed also *from* the Son, is safeguarded.

Moreover, because Spirit Christology speaks of the Son as the *giver* of the Spirit, it is also sensitive to the Western concern for placing the Son in the economic mission of the Spirit from the Father — a point that the East would concede. Yet the West also posits, in a corresponding manner, that at the level of the immanent Trinity it is also possible to say that the Son is not foreign to the procession of the Spirit from the Father. The Eastern contention that the Holy Spirit's being from the Son only applies to the economy and thus has no immanent corollary or ground does not entirely qualify as the only Eastern approach to the Son-Spirit relation. While preserving the hypostatic uniqueness of the Father, for example, Eastern fathers also speak of the place of the Son in the procession of the Holy Spirit from the Father by using *per filium* (instead of *filioque*) language.[21] Even in the context of the Western *filioque*, which tends to see the Holy Spirit with little distinction as the Spirit *of* the Father *and* the Son because of its particular way of conceiving the processions, Augustine speaks of the Holy Spirit as being from the Father and the Son, but "principally" *(principaliter)* from the Father.[22] Such language is a sign that Augustine acknowledges the personal priority of the Father in relation to his Son, who is begotten *of* the Father, in a discussion of the Holy Spirit's personal identity.

By speaking of the Son as the *bearer* of the Spirit, a pneumatological Christology also advances the discussion beyond the classic

---

21. Consider these expressions: The Spirit proceeds from the Father "through (by means of) the Son" (e.g., Maximus the Confessor, Gregory Palamas), "and receives from the Son" (e.g., St. Epiphanius), "and rests (reposes) on the Son" (e.g., Pseudo-Cyril, John of Damascus, Pope Zacharias), and "shines out through the Son" (e.g., Athanasius), or the variation "conjointly with the Son on whom he rests." The Greek fathers' variety of images for speaking of the Son's place in the eternal (not only economic) procession of the Holy Spirit from the Father suggests that the Son's share in the production of the Spirit has not been precisely defined in the Eastern tradition (thesis 4). See Congar, *I Believe in the Holy Spirit*, vol. 3, p. 213.

22. Given Augustine's *principaliter,* even the Western *filioque* must give to the Father his unique hypostatic identity as origin and source of the other two persons. *On the Holy Trinity* 15.26.47, p. 225.

filioque controversy itself by raising yet another question, namely, the place of the Spirit in the mission of the Son. Just as the Son is not foreign to the mission and procession of the Spirit from the Father, so is the Holy Spirit not foreign to the begetting of the Son from the Father. Theologians in both the East and the West speak of the Spirit's resting on the Son even at the immanent level, seeing the Jordan event as an icon of an eternal Trinitarian reality. Thus the Son both lives for us and also exists eternally "in the Spirit" or *in spiritu*.

The common contention that the Western *filioque* logically subordinates the Holy Spirit to the Father from whom he proceeds and to the Son from whom he is spirated, thus exhibiting a denial of the Holy Spirit's "active personhood," must be taken seriously.[23] Yet one must acknowledge that pneumatological depersonalization is not the only way the data can be read since the Western-Augustinian approach also views the Holy Spirit as the bond of communion or mutual love between the Father and the Son in active terms, that is, as constitutive of the immanent relation between the Father and the Son who might be said to exist for us and eternally *in spiritu*.[24]

Eastern and Western traditions could allow for an *in spiritu* model of the Trinity that complements the *per filium* and *filioque* assertions. Just as the Holy Spirit proceeds from the Father through the Son — or from the Father principally and the Son — so is the Son begotten of the Father *in spiritu*. Although contemporary theologians have submitted *spirituque* and *per spiritu* options at this point, these are less sensitive respectively to the Eastern concern for the hypostatic uniqueness of the Father as the one from whom the Son and the Holy Spirit exist and to the Western (and even Eastern) traditional interest in holding to the logical priority of the Son vis-à-vis the Holy Spirit.[25]

23. Working in an Augustinian framework, David Coffey has argued that "the Holy Spirit is the objectivization, or hypostasization, or personalization, of this mutual love [between the Father and the Son], and hence in this sense its product or outcome." *Deus Trinitas: The Doctrine of the Triune God* (New York: Oxford University Press, 1999), p. 135. For a critique of the move towards depersonalization in the Western approach, see Thomas Weinandy, *The Father's Spirit of Sonship: Reconceiving the Trinity* (Edinburgh: T & T Clark, 1995), pp. 7-9, 71-72.

24. For a development of an *in spiritu* model in terms of the Augustinian mutual love paradigm, see David Coffey, *Did You Receive the Holy Spirit When You Believed? Some Basic Questions for Pneumatology* (Milwaukee: Marquette University Press, 2005), pp. 42-74.

25. See Paul Evdokimov, *L'Esprit Saint dans la tradition orthodoxe* (Paris: Cerf, 1969), 49-78, esp. 59-60, 70-72, 75; Leonardo Boff, *Trinity and Society*, trans. Paul Burns, Theol-

Leopoldo A. Sánchez M.

The latter concern for a Trinitarian *ordo* or taxis feeds into the issue of the degree of correspondence between the economic and the immanent Trinity one is willing to concede in the biblical description of the Son of God as the giver and bearer of the Spirit of God the Father. The *per filium* and *filioque* assume a logical priority of the Son vis-à-vis the Spirit, an order that is grounded in the nature of the hypostatic union. Over against the potential danger of an adoptionist principle, such union presupposes that, logically speaking, the Son assumes a human nature before the Holy Spirit sanctifies it — or to use Thomas's language, to which I shall return later, the grace of union (*gratia unionis*) precedes habitual grace (*gratia habitualis*). Positing a *spirituque* or a *per spiritu* does not only relativize the Eastern interest in preserving the hypostatic identity of the Father as *fons divinitatis*, but also overturns the classic Trinitarian order Father-Son-Spirit grounded in the nature of the hypostatic union.

In spiritu language, on the other hand, does not have to pit itself against these Eastern and Western teachings. Its intention is actually rather humble, for in the spirit of negative theology, *in spiritu* language seeks to state something rather than nothing, namely, that the Spirit is the Son's inseparable companion in the mystery of the incarnation as well as in the mystery of the eternal triadic relations among the divine persons. By leading us to the incarnate Logos who bears and gives the Spirit of the Father, a pneumatological Christology has ecumenical potential for engaging East and West with pastoral sensitivity not only by providing a biblical and theological narrative that engages issues related to the *filioque* but also, through its *in spiritu* and *per filium* language, by offering an angle that invites all parties to a broader Trinitarian conception of the mystery of our God.

II.

When Congar explored the pneumatological dimensions of Jesus' life, his interest in restoring the reality of the *kairoi* in an account of the incarnation brought him into some tension with what might be called

ogy and Liberation Series (Maryknoll, N.Y.: Orbis, 1988), p. 205 (cf. pp. 145-47, 236); and Xabier Pikaza, *El Espíritu Santo y Jesús: Delimitación del Espíritu Santo y relaciones entre Pneumatología y Cristología* (Salamanca, Spain: Secretariado Trinitario, 1982), p. 17.

classic Logos-oriented approaches to the mystery of the incarnation. To narrow the scope of such an orientation, we might say that a Logos Christology speaks of Jesus and events in his life in terms of his individual personal (or hypostatic) inner-constitution as the God-man or incarnate Logos. Its roots can be traced back to the East, where the church struggled against the adoptionist principle in Arian and Nestorian portrayals of Christ. Arius's presentation of the Son as an exalted creature who is anointed and raised by God as a reward for his virtue and obedience forces the church in the East to speak of the Son less in terms of his being anointed or raised by God in history and more in terms of his being *homoousios* with the Father before history.

To prevent an Arian interpretation, the anointing of the Son at the Jordan begins to be read by Athanasius through the lens of the Logos's union to his body from the moment of the incarnation.[26] It is no longer the Father who anoints the Son with the Spirit at the Jordan, but rather the Son who anoints himself with his divinity (= spirit) at the moment of the incarnation.[27] To be sure, in the Alexandrian Christological tradition, which Athanasius represents, the Logos's humanity still has soteriological significance in that the Logos assumes it in order to deify it or, more concretely, bring it into the Father's presence and a share in immortality and incorruptibility. But here the interest lies more in an abstract, cosmic, or universal conceptualization of humanity (as when we use the term "human nature"), which the divine Logos assumes in order to bring all humanity into the Father's

26. When speaking of the Jordan event, Athanasius places the anointing of the Word at the incarnation: "I, being the Father's Word, I give to Myself, when becoming man, the Spirit; and Myself, become man, do I sanctify in Him, that henceforth in Me, who am Truth . . . all may be sanctified." *First Discourse Against the Arians,* in *Nicene and Post-Nicene Fathers,* 2nd series (hereafter *NPNF2*), vol. 4, ed. Philip Schaff (reprint, Peabody, Mass.: Hendrickson, 1994), 12.46.

27. "For I the Word am the chrism, and that which has the chrism from Me is the Man; not then without Me could He be called Christ, but being with Me and I in Him." *Fourth Discourse Against the Arians,* in *NPNF2,* vol. 4, 36; for a similar incarnational interpretation of anointing language, see Gregory of Nazianzus: "He is Christ, because of His Godhead. For this is the Anointing of His manhood." *Fourth Theological Oration,* in *NPNF2,* vol. 7, 21; John of Damascus also speaks of the hypostatic union as the event in which Christ "in His own person anointed Himself; as God anointed His body with His own divinity, and as Man being anointed. For He is both God and Man. And the anointing is the divinity of His humanity." *An Exact Exposition of the Orthodox Faith,* in *NPNF2,* vol. 9, 3.3.

presence. Understandably, less attention is given to the human history, becoming, and *kairoi* of the incarnate Son.

Already in the Alexandrian approach to the anointing of Jesus, we see an interest in the portrayal of the Logos as the subject of his own human body and actions — a conception that logically follows from the very notion of a union of the divine and the human in Christ. There is an interest in the question of the individuality of the Logos, his personal inner-constitution, as it were. And so one does not hear much of the Father as one who anoints the Son with the Spirit — as one might hear more readily, for example, in Irenaeus,[28] in the Cappadocian tradition represented by Basil,[29] or in a healthy Antiochene tradition like that of John Chrysostom.[30] Instead, for Athanasius, it is the Logos who anoints or chrisms his own body with his own divinity. The anointing at Jordan becomes a revelatory event that confirms what already took place at the moment of the union, or — as it was also the case for Athanasius — an exemplary event that proleptically points to Christ's giving of the Spirit to the church in baptism. In a polemic against Arian adoptionism, it is important for Athanasius to see the Son not as receiving the Spirit from the Father — not even as man at the Jordan since he has the Spirit already from the time of the union — but always as God who gives his Spirit to the church.[31]

28. On the soteriological import of Jesus' anointing as declared in Isaiah 61:1ff. (cf. Lk. 4:18 ff.), Irenaeus writes: "For in the name of Christ is implied, He that anoints, He that is anointed, and the unction itself with which He is anointed. And it is the Father who anoints, but the Son who is anointed by the Spirit, who is the unction." *Against Heresies,* in *Ante-Nicene Fathers,* ed. Alexander Roberts et al. (reprint, Peabody, Mass.: Hendrickson, 1994), vol. 1, 3.18.3, p. 446.

29. "[T]he things done in the dispensation of the coming of our Lord in the flesh; — all is through the Spirit. In the first place He [i.e., the Spirit] was made an unction, and being inseparably present was with the very flesh of the Lord. . . . After this every operation was wrought with the co-operation of the Spirit. He was present when the Lord was being tempted by the devil. . . . He was inseparably with Him while working His wonderful works. . . . And He did not leave Him when He had risen from the dead." *On the Spirit,* in *NPNF2,* vol. 8, 16.39.25; 19.49, 31.

30. See Boris Bobrinskoy's endorsement of John Chrysostom in "The Indwelling of the Spirit in Christ: 'Pneumatic Christology' in the Cappadocian Fathers," *St. Vladimir's Theological Quarterly* 28/1 (1984): esp. pp. 59-65.

31. "All other things partake of the Spirit, but He, according to you, of what is He partaker? of the Spirit? Nay, rather the Spirit Himself takes from the Son . . . and it is not reasonable to say that the latter is sanctified by the former." *First Discourse Against the Arians* 5.15, in *NPNF2,* vol. 4, p. 315.

How one confesses the union of the divine and the human in Christ became a point of controversy in the East, leading to positions we now could refer to for convenience's sake as Nestorian or extreme Antiochene (disjunctive union),[32] Eutychian, monophysite, or extreme Alexandrian (essential union), and finally Catholic (personal or hypostatic union). From Cyril of Alexandria's angle, Nestorius's approach to the humanity of the Logos — the *homo assumptus* (assumed man) of Antiochene Christology — as a relatively independent reality left open the possibility of an adoptionist conception of the union. In other words, the Spirit-endowed humanity of Christ could be logically conceived as its own independent or subjective principle of existence and thus not so much as the Spirit-endowed flesh of the divine person of the Logos.

If we grant that the Antiochene school, whom Nestorius represents on this point, has the unrealized potential of conceiving the incarnation in a more radically human and historical way — as some contemporary theologians claim — it still fails to see the divine Logos fully as the person who actually takes upon himself that human life and history. For Nestorius, the immutable is not capable of the mutable, or, to put it in other terms, the finite is not capable of containing the infinite. On the other hand, if Cyril of Alexandria, following in Athanasius's footsteps, remains strong on the inseparability of the divine Logos and his assumed flesh, he does tend to think also of human nature in a more abstract universal manner and so with less emphasis on what each *kairos* might contribute to the human life, history, or becoming of the Logos. Although Cyril's christology could in principle allow for an anointing at Jordan that affects the Logos in the flesh, it is not entirely clear whether the Alexandrian does so since his interest lies mainly in the ecclesial significance of the event.[33]

---

32. The Nestorian position could also be called historically a "conjunctive" union, but that term might give the sense today of two parts being "combined." So I use instead the term "disjunctive" to mean the tendency to divide or separate logically the two natures in the process of distinguishing them.

33. Concerning his *Declaratio Septima,* Cyril subtly underplays Jesus' passive reception of the Holy Spirit by stressing Christ's identity as *giver* of the Spirit and the implications of the event *for the church:* "But he was named also Christ, because according to his human nature he was anointed *with us* [then Cyril cites Ps. 45:8]. For although he was the *giver* of the Holy Spirit, . . . nevertheless as he is man he was *called* anointed economically, the Holy Spirit resting upon him spiritually . . . in order that he might abide *in us*" (italics mine). See *The XII. Anathematisms of St. Cyril against Nestorius,* in *NPNF2,* vol. 14, p. 214.

Following Irenaeus, the anointing of the Logos has an ecclesial trajectory in that he restores the Spirit lost to humanity since Adam's fall. However, unlike Irenaeus, and following Athanasius, it is not important for Cyril to anchor the Logos's giving of his Spirit in his being anointed at Jordan per se since the Logos already has his Spirit from the moment of the hypostatic union. It is clear enough, therefore, over against the logical adoptionist principle in Nestorianism, that Cyril focuses instead on the revelatory (or proclamatory) and exemplary (or ecclesial) nature of the Jordan event.[34] When joined to the Alexandrian tradition's anti-Arian emphasis on the Logos as the giver (as opposed to receiver) of the Spirit, the school's anti-Nestorian focus on the Logos as personal subject of his own actions yields Cyril's statements concerning the Holy Spirit as the Logos's own Spirit. It is then more amenable to Alexandrian Christology to speak of the Logos as one who works through his own Spirit in the mystery of the incarnation. Less so to speak of the Logos as one through or upon whom the Spirit of the Father works. However, it is possible to bring these kinds of seemingly opposite expressions closer to one another in a Spirit Christology that affirms the incarnate Logos as both the bearer and the giver of the Holy Spirit.

The sixteenth-century Lutheran-Reformed controversy on the mode of Christ's presence in the Lord's Supper can be framed in terms of Cyril's teaching against Nestorius. The Lutherans claimed that the Reformed teaching of a spiritual (as opposed to bodily) presence of the Logos in his body and blood — one in which we receive Christ's body and blood spiritually by faith but not orally — assumed a disjunctive Nestorianizing Christological paradigm in which the Logos and his body in heaven did not have the kind of communion that would allow for the Logos to communicate his divine power and forgiveness to us in and through his assumed human nature *(genus maiestaticum).*[35] Through

---

34. On Cyril's position, see José Miguel Odero, "La Unción de Cristo según S. Cirilo Alejandrino," in *Credo in Spiritum Sanctum: Atti del Congresso Teologico Internazionale di Pneumatologia,* vol. 1, ed. José Saraiva Martins (Rome: Librería Editrice Vaticana, 1983), pp. 203-08, and his more extensive study "La Unción y el Bautismo de Cristo en S. Cirilo de Alejandría," in *Cristo, Hijo de Dios y Redentor del Hombre: III Simposio Internacional de Teología de la Universidad de Navarra,* ed. Lucas F. Mateo-Seco et al. (Spain: Navarra, 1982), pp. 519-40.

35. See *Formula of Concord* (hereafter *FC*), Ep VII and SD VII, in *The Book of Concord: The Confessions of the Evangelical Lutheran Church,* ed. Robert Kolb and Timothy J. Wengert (Minneapolis: Fortress, 2000).

the lens of the Nestorian controversy, one could see that, from a Reformed perspective, the Lutheran argument for the bodily presence of the divine Logos in the sacrament and therefore the oral reception of the same amounted to a Eutychianizing move towards an ill-conceived union (a confusion) that did not respect the proper Chalcedonian distinction between the divine and the human in the person Christ. The Lutherans are aware of such criticism. They respond by admitting that the ontological question concerning *how human a human nature through which the divine Logos operates should be* is ultimately less important than the soteriological benefit of the *genus maiestaticum,* namely, that the Logos is able to communicate his forgiveness through his own body and blood anywhere the sacrament is orally received.[36]

It is clear that the Lutheran position assumes the Alexandrian Christology of Cyril, but should the Reformed position be seen merely through Eastern eyes and thus only as adoptionistic in a Nestorianizing way? In his classic treatment of Lutheran Christology, Martin Chemnitz delves at length into the supernatural or infused created gifts that dwell in Christ's humanity.[37] Such gifts make Christ like the saints with the exception that he, unlike the saints, is also the source of the gifts and thus has them in greatest measure. Yet the presence of such gifts that inhere in the humanity of Christ do not reach the level of the *genus maiestaticum.* Infused gifts are capable of making Christ different from the saints by degree, but not by nature. While the supernatural or infused gifts are said to be the external effects of the Logos's divine nature upon his human nature, the *genus maiestaticum* refers to the communication of the Logos's divine attributes to his human nature.[38] Chemnitz refers to su-

36. *FC,* SD, p. 53: "No one can know better and more completely than the Lord Christ himself what Christ has received through the personal union and through his glorification or exaltation according to his assumed human nature, and of what this assumed human nature is capable above and beyond its natural characteristics without being destroyed." *FC,* SD, p. 92: "Through his divine omnipotence Christ can be present in his body, which he has placed at the right hand of the majesty and power of God, wherever he wishes, especially where he has promised his presence in his Word, such as in the Holy Supper. His omnipotence and wisdom can surely accomplish this without changing or destroying his true human nature."

37. See especially "Gifts Conferred on Christ's Human Nature," in *The Two Natures in Christ,* trans. J. A. O. Preus (St. Louis: Concordia, 1971), pp. 247-55.

38. Chemnitz notes: "these infused gifts are not actually the essential attributes of the divine nature. Rather, they are His workings outside the divine nature which are infused into the human nature of Christ in such a way that they inhere in it, as they say

pernatural created gifts as "habitual" (a term used by Western scholastic theologians) and attributes them at times to the presence of the Holy Spirit in the Logos's own humanity or, to use Alexandrian language, to the Logos's communication of his own Spirit to his flesh.[39]

Chemnitz's distinction between Christ's communication of his divine majesty to his human nature (unique to his person and thus non-transferable to the saints) and the communication of his supernatural gifts to his human nature (something he shares with the saints, but also has in inexhaustible measure) has roots in Western Christology and would have been known in the scholastic tradition. While Chemnitz uses the distinction primarily to avoid an adoptionist Christology that would reduce Christ to one of the saints, or a Nestorianizing one that would think of the Spirit-indwelt humanity of Christ separately from the Logos as subject of his own acts in and through his body and blood,[40] the use of the distinction also allows us to understand the Western perspective that at least some Reformed theologians might have had in their approach to Christology and sacramentology. It is partly a pneumatologically-informed perspective.

In the Western scholastic tradition, Thomas Aquinas distinguishes between the *gratia unionis* (grace of union), which is a synonym for the hypostatic union, and the *gratia habitualis* (habitual grace), which he associates with Christ's special holiness.[41] Whether one speaks of habitual grace or infused gifts, Chemnitz is aware of this distinction and, by using it in part to be critical of the Reformed, acknowledges that Reformed Christology can also be read through Western scholastic eyes and not only through Eastern-Alexandrian eyes. While

---

in the schools, formally, habitually, and subjectively, by which the very humanity of Christ in itself and according to itself is formed and perfected, so that it can be an instrument characteristic of, suitable for, and properly disposed for the deity, through which and in communion with and in cooperation with which the divine power of the Logos can exercise and carry out the workings of His divine majesty." *The Two Natures in Christ*, p. 248.

39. *The Two Natures in Christ*, p. 249. Passages include Luke 2:40 and Isaiah 11:1-2. But see also the use of Lk. 1:35 (pp. 56-57).

40. See, for example, *FC*, SD VIII, 51-55, 67-76.

41. Thomas describes the distinction between *gratia unionis* and *gratia habitualis*: "The grace of union is precisely God's free gift to the human nature of having personal existence in the Word, and that is the term of the assumption. Habitual grace, forming part of the special holiness of this man, is an effect following upon the union." *Summa Theologiae* 3a, q. 6, a. 6.

one can speak of Christ's presence in his body and blood through his Spirit (something the Reformed would agree to), Chemnitz's point is that such affirmation concerning habitual gifts (or supernatural gifts of the Spirit) does not yet reach the level of the type of statement that confesses Christ's communication of his own divine power to and through his body and blood to us in his Supper. Chemnitz's point is that Lutherans do not *only* speak of a spiritual participation by faith in Christ's gift of his Spirit (and/or of his divine nature) when we have his Supper (such spiritual presence of Christ in the Supper is not denied by Lutherans), but also that we receive Christ himself in and through his own body and blood orally for our salvation.[42]

While the Reformed would not disagree in principle with the grace of union or the communion of properties *(communicatio idiomatum)*, Reformed theologian McCormack has noted that such communion is typically mediated through the Holy Spirit's place in the humanity of the God-man.[43] That dimension of Reformed thought sees the Logos's unique or immediate work, strictly speaking, as the assumption of a human nature, and then leaves the history of the Logos to a description of the Holy Spirit's immediate presence and activity in and through his assumed human nature.[44] If the pneumatic dimension of the incarnation wins in the effort, the union of the Logos and his humanity seems to be more of a formal assertion than one that applies to what the Logos actually does as the subject of his own life and mission.

On the other hand, Lutheran Christology is strongest on the grace of union. It sees such union in an unmediated manner simply as the human life and history of the person of the Logos per se, although it has not entirely developed the pneumatic dimensions of such Chris-

42. FC, Ep VII, 15: "We believe, teach, and confess that the body and blood of Christ are received *not only* spiritually through faith *but also* orally with the bread and wine, though not in Capernaitic fashion but rather in a supernatural, heavenly way . . ." (italics mine).

43. "The agent who healed the human nature was not the Logos; it was the Holy Spirit. Such a teaching coheres nicely with the view advanced earlier that the communion of natures was a mediated union and not an immediate one." Bruce L. McCormack, *For Us and For Our Salvation: Incarnation and Atonement in the Reformed Tradition*. Studies in Reformed Theology and History (Princeton: Princeton Theological Seminary, 1993), p. 19 (cf. p. 36).

44. The Reformed theologian, John Owen (1616-1683), argues for the Holy Spirit's mediating role in the incarnation while arguing against the *genus maiestaticum*. *The Holy Spirit* (Grand Rapids, Michigan: Sovereign Grace, 1971), pp. 160-62.

tology, which may be more accessible through the Western Christological language of *gratia habitualis* or Chemnitz's created gifts. The Eastern-Alexandrian tradition provides the rationale for the Lutheran Logos-oriented *genus maiestaticum,* but the Western tradition, which is congenial to some aspects of Reformed Christology, might complement it with something like a *genus habitualis* or *genus pneumatikon.*

There is room in Lutheran Christology for such a move towards complementarity. For instance, Chemnitz speaks of the growth, perfection, or fulfillment of the Son's humanity under the category of habitual grace or *gratia habitualis,* which is concerned precisely with the supernatural qualities or infused gifts of his assumed human nature. Unlike the grace of union *(gratia unionis),* which concerns the person of the Logos's communication of his divine power to his assumed human nature, the *gratia habitualis* allows us to speak in a complementary way of the Logos's giving of supernatural created gifts to his human nature. At times, Chemnitz describes such gifts as the workings or effects of the Logos's divine nature in and through his humanity, but at other times, as previously noted, he explicitly uses biblical passages that associate such qualities and gifts with the presence and activity of the person of the Holy Spirit in the incarnate Logos. A *genus habitualis* allows us to affirm that the Holy Spirit's presence in the incarnate Logos disposes his humanity to work in unity with the Logos himself in bringing about the work of salvation for us, and thus that the Spirit's presence in the incarnate Logos perfects or brings to fulfillment (to its goal) his human life and history for us.[45]

Genus maiestaticum and *genus habitualis* language do not have to be pitted against each other. Their Eastern and Western roots can be honored. The former will emphasize the Logos-oriented dimension of the mystery of the incarnation, namely, the Logos's self-giving of divine majesty in and through His assumed humanity, in and through His body and blood, for us and for our salvation. The latter will emphasize the Spirit-oriented aspect of the mystery of the incarnation, which can be phrased as the Father's giving of his Spirit to his incarnate Son (Eastern Cappadocian), the Logos's giving of his Spirit to his assumed flesh (Eastern Alexandrian), or the Spirit's sanctification and perfection of the Logos's humanity or *gratia habitualis* (Western scholastic).

Furthermore, besides developing the pneumatological dimen-

---

45. See n. 38 above.

sions of the Logos's human life and work in the economy of salvation, to avoid the Reformed charge of Eutychianism, Lutherans must be careful to anchor the Logos's communication of divine properties to the assumed human nature *(genus maiestaticum)* in the person or hypostasis of the Logos and not in the divine nature as such.[46] To avoid the charge of Nestorianism, however, the Reformed will have to consider developing further the Logos-oriented dimensions of its approach to the incarnation and the Lord's Supper. Such a fuller Trinitarian approach to Christology would allow for both the Holy Spirit *and* the Logos himself to be present for us and for our salvation in and through the assumed flesh.

Both the Logos and the Holy Spirit are given by God the Father, according to what is proper to each person, through Christ's body and blood.[47] If the Lutheran tradition will have to reflect further on the Logos's giving *of the Holy Spirit* in his Supper along Western scholastic lines, the Reformed tradition will have to reflect further on the divine Logos's giving *of himself* in the Supper along Eastern Alexandrian lines. Needless to say, the conversation will continue, but this brief look at Lutheran-Reformed controversies over Christology and the Lord's Supper suggests that a pneumatological Christology in Nicene-Chalcedonian key (and thus one that works together with a Logos-oriented one) has ecumenical potential for bringing closer to one another Eastern and Western elements present in both traditions in the service of a fuller Trinitarian Christology and soteriology.

III.

The productivity of pneumatology in the promotion of an ecumenically sensitive ecclesiology has been explored from a variety of angles.

46. McCormack argues that the Reformed tradition's emphasis on the distinction of natures comes out of a reaction against what they perceive as a Lutheran teaching of *communio naturarum. For Us and For Our Salvation,* p. 13.

47. What Clark has suggested for the Roman Catholic tradition on what is proper to the Son and the Spirit in the Eucharist — respectively, the words of institution and the epiclesis — needs to be worked out also from confessional Lutheran and Reformed perspectives. In contrast to Catholics, Lutherans will tie the Spirit much more closely to the actual words of institution, but the Trinitarian framework of this exercise is correct. See Neville S. Clark, "Spirit Christology in the Light of Eucharistic Theology," *Heythrop Journal* 23, no. 3 (1982): 270-284.

For instance, the unity of God in the communion of three persons has been presented as the immanent ground *(theologia)* and source for living out the unity of the church catholic in various forms of *koinōnia* among the churches.[48] The East's eschatological conception of the Holy Spirit as the one in whom the Father perfects or brings to completion all things through the Son in the economy *(oikonomia)* offers yet another source for contemporary reflection on the Holy Spirit's role in driving local churches towards the divinely intended goal of *koinōnia*.[49] Forms of *koinōnia* among churches may encompass anything from dialogue to doctrinal consensus to tangible institutional forms and commitments — all of which reflect at various stages the goals and fruits of the ecumenical task.[50]

While everyone agrees *that* unity in Christ is both a gift of the Spirit and a task led by the Spirit, questions on *how* such unity should translate into some visible forms of communion or *koinōnia* remain. A sticky issue is where the locus of authority should be placed within an ordered communion. This question has been a particularly divisive one in the history of the Western church since the sixteenth century. The Reformation may be seen pneumatologically as a struggle over the privileged locus of the Spirit in defining ecclesial authority. Is such privileged locus the one who holds this or that teaching office? If so, what happens when the Pope, bishops, the *magisterium,* or church councils err? Or is the Holy Spirit's primary locus the heart and mind of each individual believer? But if so, then what about old and new enthusiasts who ultimately look for God and his will in their inner thoughts, feelings, and subjective experiences?

While not denying that the Holy Spirit dwells in each individual believer's heart and guides the church catholic and her teachers into all

48. See Lorelei F. Fuchs, "The Holy Spirit and the Development of Communio/ Koinōnia Ecclesiology as a Fundamental Paradigm for Ecumenical Engagement," in *The Holy Spirit, the Church, and Christian Unity: Proceedings of the Consultation held at the Monastery of Bose, Italy, 14-20 October 2002,* ed. D. Donnelly, A. Denaux, and J. Fameree (Leuven, Belgium: Leuven University Press, 2005), pp. 159-75.

49. See John Zizioulas, "The Holy Spirit and the Unity of the Church: An Orthodox Approach," in *The Holy Spirit, the Church, and Christian Unity,* pp. 35-46; also Nikos A. Nissiotis, "Pneumatological Christology as a Presupposition of Ecclesiology," in *Oecumenica,* ed. F. W. Kantzenbach and Vilmos Vajta (Minneapolis: Augsburg, 1967), pp. 235-52.

50. See Adelbert Denaux, "Holy Spirit, Authority, and Unity: Preliminary Remarks," in *The Holy Spirit, the Church, and Christian Unity,* pp. 267-87.

truth, the Lutheran Reformers ultimately see the external Word (*verbum externum*) as the privileged locus of the Holy Spirit and thus of normative authority in the church.[51] To use another language, there is a certain priority given in the Reformation to the Spirit-Word relationship as the basis for and way into Spirit-office, Spirit-charisma, and thus Spirit-church questions. Braaten readily acknowledges that office-bearers can indeed "betray their witness to the gospel" (the Reformation concern), but also argues in the face of the Western fragmentation of Protestantism for the need to establish a "concrete official and public locus of authority whose task is to implement the authority of the normative sources of the faith."[52] To put it in other terms, Braaten contends that the invisible unity of the church grounded in the freedom of the gospel and the means of grace must not necessarily be pitted against the church's visible witness to its unity in Christ through office, order, and structure.[53]

Among Roman Catholic theologians, and in the context of a response to the Renewal (Charismatic) movement in Roman Catholicism, Congar argues for the complementarity of institution and charisma in an account of the church.[54] The gifts of the Holy Spirit are seen not only as "charismatic," or coming from the priesthood of all believers due to their common baptismal dignity, but also as "hierarchical," or dealing with the service of its ordained ministers. There is a recognition that the "charismatic" dimension, though "extra-sacramental" per se, still brings vitality to the institutional church's internal life and service to the world — especially when the church has become too rationalistic, clergy-centered, or bureaucratic. Yet the "hierarchical" or institutional gifts are still seen as necessary in order to

51. See Inge Lønning, "The Reformation and the Enthusiasts," in *Conflicts about the Holy Spirit,* eds. Hans Küng and Jürgen Moltmann (New York: Seabury, 1979), pp. 33-40, and Harding Meyer, "A Protestant Attitude," in the same volume, pp. 83-92.

52. Braaten, *Mother Church,* pp. 80, 96.

53. Braaten, *Mother Church,* pp. 16-17.

54. See Congar's reflections on *Lumen Gentium*'s recognition of the necessary tension and complementarity between the charismatic and institutional character of the church in *I Believe in the Holy Spirit,* vol. 2, pp. 149-60. The key text from *LG* 8 is: "As the assumed nature, inseparably united to him serves the divine Word as a living organ of salvation, so, in a somewhat similar way, does the social structure of the Church serve the Spirit of Christ who vivifies it, in the building up of the body" (cf. Eph. 4,15); see also L. F. Fuchs, "The Holy Spirit and the Development of Communio/Koinōnia Ecclesiology," pp. 170-72.

express the sacramental character of the church, which deals with the delivery of the instituted means of grace through the successors of the apostles.

Congar argues that the unity of the churches cannot be ultimately anchored in our spiritual communion (the church's pneumatological dimension), but must include unity grounded in the church's Word, sacraments, confession or creed, and teaching of the faith, as well as in the ordained ministries that see to their implementation (incarnational or Christological aspect).[55] Within an institution-charisma framework, Congar places the Word and its ministries (including the Petrine office with the apostolic college of bishops) on the side of the incarnational-Christological dimension of the church over against an ecclesial (or more explicitly, Charismatic) reductionism that does away with Word and office in favor of "an immediate experience of the Spirit and its fruits."[56] The Spirit is not conceived merely in terms of communion with God through faith in Christ or in terms of spiritual gifts, for the Spirit is also the inner life and the power of the Word that brings us to Christ and his sacraments "so that the Word becomes present, inward and dynamically active."[57]

Although Congar does not explicitly use a Spirit Christology to lay out a theology of the church and ecumenism, he clearly applies a Trinitarian narrative to the task. Ralph Del Colle more explicitly reflects on the church via a Spirit Christology, arguing by way of analogy that the missions of the Son and the Holy Spirit in relationship to created human reality — respectively, the Son's assumption of a human nature and the Holy Spirit's indwelling of the incarnate Son (and the saints) — promote an appreciation for the church's identity as both an incarnational visible reality and a spiritual fellowship.[58] Del Colle begins with the distinction between the two missions and speaks of Christological aspects of the church's life such as Word and sacrament, discipline and order, and of pneumatological aspects such as gifts and spirituality.

Del Colle argues that, while the *Christus praesens* (the presence of the risen Christ in the church) is the incarnational "form of the

---

55. Congar, *I Believe in the Holy Spirit,* vol. 2, p. 207.
56. Congar, *I Believe in the Holy Spirit,* vol. 2, p. 211.
57. Congar, *I Believe in the Holy Spirit,* vol. 2, p. 211.
58. Ralph Del Colle, "The Outpouring of the Holy Spirit: Implications for the Church and Ecumenism," in *The Holy Spirit, the Church, and Christian Unity,* pp. 247-65.

Church" as a reality in the world that is "seen and heard," the *Spiritus praesens* accounts for the communion and diversity of the church.[59] While each church will have a different conception of its incarnational form or *gestalt,* of *how* the institutional form of the *Christus praesens* appears in its life, Del Colle argues that all communions explicitly or implicitly recognize the presence of the risen Christ in the visible life or form of the church.[60] In terms of the *Spiritus praesens,* we acknowledge each other's gifts and callings as these are expressed through the various "Christologically-oriented forms" of the church. Thus even in the face of an "imperfect communion," some sort of real communion can still be posited based on the joint mission of the Son and the Spirit in the church.[61]

Acknowledging Del Colle's points, it remains the case that an integral vision of the church as a reality grounded in the joint mission of Christ and the Spirit still benefits from the Reformation's insight concerning the priority of the Spirit-Word relationship over the Spirit-Church relationship in establishing ecclesial authority. No one disputes that the Holy Spirit leads the church into all truth. But how does one discern the spirits? After the Reformation, there is really no turning back on the mediation of the Word in the discernment of spirits, and any pneumatological legitimization of ecclesial authority must account for the real problem of putting too much trust in the church and her offices.[62]

At the same time, making the external Word *(verbum externum)* the normative locus of the Spirit should not be seen as a fundamentalist or Biblicist approach to the Word divorced of church and office — a concern Braaten eloquently argues against a sort of common Protestant ecclesial minimalism. Instead, such normativity must be seen as an attempt to link the work of the Spirit in the office holder (and the individual believer, for that matter) to the *personal* Word of God who is Jesus Christ. From a Trinitarian perspective, therefore, the Reformers' insistence on the normativity of the Word must be seen as an attempt to ground not only the church's spiritual fellowship by faith, but also

59. Del Colle, "The Outpouring of the Holy Spirit," pp. 254-257; for the distinction between the *Christus praesens* and the *Spiritus praesens,* see also Ralph Del Colle, *Christ and the Spirit: Spirit-Christology in Trinitarian Perspective* (New York: Oxford, 1994), pp. 174-79.
60. "The Outpouring of the Holy Spirit," p. 256.
61. "The Outpouring of the Holy Spirit," pp. 264-65.
62. See Meyer, "A Protestant Attitude," p. 86.

her visible form of life and witness (e.g., Word and sacrament, divinely-ordained or humanly-established offices in the church, good works and gifts of the Spirit) in the incarnate Word upon whom the Spirit rests, through whom the Spirit is given, and to whom the Spirit points for life.

Although Scripture is the Word of God, the written Word is, for Luther, a servant of the Gospel proclamation, which in turn points to Jesus Christ as our gift and example.[63] As Luther puts it, the church is not finally a "pen-house," but a "mouth-house." Holy Scripture is normative for the sake of the Gospel. This means that Scripture is meant to serve the church's discernment of the legitimacy of what is being proclaimed and taught in her midst by both office bearers and individual believers. It also means that there is a practical use of Scripture, which serves the church's discernment of what is lived out by her members in response to the Gospel. Ultimately, both the written and the spoken Word are servants of Christ so that all Scripture tends towards him as our gift, to be received by that faith which justifies us, and as our example, which exercises our good works or shapes our lives after Christ's own service unto death for others.

What is crucial yet underdeveloped in Luther's claim for the priority of the authority of the external Word vis-à-vis the authority of the office-bearer and the inner testimony of the Spirit in the believer's heart is that such priority can only be guaranteed and thus confessed on the basis of the inseparability of Jesus Christ and the Holy Spirit. The Holy Spirit's presence in and activity through the written, spoken, and sacramental forms of the Word derive precisely from the Spirit's presence in and activity through and with the Son, who in the language of John, is the incarnate and glorified Word upon whom the Spirit of the Father remains, through whom the Spirit of the Father is given to the church to remit and retain sins, and to whom the Spirit of truth points for eternal life and to norm the church's proclamation and teaching in a world hostile to Christ.

The Son and the Spirit are inseparably united in the written, spo-

---

63. See Martin Luther, *A Brief Instruction on What to Look for and Expect in the Gospels,* in *Luther's Works,* American Edition, vol. 35 (Philadelphia: Fortress/Muhlenberg, 1960), pp. 117-24; David W. Lotz, "The Proclamation of the Word in Luther's Thought," *Word & World* 3, no. 4 (1983): 344-54, and "Sola Scriptura: Luther on Biblical Authority," *Interpretation* 35, no. 3 (1981): 258-73; Uuras Saarnivaara, "Written and Spoken Word," *Lutheran Quarterly* 2 (May 1950): 167-79.

ken, and sacramental forms of the church's life. The Son and the Holy Spirit are also inseparably united in and at work through the church's offices and institutional life, the charisms or gifts of all her members, and their holiness and good works. Yet these other marks of the joint mission of the Son and the Spirit in the church must be continually discerned on the basis of the church's prior commitment to the Spirit of Christ's work "for us and for our salvation" through Scripture, the Gospel, and the sacraments. With this proviso in place, and because the Son and the Spirit are at work through the church at all times and places, one can also argue for the need for order and office in the safe-guarding of the faithful interpretation of Scripture according to the rule of faith and creed, the implementation of the proper administra-tion of the Gospel and sacraments, and the establishment of various forms of discipline to guide members in the way of good works in the world.

Roman Catholics and Eastern Orthodox theologians will con-tinue to approach the Spirit-Word relationship through Spirit-church-office lens. Evangelicals and Pentecostals will tend to approach the Spirit-Word relationship through Spirit-charism or Spirit-holiness lens. Lutherans will continue to approach church and office, as well as charism and holiness, through the lens of a more fundamental and therefore prior economic Trinitarian commitment to the joint mission of the Son and the Spirit in the economy of the Spirit-breathed Word in its spoken, written, and sacramental forms. Such Spirit-breathed Word cannot be reduced to office or charism, but, as Braaten reminds us, neither can church-office and charism-holiness be taken away from the life of the church and her ministers — even if such marks of the church remain servants of the Spirit-breathed Word.

Excessive forms of congregationalism evade accountability to other churches, even within the same church bodies, and can lead to sectarianism. The same can happen, oddly enough, with episcopal church orders that fail to work with the local churches and listen to what the Spirit is doing in them through Word and sacrament and through the gifts of God's people. While a Spirit Christology argues for no particular form of church government or order, it teaches us to con-fess and rejoice in the Father's commitment to preserve the church in spite of and in the midst of the errors of her office bearers in all forms of church order by reminding us of the continuous activity of the Son and the Spirit in the church through Word and sacrament, as well as through her holiness and gifts. At the same time, a Spirit Christology also challenges separated churches to confess and celebrate the unity of the church already achieved through the Gospel as the Spirit's gift even in the absence of perfect visible communion.

While a Spirit Christology does not actually discourage work towards a more perfect visible unity in terms of order and structure, the priority it gives to the Spirit-Word relationship vis-à-vis the Spirit-church relationship does not make achieving visible unity a condition for being church proper. And yet a Spirit Christology challenges us to attend to what the Son and the Spirit are doing among the separated churches through their incarnational audible and visible forms of service such as the proclamation of the Word and giving of the sacraments, faithful teaching and confession of office bearers, concrete manifestations of charisms, and the holy lives and virtues of God's people. Even in the face of an imperfect communion, therefore, a Spirit Christology still calls us to discern, acknowledge, learn from, and even celebrate those ways in which the churches are seeking to express the invisible unity all Christians have through the Gospel in visible forms that serve that Gospel and the unity it engenders by the power of the Spirit.

Bibliography of the Publications of Carl E. Braaten 1962-2010

Books Authored

History and Hermeneutics, New Directions in Theology Today, Volume 2. Westminster Press, 1966.

The Ethics of Conception and Contraception: Studies in Man, Medicine and Theology. Board of Social Ministry, Lutheran Church in America, 1967.

The Future of God: The Revolutionary Dynamics of Hope. Harper & Row, 1969.

Spirit, Faith, and Church. Coauthored with Wolfhart Pannenberg and Avery Dulles. Westminster, 1970.

The Futurist Option. Coauthored with Robert W. Jenson. Paulist Press, 1970.

Christ and Counter-Christ: Apocalyptic Themes in Theology and Culture. Fortress, 1972.

Eschatology and Ethics: Essays on the Theology and Ethics of the Kingdom of God. Augsburg Publishing House, 1974.

The Whole Counsel of God. Sermons by Carl E. Braaten. Fortress, 1974.

The Living Temple: A Practical Theology of the Body and the Foods of the Earth. Coauthored with LaVonne Braaten. Harper and Row, 1976.

The Flaming Center: A Theology of the Christian Mission. Fortress, 1977.

Stewards of the Mysteries: Sermons for Festivals and Special Occasions. Augsburg, 1983.

Principles of Lutheran Theology. Fortress, 1983.

The Apostolic Imperative: Nature and Aim of the Church's Mission and Ministry. Augsburg, 1985.

Justification: The Article by Which the Church Stands or Falls. Fortress, 1990.

No Other Gospel! Christianity among the World's Religions. Fortress, 1992.

Mother Church, Eschatology and Ecumenism. Fortress Press, 1998.

That All May Believe, Theology of the Gospel and the Mission of the Church. Eerdmans, 2008.

Because of Christ: Memoirs of a Lutheran Theologian. Eerdmans, 2008.

Books Edited

Kerygma and History: A Symposium on the Theology of Rudolf Bultmann. Translated and edited by Carl E. Braaten and Roy A. Harrisville. Abingdon, 1964.

The Historical Jesus and the Kerygmatic Christ, by Rudolf Bultmann. Translated and edited by Carl E. Braaten and Roy A. Harrisville. Abingdon, 1964.

The So-Called Historical Jesus and the Historic Biblical Christ, by Martin Kähler. Translated, edited and with an introduction by Carl E. Braaten. Fortress, 1964.

Perspectives on Nineteenth and Twentieth Century Protestant Theology, by Paul Tillich. Edited with an introduction by Carl E. Braaten. Harper and Row, 1967.

A History of Christian Thought, by Paul Tillich. Edited and with a preface by Carl E. Braaten. Harper and Row, 1968.

The New Church Debate: Issues Facing American Lutheranism. Edited with an introduction by Carl E. Braaten. Fortress, 1983.

Christian Dogmatics. Volumes 1 and 2. Edited by Carl E. Braaten and Robert W. Jenson. Fortress, 1984.

The Theology of Wolfhart Pannenberg. Edited by Carl E. Braaten and Philip Clayton. Augsburg, 1988.

Our Naming of God: Problems and Prospects of God-Talk Today. Edited by Carl E. Braaten. Fortress, 1989.

A Map of Twentieth Century Theology: Readings from Karl Barth to Radical Pluralism. Edited and introduced by Carl E. Braaten and Robert W. Jenson. Fortress, 1995.

Either/Or: The Gospel or Neopaganism. Edited by Carl E. Braaten and Robert W. Jenson. Eerdmans, 1995.

Reclaiming the Bible for the Church. Edited by Carl E. Braaten and Robert W. Jenson. Eerdmans, 1995.

The Catholicity of the Reformation. Edited by Carl E. Braaten and Robert W. Jenson. Eerdmans, 1996.

The Two Cities of God: The Church's Responsibility for the Earthly City. Edited by Carl E. Braaten and Robert W. Jenson. Eerdmans, 1997.

Union with Christ: The New Finnish Interpretation of Luther. Edited by Carl E. Braaten and Robert W. Jenson. Eerdmans, 1998.

The Marks of the Body of Christ. Edited by Carl E. Braaten and Robert W. Jenson. Eerdmans, 1998.

Sin, Death and the Devil. Edited by Carl E. Braaten and Robert W. Jenson. Eerdmans, 2000.

Church Unity and the Papal Office. Edited by Carl E. Braaten and Robert W. Jenson. Eerdmans, 2001.

The Strange New World of the Gospel: Re-Evangelizing in the Postmodern World. Edited by Carl E. Braaten and Robert W. Jenson. Eerdmans, 2002.

The Last Things: Biblical and Theological Perspectives on Eschatology. Edited by Carl E. Braaten and Robert W. Jenson. Eerdmans, 2003.

Jews and Christians: People of God. Edited by Carl E. Braaten and Robert W. Jenson. Eerdmans, 2003.

In One Body Through The Cross: The Princeton Proposal for Christian Unity. Edited by Carl E. Braaten and Robert W. Jenson. Eerdmans, 2003.

Mary, Mother of God. Edited by Carl E. Braaten and Robert W. Jenson. Eerdmans, 2004.

The Ecumenical Future. Edited by Carl E. Braaten and Robert W. Jenson. Eerdmans, 2004.

I Am the Lord Your God: Christian Reflections on the Ten Commandments. Edited by Carl E. Braaten and Christopher R. Seitz. Eerdmans, 2005.

Articles and Chapters

1962

"The Crisis of Confessionalism." *dialog: A Journal of Theology* 1, no. 1 (Winter 1962): 38-48.

"Radical Laicism." *Koinonia* (Journal of the Chicago Lutheran Theological Seminary Student Association) (March 1962): 3-5.

"Grace." *Resource* 3, no. 7 (April 1962): 2-6.

"Jesus and the Kerygma in Rudolf Bultmann's Theology." *Koinonia* (Journal of the Chicago Lutheran Theological Seminary) (December 1962): 11-13.

"Paul Tillich as a Lutheran Theologian." *Record* (Chicago Lutheran Theological Seminary) 67, no 3 (August 1962): 34-42.

"The Correlation between Justification and Faith in Classical Lutheran Dogmatics." In *The Symposium on Seventeenth Century Lutheranism,* Selected Papers, vol. I, pp. 77-90. St. Louis, 1962.

"New Frontiers in Theology." *Record* (Chicago Lutheran Theological Seminary) 67, no. 4 (November 1962): 29-40.

1963

"A New Order of Relations." *Frontiers* 14, no. 6 (February 1963): 14-19.

"Christ Today: The Lord of History." *Lutheran World* 10, no. 3 (July 1963): 257-66.

"Christus Heute: Der Herr der Geschichte." *Lutherische Rundschau* 13, no. 3 (July 1963): 183-298.

"Modern Interpretations of Nestorius." *Church History* 32, no. 3 (September 1963): 251-67.

"The Context and Scope of Theological Education." *Record* (Chicago Lutheran Theological Seminary) 68, no. 4 (November 1963): 22-27.

"Incarnation and Demythologizing," *Koinonia* (December 1963): 1-6.

1964

"The Interdependence of Theology and Preaching." *dialog: A Journal of Theology* 3, no. 1 (Winter 1964): 12-20.

"The Dynamics of a Responding Church in a Changing World." In *The Challenge of Change*. Luther College Press, 1964.

"Obedient Love in Human Relations." *National Lutheran* 32, no. 3 (March 1964): 6-8.

1965

"Comment on Caemmerer's Paper" (A Theological Examination of the Concepts of the Church and the Church's Educational Institutions — Richard R. Caemmerer). In *Educational Integrity and Church Responsibility,* Papers of the 51st Annual Meeting of the National Lutheran Educational Conference, January 1965, pp. 9-11.

"The Tragedy of the Reformation." *The Bell,* Thiel College Bulletin, Greenville, Pa., Vol. 55, No. 3 (March 1965): 3-5.

"The Current Controversy on Revelation: Pannenberg and His Critics." *The Journal of Religion* 45, no. 3 (July 1965): 225-37.

"How New Is the New Hermeneutic?" *Theology Today* 22, no. 2 (July 1965): 218-35.

"The Lordship of Christ in Modern Theology." *dialog: A Journal of Theology* 4, no. 3 (Summer 1965): 259-67.

"The Tragedy of the Reformation and the Return to Catholicity." *Record* (Chicago Lutheran Theological Seminary) 70, no. 3 (August 1965): 5-16.

"Un 'Sic et Non' Protestant." *Lumière et Vie* 24, no. 74 (August-October 1965): 20.

1966

"Reflections on the Lutheran Doctrine of the Law." *The Lutheran Quarterly* 18, no. 1 (February 1966): 72-84.

"Rome, Reformation, and Reunion." *Una Sancta* 23, no. 2 (1966): 3-8.

"Reunion, Yes; Return, No." *Una Sancta* 23, no. 3 (1966): 27-33.

"The Theme of the Future in Current Eschatologies." *Record* (Chicago Lutheran Theological Seminary) 71, no. 3 (August 1966): 5-10.

1967

"The Reunited Church of the Future." *Journal of Ecumenical Studies* 4, no. 4 (1967): 611-28.

"Toward a Theology of Hope." *Theology Today* 24, no. 2 (1967): 208-26.

"Speaking of God in a Secular Age." *Context* I, no. 1 (Autumn 1967): 3-17.

1968

"Toward a Theology of Hope." *Theology Digest* 16, no. 2 (Summer 1968): 151-54.

"Radikale Theologie in Amerika." *Lutherische Monatshefte,* no. 2 (February 1968): 55-59.

"Zur Theologie der Revolution." *Lutherische Monatshefte,* no. 5 (Mai 1968): 215-20.

1969

"The Church on the Frontier of History." *Lutheran Quarterly* 21, no. 1 (February 1969): 12-16.

"Ecumenism and Theological Education in the United States." *Oecumenica* (1969): 199-208.

"The Phenomenology of Hope." In *Christian Hope and the Future of Humanity,* edited by Franklin Sherman. Augsburg, 1969.

1970

"Who Is Bernard Lonergan?" *Lutheran World* 17, no. 4 (1970): 372-76.

"Wer Ist Bernard Lonergan?" *Lutherische Rundschau* (October 1970): 372-76.

"American Historical Experience and Christian Reflection." In *Projections: Shaping an American Theology for the Future,* edited by Thomas F. O'Meara & Donald M. Weisser, pp. 86-108. Doubleday, 1970.

1971

"The Future as the Source of Freedom." *Theology Today* 27, no. 4 (January 1971): 382-93.

"Untimely Reflections on Women's Liberation." *dialog: A Journal of Theology* 10, no. 2 (Spring 1971): 104-11.

"Ecumenism: Where Do We Go from Here?" *dialog: A Journal of Theology* 10, no. 4 (Autumn 1971): 288-91.

"The Significance of Apocalypticism for Systematic Theology." *Interpretation* 25, no. 4 (October 1971): 480-99.

"Theology of Hope." In *Philosophical and Religious Issues,* edited by L. Miller. Dickenson Publishing Company, 1971.

1972

"Ambiguity and Hope in the Ecumenical Movement." *dialog: A Journal of Theology* 11, no. 3 (Summer 1972): 209-15.

"Die Bedeutung der Zukunft." *Evangelische Theologie* 32, no. 4 (July/August 1972): 209-15.

"A Theological Conversation with Wolfhart Pannenberg." *dialog: A Journal of Theology* 11, no. 4 (Autumn 1972): 286-95.

"A Lutheran View of the Catholic Dialog with Luther." *dialog: A Journal of Theology* 11, no. 4 (Autumn 1972): 299-303.

"Theology and Our Common World." *Worldview* 15, no. 9 (September 1972): 22-27.

"Theology and Welfare." *Lutheran Social Concern* 12, no. 3 (Fall 1972): 31-38.

"A Response to a Critique of Braaten's Review of Pannenberg's *Basic Questions in Theology*." *Worldview* 15, no. 2 (December 1972): 56-57.

"The Significance of the Future: An Eschatological Perspective." In *Hope and the Future of Man,* edited by Ewert H. Cousins, pp. 40-54. Fortress, 1972.

"Religion as Patriotism or Protest." *Event* 12, no. 10 (November 1972): 4-7.

1973

"Die Botschaft vom Reiche Gottes und die Kirche." In *Evangelium und Geschichte. Das Evangelium und die Zweideutigkeit der Kirche,* vol. 3, edited by Vilmos Vajta, pp. 11-54. Vandenhoeck und Ruprecht, 1973.

"A Theology of the Body." *Lutheran* 2, no. 7 (April 1973): 12-15.

1974

"A Decade of Ecumenical Dialogues." *dialog: A Journal of Theology* 13, no. 2 (Spring 1974): 142-48.

"The Gospel of the Kingdom of God and the Church." In *The Gospel and the Ambiguity of the Church,* edited by Vilmos Vajta, pp. 3-26. Fortress, 1974.

"Response to Professor Carl Peter" (Carl Peter, *The Quest of a Credible Eschatology*) in *The Catholic Theological Society of America, Proceedings of the 29th Annual Convention,* vol. 29, pp. 273-78. Chicago, Illinois, 1974.

"From Apocalyptic to Somatic Theology." *dialog: A Journal of Theology* 13, no. 4 (Autumn 1974): 279-301.

"Caring for the Future: Where Ethics and Ecology Meet." *Zygon* 9, no. 4 (December 1974): 311-22.

"The Cancellation of Hope by Myth." In *Philosophy of Religion,* edited by Norbert O. Schedler. Macmillan, 1974. (Excerpted from *The Future of God,* pp. 42-46.)

1975

"Theology of Mission and Service," *Contact* (Lutheran Social Services Chaplaincy Newsletter) 8, no. 1 (Spring 1975): 3-14.

1976

"The Challenge of Liberation Theology — A Lutheran Perspective." In *Consultation on Theological Presuppositions Implicit in the Current Theories of Education,* a Study by the USA National Committee of the Lutheran World Federation, pp. 63-82. 1976.

"The Christian Mission and American Imperialism." In *Religion and the Dilemmas of Nationhood*, Bicentennial Years of the Knubel-Miller-Greever Lectures, edited by Sydney E. Ahlstrom, pp. 64-72. Lutheran Church in America, 1976.

"The Christian Mission and American Imperialism." *dialog: A Journal of Theology* 15, no. 1 (Winter 1976): 70-78.

"American Imperialism and the Christian Mission" (abridged version). *World Encounter* (June 1976): 1-5.

"A Trinitarian Theology of the Cross." *Journal of Religion* 56, no. 1 (January 1976): 113-21.

"Taking Our Bodies Seriously." *Faith at Work* 89, no. 4 (June 1976): 6-7.

"Lutherans on Liberty and Liberation." *dialog: A Journal of Theology* 15, no. 3 (Summer 1976): 166-68.

"The Gospel of Justification *Sola Fide.*" *dialog: A Journal of Theology* 15, no. 3 (Summer 1976): 207-13.

1977

"A Personal Odyssey." *Kirche og Folk* 26, no. 19 (November 1977): 43-44.

1978

"Theology and the Body." *Physical Activity and Human Well-being*, edited by Fernand Landry and William A. R. Orban. Symposia Specialists, 1978. A collection of the papers presented at the International Congress of Physical Activity Sciences held in Quebec City, July 11-16, 1976.

1979

"The One Universal Church." *Schola: A Pastoral Review of Sacred Heart School of Theology* 2 (1979): 19-32.

"Sex, Marriage, and the Clergy." *dialog: A Journal of Theology* 18, no. 3 (Summer 1979): 169-74.

1980

"Who Do We Say That He Is? On the Uniqueness and Universality of Jesus Christ." *Occasional Bulletin* 4, no. 1 (January 1980): 2-9.

"The Universal Meaning of Jesus Christ." LCA *Partners* 2, no. 6 (December 1980): 13-16.

1981

"The Ordination of Deacons." *dialog: A Journal of Theology* 20, no. 2 (Spring 1981): 101-5.

"Open Letter to David Preus." *dialog: A Journal of Theology* 20, no. 2 (Spring 1981): 136-37.

"The Christian Doctrine of Salvation." *Interpretation* 35, no. 2 (April 1981): 117-31.

"Braaten Responds" (to the critique of Braaten's position regarding universalism). *Partners* 3, no. 3 (June 1981): 20-21.

"Can We Still Hold to the Principle of '*Sola Scriptura*'?" *dialog: A Journal of Theology* 21, no. 3 (Summer 1981): 189-94.

"The Lutheran Confessional Heritage and Key Issues in Theology Today." *Currents in Theology and Mission* 8, no. 5 (October 1981): 260-68.

"Toward an Ecumenical Theology of Human Rights." In *How Christian Are Human Rights?* edited by Eckehart Lorenz, pp. 36-54. Lutheran World Federation, 1981.

"Auf dem weg zu einer Okumenische Theologie der Menschenrechte." In *Zur Sache* 22, pp. 52-79. Lutherisches Verlagshaus, 1981.

"The Uniqueness and Universality of Jesus Christ." In *Mission Trends, No. 5,* edited by Gerald H. Anderson and Thomas F. Stransky, C.S.P., pp. 69-89. Eerdmans, 1981.

"Carl Braaten responds to critiques of his December 1980 *LCA Partners* article on the uniqueness of Christ." *LCA Partners* 3, no. 3 (June 1981): 20-21.

1982

"The Contextual Factor in Theological Education." *dialog: A Journal of Theology* 21, no. 3 (Summer 1982) 169-74.

"The Future of the Ecumenical Movement." *Theology Digest* 30, no. 4 (Winter 1982): 303-12.

1983

"Reflections on the St. Louis Forum: Authority and Power in the Church." *ATS Theological Education* 19, no. 2 (Spring 1983): 101-5.

"Ecclesiological Perspectives." *The Covenant Quarterly* 41, no. 3 (August 1983): 53-58.

"Evangelization in the Modern World." In *Consulting on Evangelism*. A Document of the Division for World Mission and Ecumenism for the Lutheran Church in America, pp. 33-50. 1983.

"Jesus Among the Jews and Gentiles." *Currents in Theology and Mission* 10, no. 4 (August 1983): 197-209.

"Shadows of the Cross: On the Contemporary Significance of Luther's Theology." Chancellor's Address, delivered at Regis College, Toronto, November 21, 1983.

1984

"Praxis: The Trojan Horse of Liberation Theology." *dialog: A Journal of Theology* 23, no. 3 (Summer 1984): 276-80.

"Romans 12:14-21." *Interpretation* 38, no. 3 (July 1984): 291-95.

"Evangelization in the Modern World." In *The Continuing Frontier: Evangelism.* A Document of the Division for World Mission for the Lutheran Church in America (September 1984): 30-45.

"Prolegomena to Christian Dogmatics." In *Christian Dogmatics,* First Locus, vol. I, edited by Carl E. Braaten and Robert W. Jenson, pp. 5-78. Fortress, 1984.

"The Person of Jesus Christ." In *Christian Dogmatics,* Sixth Locus, vol. I, edited by Carl E. Braaten and Robert W. Jenson, pp. 465-569. Fortress, 1984.

1985

"The Question of God and the Trinity." In *Festschrift: A Tribute to Dr. William Hordern,* edited by Walter Freitag, pp. 6-16. University of Saskatchewan, 1985.

1986

"Whole Person and Whole Earth." *Lutheran Women* (May 1986): 6-9.

"The Problem of the Absoluteness of Christianity." *Interpretation* 40, no. 4 (October 1986): 341-53.

"Theological Perspectives in the Christian Mission among Muslims." In *God and Jesus: Theological Reflections for Christian-Muslim Dialog,* Division for World Mission and Interchurch Co-operation of the American Lutheran Church, 8-19. 1986.

1987

"Whatever Happened to Law and Gospel?" *Currents in Theology and Mission* 14, no. 2 (Spring 1987): 111-18.

"Let's Talk about the Death of God." *dialog: A Journal of Theology* 26, no. 3 (Summer 1987): 209-14.

"Men, Women, and the Trinity." *Cresset* 51, no. 1 (November 1987): 23-25.

"Christocentric Trinitarianism v. Unitarian Theocentrism: A Response to S. Mark Heim." *Journal of Ecumenical Studies* 24, no. 1 (Winter 1987): 17-21.

"The Problem of the Absoluteness of Christianity: An Apologetic Reflection." In *Worldviews and Warrants,* edited by William Schweiker and Per M. Anderson, pp. 51-70. University Press of America, 1987.

"A Look at CPE from a Lutheran Theological Perspective." *SPC Journal,* 10 (1987): 30-33.

1988

"The Doctrine of the Two Kingdoms Re-Examined." *Currents in Theology and Mission* 15, no. 6 (December 1988): 497-505.

"The Meaning of Evangelism in the Context of God's Universal Grace." *Journal of the Academy for Evangelism in Theological Education* 3 (1987-1988): 9-19.

"Preaching Both Law and Gospel." *International Christian Digest* 2, no. 4 (May 1988): 37-41.

"Salvation through Christ Alone." *Lutheran Forum* 22, no. 4 (November 1988): 8-12.

"Lutheran Theology and Religious Pluralism." *LWF* [Lutheran World Federation] *Report* 23/24 (January 1988): 105-28.

1989

"Preaching Christ in an Age of Religious Pluralism." *Word and World* 9, no. 3 (Summer 1989): 244-50.

"Jesus and World Religions." *World Encounter,* no. 3 (1989): 4-7.

"The Mind and Heart of the Lutheran Pastor." *dialog: A Journal of Theology* 28 (Spring 1989): 117-19.

"Introduction: Naming the Name" and "The Problem of God-Language Today." In *Our Naming of God: Problems and Prospects of God-Talk Today,* edited by Carl E. Braaten, pp. 1-34. Fortress, 1989.

1990

"Whole Person and Whole Earth." In *The Parish Nurse,* edited by Granger Westberg, pp. 77-81. Augsburg, 1990.

"The Triune God: The Source of Unity and Mission." *Missiology, An International Review* 18, no. 4 (October 1990): 417-27.

"God in Public Life — A Rehabilitation of the Lutheran Idea of the 'Orders of Creation.'" *Lutheran Theological Seminary Bulletin* 70, no. 1 (Winter 1990): 34-52.

"God in Public Life: Rehabilitating the 'Orders of Creation.'" *First Things,* no. 8 (December 1990): 32-38.

"Paul Tillich's Message for Our Time." *Anglican Theological Review* 72, no. 1 (Winter 1990): 16-25.

"Gott und das Evangelium: Pluralismus und Apostasie in der amerikanischen Theologie." *Kerygma und Dogma* 36, no. 1 (January/March 1990): 56-71.

"The Identity and Meaning of Jesus Christ." In *Lutherans and the Challenge of Religious Pluralism,* edited by Frank Klos, C. Lynn Nakamura, and Daniel F. Martensen, pp. 103-38. Augsburg, 1990.

1991

"God and the Gospel: Pluralism and Apostasy in American Theology." *Lutheran Theological Journal* 25, no. 1 (May 1991): 38-50.

"The Mission of the Gospel." *F.O.C.L. Point* 2, no. 2 (Fall 1991): 1-2.

1992

"Christian Theology and the History of Religions." *Currents in Theology and Mission* 19, no. 1 (February 1992): 5-13.

"No Other God." *Evangelical Catholic* (Theological and Opinion Journal of the Episcopal Synod of America) 15, no. 2 (November/December 1992): 1-3.

"Response to Paul F. Knitter" ("Religious Pluralism in Theological Education"). *Anglican Theological Review* 74, no. 4 (Fall 1992): 438-42.

1994

"Jesus and the Church." *Ex Auditu: An International Journal of Theological Interpretation of Scripture* 10 (1994): 59-72.

"The Il/Legitimacy of Lutheranism in America?" *Lutheran Forum* 28, no. 1 (February 1994): 38-44.

"Response to Manfred K. Bahmann." *Lutheran Forum* 28, no. 3 (August 1994): 11-12.

"Ecumenical Orthodox Dogmatics?" *Touchstone* 7, no. 1 (Winter 1994): 10-11.

1995

"The Gospel for a Neopagan Culture." In *Either/Or: The Gospel or Neopaganism,* edited by Carl E. Braaten and Robert W. Jenson, pp. 7-22. Eerdmans, 1995.

"No Other Gospel." *Lutheran* 8, No. 10 (October 1995): 20-23.

"Introduction: Gospel, Church, and Scripture." In *Reclaiming the Bible for the Church,* edited by Carl E. Braaten and Robert W. Jenson, pp. ix-xii. Eerdmans, 1995.

1996

"Scripture, Church, and Dogma, An Essay on Theological Method." *Interpretation* 50, no. 2 (April 1996): 142-55.

"Katolicita a reformacia." *Cirkevne Listy* (October 1996): 152-54.

"Die Katholizität der Reformation." *Kerygma und Dogma* 42 (July/September 1996): 186-201.

"The Problem of Authority in the Church." In *The Catholicity of the Reformation,* edited by Carl E. Braaten and Robert W. Jenson, pp. 53-66. Eerdmans, 1996.

"Confessional Integrity in Ecumenical Dialogue." *Lutheran Forum* 30, no. 3 (1996): 24-30.

"A Harvest of Evangelical Theology." *First Things,* no. 63 (May 1996): 45-48.

1997

"Creation, Eschatology, Ecology." In *Caritas Dei, Beiträge zum Verständnis Luthers und der gegenwärtigen Ökumene,* Festschrift for Tuomo Mannermaa on His Sixtieth Birthday, edited by Oswald Bayer, Robert W. Jenson, and Simo Knuuttila, pp. 128-38. Luther-Agricola Gesellschaft. Helsinki, 1997.

"The Cultural Captivity of Theology: An Evangelical Catholic Perspective." The Inaugural Margaret McKinnon Memorial Lecture on Christianity and Culture, published by The Nepean Presbytery of the Uniting Church in Australia, pp. 1-19. Melbourne, 1997.

"Hearing the Other: The Promise and Problem of Pluralism." *Currents in Theology and Mission* 24, no. 5 (October 1997): 393-400.

"The Role of Dogma in Church and Theology." In *The Task of Theology Today*, edited by Victor Pfitzner and Hilary Regan, pp. 25-57. Australian Theological Forum, 1998.

"Natural Law in Theology and Ethics." In *The Two Cities of God: The Church's Responsibility for the Earthly City*, edited by Carl E. Braaten and Robert W. Jenson, pp. 42-58. Eerdmans, 1977.

"A Response" (to Russell Hittinger on "Natural Law and Catholic Moral Theology"). In *A Preserving Grace, Protestants, Catholics, and Natural Law*, edited by Michael Cromartie, pp. 31-40. Eerdmans, 1997.

Epilogue: "Theology *Pro Ecclesia* — Evangelical, Catholic & Orthodox." In *Reclaiming the Great Tradition*, edited by James S. Cutsinger, pp. 185-98. InterVarsity, 1997.

1998

"The Finnish Breakthrough in Luther Research." In *Union With Christ*, edited by Carl E. Braaten and Robert W. Jenson, pp. vii-ix. Eerdmans, 1988.

1999

"Foreword." *Christ and Culture in Dialogue*, edited by Angus J. L. Menuge, Alberto L. García, and William Cario, pp. 7-13. Concordia Academic Press, 1999.

"The Special Ministry of the Ordained." In *Marks of the Body of Christ*, edited by Carl E. Braaten and Robert W. Jenson, pp. 123-36. Eerdmans, 1999.

"The Significance of New Testament Christology for Systematic Theology." In *Essays on Christology: Who Do You Say That I Am?* edited by Mark Allan Powell and David R. Bauer, in Honor of Jack Dean Kingsbury, pp. 216-27. Westminster John Knox, 1999.

"The Last Things." *The Christian Century* 116, no. 33 (December 1, 1999): 1174-75.

"The Gospel Proviso: Lessons from 20th-Century Theology for the Next Millennium." *dialog: A Journal of Theology* 38, no. 4 (Fall 1999): 245-52.

"The Resurrection Debate Revisited." *Pro Ecclesia* 8, no. 1 (Spring, 1999).

2000

"Powers in Conflict: Christ and the Devil." In *Sin, Death, & the Devil*, edited by Carl E. Braaten and Robert W. Jenson, pp. 94-107. Eerdmans, 2000.

"Robert William Jenson — A Personal Memoir" and "Eschatology and Mission in the Theology of Robert Jenson." In *Trinity, Time, and Church: A Response to the Theology of Robert W. Jenson,* edited by Colin E. Gunton, pp. 1-9 and 298-311. Eerdmans, 2000.

"The Evangelical and Catholic Theology of Paul Tillich: A Lutheran Appreciation." *The North American Paul Tillich Society Newsletter* 26, no. 1 (Winter 2000): 2-7.

"*Nullus Diabolus — Nullus Redemptor:* Apocalyptic Perspectives on the Struggle for Life against Death." In *Thinking Theologically about Abortion,* edited by Paul T. Stallsworth, pp. 51-72. Bristol House, 2000.

"Augsburg Confession, Article VII: Its Implications for Church Fellowship and Structure." *Certus Sermo* (an Independent Monthly Review of the Northwest Washington Synod of the Evangelical Lutheran Church in America), no. 119 (March 2000), 1-(4). Continued in no. 120 (April 2000): 1-3.

2001

"Introduction." Co-authored with Robert W. Jenson. In *Church Unity and the Papal Office,* pp. 1-9. Eerdmans, 2001.

"The Reality of the Resurrection." In *Nicene Christianity: The Future for a New Ecumenism,* edited by Christopher R. Seitz, pp. 107-18. Brazos, 2001.

"A Shared Dilemma: Catholics and Lutherans on the Authority and Interpretation of Scripture." *Pro Ecclesia* 10, no. 1 (Winter 2001): 63-75.

2002

"The Future of the Apostolic Imperative: At the Crossroads of World Evangelization." In *The Strange New Word of the Gospel: Re-Evangelizing in the Postmodern World,* edited by Carl E. Braaten and Robert W. Jenson, pp. 159-74. Eerdmans, 2002.

"Christology and the Missionary Crisis of the Church." In *Story Lines, Chapters on Thought, Word, and Deed* (for Gabriel Fackre), edited by Skye Fackre Gibson, pp. 106-12. Eerdmans, 2002.

2003

"Apocalyptic Imagination in Theology." In *The Last Things, Biblical and Theological Perspectives on Eschatology,* edited by Carl E. Braaten and Robert W. Jenson, pp. 14-32. Eerdmans, 2003.

2004

"The Christian Faith in an Inter-Faith Context." *dialog: A Journal of Theology* 43, no. 3 (Fall 2004): 233-37.

2005

"Sins of the Tongue." In *I Am the Lord Your God: Christian Reflections on the Ten*

Commandments, edited by Carl E. Braaten and Christopher R. Seitz, pp. 206-17. Eerdmans, 2005.

"The Reality of the Resurrection." *Good News* (The Magazine for United Methodist Renewal) (September/October 2005): 28-30.

2006

"A Response to My Lutheran *Dialog* Responders." *dialog: A Journal of Theology* 45, no. 3 (Summer 2006): 192-96.

2007

"Sexuality and Marriage." In *The Ten Commandments for Jews, Christians, and Others,* edited by Roger E. Van Harn, pp. 135-47. Eerdmans, 2007.

"Reclaiming the Natural Law for Theological Ethics." *Journal of Lutheran Ethics* 7, no. 10 (October, 2007).

2008

"A Critique of the 'Draft Social Statement on Human Sexuality' Prepared by the Task Force for ELCA Studies on Sexuality, Church in Society" (Evangelical Lutheran Church in America). *Journal of Lutheran Ethics* 8, no. 7 (July, 2008).

2009

"On Flunking the Theological Test in the ELCA." *dialog: A Journal of Theology* 47, no. 1 (Winter 2009).

Editorials

"Communion Before Confirmation?" *dialog: A Journal of Theology* 1, no. 3 (Summer 1962): 61-62.

"Against the Becker Amendment." *dialog: A Journal of Theology* 3, no. 4 (Autumn 1964): 295-97.

"The Second Vatican Council's Constitution on the Church." *dialog: A Journal of Theology* 4, no. 2 (Spring 1965): 136-39.

"The Theological Mandate of the Church College." *dialog: A Journal of Theology* 4, no. 3 (Summer 1965): 218-21.

"Dialog — The Fifth Year." *dialog: A Journal of Theology* 5, no. 1 (Winter 1966): 4-6.

"Paul Tillich: Lutheran and Catholic." *dialog: A Journal of Theology* 5, no. 1 (Winter 1966): 6-7.

"The New Social Gospel Movement." *dialog: A Journal of Theology* 5, no. 2 (Spring 1966): 133-35.

"The Next 450 Years." *dialog: A Journal of Theology* 6, no. 4 (Autumn 1967): 244-45.

"Intercommunion." *dialog: A Journal of Theology* 8, no. 2 (Spring 1969): 88.

"Theology and Student Politics." *dialog: A Journal of Theology* 9, no. 1 (Winter 1970): 5-6.

"On Polarization." *dialog: A Journal of Theology* 9, no. 3 (Summer 1970): 167-68.

"Luther at Worms — Some Kind of Revolutionary." *dialog: A Journal of Theology* 10, no. 1 (Winter 1971): 4-5.

"The Grand Inquisitor of Missouri." *dialog: A Journal of Theology* 10, no. 2 (Spring 1971): 84-86.

"Hanoi Ploy." *dialog: A Journal of Theology* 10, no. 2 (Spring 1971): 89.

"Dialog after Ten Years." *dialog: A Journal of Theology,* vol. 11, no. 1 (Winter 1972): 4-5.

"The Future Is Not What It Used To Be." *dialog: A Journal of Theology* 11, no. 1 (Winter 1972): 5-8.

"Churches of the Reformation, Unite!" *dialog: A Journal of Theology* 11, no. 1, (Winter 1972): 11-12.

"The Colliding of Eschatology and Establishment." *dialog: A Journal of Theology* 11, no. 1 (Winter 1972): 18-22.

"How Christian Is the New Ethnicity?" *dialog: A Journal of Theology* 11, no. 3 (Summer 1972): 166-67.

"On Leaving America." *dialog: A Journal of Theology* 11, no. 4 (Autumn 1972): 245-46.

"On Getting Keyed Up for Key 73." *dialog: A Journal of Theology* 11, no. 4 (Autumn 1972): 1972.

"Garbage In, Garbage Out! The Press Report on the St. Louis Faculty." *dialog: A Journal of Theology* 11, no. 4 (Autumn 1972): 249-50.

"Which Key?" *dialog: A Journal of Theology* 12, no. 1 (Winter 1973): 4.

"The Lutheran Church in America's Affirmation of Faith." *dialog: A Journal of Theology* 12, no. 2 (Spring 1973): 92-93.

"The Retreat to Conservatism." *dialog: A Journal of Theology* 12, no. 3 (Summer 1973): 12-15.

"Providence and Watergate." *dialog: A Journal of Theology* 12, no. 4 (Autumn 1973): 249-50.

"The Charismatic Phenomenon." *dialog: A Journal of Theology* 13, no. 1 (Winter 1974): 6-7.

"The Current Controversy in the Missouri Synod." *dialog: A Journal of Theology* 13, no. 2 (Spring 1974): 84-85.

"An Evangelical Papacy?" *dialog: A Journal of Theology* 13, no. 2 (Spring 1974): 90.

"Dialog in Transition." *dialog: A Journal of Theology* 13, no. 4 (Autumn 1974): 244-45.

"The Enemy of My Enemy Is My Friend: On the Hartford Theses." *dialog: A Journal of Theology* 14, no. 2 (Spring 1975): 84-85.

"Goodbye, Lutheran Unity." *dialog: A Journal of Theology* 14, no. 4 (Autumn 1975): 244-46.

"Lutherans Split in Chile." *dialog: A Journal of Theology* 14, no. 4 (Autumn 1975): 250-51.

"Sixty Millions for Missions." *dialog: A Journal of Theology* 16, no. 3 (Summer 1977): 164-65.

"What's Going on in Theology." *Lutheran School of Theology Epistle* 13, no. 1 (Fall 1977): 2, 4.

"The Myth of the Chicago School." *dialog: A Journal of Theology* 17, no. 2 (Spring 1978): 85-87.

"On Mixing Religion and Politics." *dialog: A Journal of Theology* 19, no. 4 (Autumn 1980): 244-45.

"Beyond Ecumenism, What?" *dialog: A Journal of Theology* 20, no. 1 (Winter 1981): 7-10.

"Where Is the Magisterium?" *dialog: A Journal of Theology* 22, no. 1 (Winter 1983): 4-5.

"What's in a Name?" *dialog: A Journal of Theology* 22, no. 1 (Winter 1983): 7.

"The Future of *dialog*." *dialog: A Journal of Theology* 23, no. 4 (Autumn 1984): 244-45.

"No Breakthrough Whatever" (on the Lutheran-Catholic Dialogue on "Justification by Faith"). *dialog: A Journal of Theology* 23, no. 4 (Autumn 1984): 245-46.

"The Crisis of Authority." *dialog: A Journal of Theology* 23, no. 4 (Autumn 1984): 247-48.

"The New Inquisition." *dialog: A Journal of Theology* 24, no. 1 (Winter 1985): 4-5.

"Is Liberation Theology a Heresy?" *dialog: A Journal of Theology* 24, no. 1 (Winter 1985): 5-6.

"How to Save the Lutheran Church." *dialog: A Journal of Theology* 24, no. 2 (Spring 1985): 84-85.

"Lutheran School of Theology and the Pittsburgh Crisis." *dialog: A Journal of Theology* 24, no. 3 (Summer 1985): 164-65.

"Merger Watch: Theological Education in the New Lutheran Church." *dialog: A Journal of Theology* 24, no. 3 (Summer 1985): 206-7.

"The Bishops Commission and the Pittsburgh Confession." *dialog: A Journal of Theology* 24, no. 4 (Autumn 1985): 243-47.

"Reunion in Our Lifetime?" *dialog: A Journal of Theology* 24, no. 4 (Autumn 1985): 242-43.

"Lutheran Schizophrenia." *dialog: A Journal of Theology* 24, no. 4 (Autumn 1985): 247.

"The Melanchthonian Blight." *dialog: A Journal of Theology* 25, no. 2 (Spring 1986): 82-83.

"Who's the Phony? Tutu, Falwell, and Apartheid." *dialog: A Journal of Theology* 25, no. 2 (Spring 1986): 83.

"Lutherans Concerned Issue Call for Dialogue." *dialog: A Journal of Theology* 25, no. 2 (Spring 1986): 83-84.

"The Name Will Change but the Game Will Remain the Same." *dialog: A Journal of Theology* 25, no. 2 (Spring 1986): 84-85.

"Tourists and Terrorists." *dialog: A Journal of Theology* 25, no. 3 (Summer 1986): 162.

"The Centenaries of Karl Barth and Paul Tillich." *dialog: A Journal of Theology* 25, no. 3 (Summer 1986): 164.

"Those Lutheran Church in America Bishops." *dialog: A Journal of Theology* 25, no. 3 (Summer 1986): 214-15.

"True and False Thinking on Repristination." *dialog: A Journal of Theology* 25, no. 4 (Summer 1986): 247-48.

"Does God Cause Aids?" *dialog: A Journal of Theology* 25, no. 4 (Autumn 1986): 246-47.

"Quotas: The New Legalism." *dialog: A Journal of Theology* 25, no. 1 (Winter 1986): 3-4.

"Berger Speaks Out on Apostasy." *dialog: A Journal of Theology* 26, no. 2 (Spring 1987): 82.

"The Ecumenical Impasse and Beyond." *dialog: A Journal of Theology* 26, no. 2 (Spring 1987): 83-87.

"We Have a Bishop." *dialog: A Journal of Theology* 26, no. 3 (Summer 1987): 162.

"God and/or Christ." *dialog: A Journal of Theology* 26, no. 4 (Autumn 1987): 242-43.

"Ecclesiogenesis: On Giving Birth to a New Church." *dialog: A Journal of Theology* 26, no. 4 (Autumn 1987): 243-44.

"The Six Year Study of Ministry." *dialog: A Journal of Theology* 26, no. 1 (Winter 1987): 5-6.

"Theological Issues Facing the Evangelical Lutheran Church in America." *dialog: A Journal of Theology* 27, no. 2 (Spring 1988): 87-89.

"Can the Church Be Saved?" *dialog: A Journal of Theology* 27, no. 3 (Summer 1988): 162.

"Liberation Theology Coming of Age." *dialog: A Journal of Theology* 27, no. 4 (Autumn 1988): 241.

"Neuhaus and the Bishops on Contra Aid." *dialog: A Journal of Theology* 27, no. 4 (Autumn 1988): 242.

"Let's Reorganize the ELCA." *dialog: A Journal of Theology* 28, no. 2 (Spring 1989): 164-65.

"Should the ELCA Join the WCC and the NCC?" *dialog: A Journal of Theology* 28, no. 2 (Spring 1989): 166-67.

"The Making of an American Protestant Church." *dialog: A Journal of Theology* 28, no. 4 (Autumn 1989): 243-44.

"A Call to Faithfulness." *dialog: A Journal of Theology* 28, no. 4 (Autumn 1989): 246.

"Inappropriate." *dialog: A Journal of Theology* 29, no. 1 (Winter 1989): 3.

"Ecumenical Bottom Lines." *dialog: A Journal of Theology* 29, no. 2 (Spring 1990): 82.

"On Higgins Bashing." *dialog: A Journal of Theology* 29, no. 2 (Spring 1990): 84-85.

"The Outrage of the Season." *dialog: A Journal of Theology* 29, no. 3 (Summer 1990): 164.

"Uncivil War on Ecumenism." *dialog: A Journal of Theology* 29, no. 3 (Summer 1990): 165-66.

"Can You Top This One?" *dialog: A Journal of Theology* 29, no. 4 (Autumn 1990): 246-47.

"Richard John Neuhaus: A Tribute to a Friend and Colleague." *dialog: A Journal of Theology* 29, no. 4 (Autumn 1990): 248-49.

"We Believe in the One Church." *Taking the Lead* (a Publication of the Rocky Mountain Continuing Education Center — ELCA) 2, no. 2 (1994): 8-11.

"What Price Unity?" *Pro Ecclesia: A Journal of Catholic and Evangelical Theology* 3, no. 4 (Fall 1994): 407-10.

"The Historical Jesus and the Church." *Pro Ecclesia: A Journal of Catholic and Evangelical Theology* 4, no. 1 (Winter 1995): 11-12.

"The House of God." *Lutheran Forum* 39, no. 2 (Summer 2005): 8-11.

Contributors

THE REV. JAMES M. CHILDS, JR., PH.D., assumed the position of Edward C. Fendt Professor of Systematic Theology in 2004. Prior to that he was Joseph A. Sittler Professor of Theology and Ethics. For twenty of his twenty-six years at Trinity he served as Academic Dean. From 2002 to 2005 he served in the capacity of Director for ELCA Studies on Sexuality. He is also a member of the Society of Christian Ethics and recently served on its Board of Directors. He is the author of seven books in the area of Christian ethics. Among his ethical contributions we find *Greed: Economics and Ethics in Conflict*, Fortress, 2000; *Preaching Justice: The Ethical Vocation of Word and Sacrament Ministry*, Trinity Press International, 2000; *What It Means to Be Lutheran in Social Ministry*, Lutheran Services in America, 2000; *Faithful Conversations: Christian Perspectives on Homosexuality*, Fortress, 2003, for which he was editor and contributor. Most recently he published the second edition of *Faith, Formation, and Decision*, newly titled *Ethics in the Community of Promise*, Fortress, 2006, and *The Way of Peace*, Fortress, 2008.

GABRIEL FACKRE is Abbot Professor of Christian Theology Emeritus at Andover Newton Theological School. He is the author of thirty books in the fields of theology and ethics and past president of the American Theological Society. Active in ecumenical venues, he attended the first and second assemblies of the World Council of Churches and represented the United Church of Christ in various full communion dialogues. Before seminary teaching he served for twelve years as a mission pastor in industrial areas of Chicago and Greater Pittsburgh. He is married to Dorothy Fackre. The couple have five children and eight grandchildren.

ALBERTO L. GARCÍA is Professor of Theology and Director of the Lay Ministry Program at Concordia University, Wisconsin. He has also taught at the Concordia Seminaries in Fort Wayne and St. Louis and at Florida International University, Miami, Florida. He is the author of six books in the areas of systematic theology, missions and faith in relationship to culture. He received his Doctor of Theology under the direction of the Rev. Dr. Carl E. Braaten at the Lutheran School of Theology at Chicago. He is an active member of the Asociación para la Educación Teológica Hispana (AETH). He is also an ordained Lutheran minister who has planted two Hispanic congregations in Chicago and Hollywood, Florida. He is married to Mori and they have two grown children and a granddaughter.

TIMOTHY GEORGE is the founding dean of Beeson Divinity School of Samford University and a senior editor of *Christianity Today*. He also serves as general editor of the Reformation Commentary on Scripture, a 28-volume series of sixteenth-century exegetical comment. He is a member of the International Baptist-Catholic Dialogue sponsored by the Baptist World Alliance and the Pontifical Council for Promoting Christian Unity.

ROBERT W. JENSON is Carl Braaten's career-long collaborator: in the writing and editing of books, in the founding and editing of the journals *Dialog* and *Pro Ecclesia,* in the founding and direction of the Center for Catholic and Evangelical Theology, and in decades of theological discussion and occasional spirited argument. He holds a Dr. Theol. from Heidelberg, and studied also at the universities of Minnesota and Basel. He is the author of a small shelf of books, perhaps his *Systematic Theology* and commentary on Ezekiel should be especially mentioned — together with *Conversations with Poppi about God,* a record of theological converse with his eight-year-old granddaughter. He now lives in Princeton, New Jersey, and sometimes teaches in the local university.

JOSEPH L. MANGINA is Associate Professor of Theology at Wycliffe College, Toronto School of Theology. A native of New Jersey, he received his M.Div. and his Ph.D. from Yale University. He is the author of two books on the theology of Karl Barth, and of the volume *Revelation* in the Brazos Theological Commentary series. He is married and has two children. When he is not teaching theology he may be found cycling, hiking, or in the kitchen indulging his love of Italian cooking.

CHERYL M. PETERSON is Associate Professor of Systematic Theology at Trinity Lutheran Seminary in Columbus, Ohio. An ordained pastor in the Evangelical Lutheran Church in America, she has served congregations in Tyrone, Pennsylvania and Milwaukee, Wisconsin. She received the M.Div. from the Lutheran School of Theology at Chicago and the Ph.D. from Marquette University in Milwaukee. She is a member of the U.S. Lutheran–Roman Catholic Dialogue and has participated in several seminars sponsored by the Lutheran World Federation. Her primary research interests are in the areas of pneumatology and ecclesiology.

MICHAEL ROOT is Professor of Systematic Theology at Lutheran Theological Southern Seminary in Columbia, South Carolina, where he served as Dean from 2003 to 2009. He served ten years as Research Professor at the Institute for Ecumenical Research in Strasbourg, France, and has taught at Davidson College in Davidson, North Carolina, and Trinity Lutheran Seminary in Columbus, Ohio. Since January 2006, he has been Executive Director of the Center for Catholic and Evangelical Theology. He was a member of the US and international Lutheran-Catholic dialogues, the US Lutheran–United Methodist dialogue, the Anglican-Lutheran International Working Group, and the Anglican-Lutheran International Commission. He served on the drafting teams that produced the Lutheran–Roman Catholic *Joint Declaration on the Doctrine of Justification* and *Called to Common Mission,* which established full communion between the Evangelical Lutheran Church in America and the Episcopal Church. He is the author (with Gabriel Fackre) of *Affirmations and Admonitions* (Eerdmans, 1998) and editor of *Justification by Faith* (with Karl Lehmann and William Rusch, Continuum, 1997), *Baptism and the Unity of the Church* (with Risto Saarinen, Eerdmans, 1998), and *Sharper than a Two-Edged Sword: Preaching, Teaching, and Living the Bible* (with James Buckley, Eerdmans, 2008).

LEOPOLDO A. SÁNCHEZ M. is Assistant Professor of Systematic Theology and Director of the Center for Hispanic Studies in the Werner R. H.

Krause and Elizabeth Ringger Krause Endowed Chair for Hispanic Ministries at Concordia Seminary, St. Louis. His areas of research are pneumatology, Trinitarian theology, and issues in Hispanic/Latino theology and missions. He is married to Tracy. They have two children, Lucas and Ana.

FRANK C. SENN, STS is Pastor of Immanuel Lutheran Church, Evanston, Illinois, and Senior of the Society of the Holy Trinity, a ministerium and oratory for Lutheran pastors. He was a student and later a faculty colleague of Carl Braaten's at the Lutheran School of Theology at Chicago. He earned a Ph.D. in liturgical studies from the University of Notre Dame. Dr. Senn is the author of nine books, of which *Christian Liturgy — Catholic and Evangelical* (Fortress, 1997) is his magnum opus, as well as numerous journal and encyclopedia articles. His research interests are in the areas of the history, theology, and practice of Christian worship. He is a past president of the North American Academy of Liturgy and The National Liturgical Conference. He is married to Mary Elizabeth and has three grown children.

SUSAN K. WOOD is Professor of Systematic Theology at Marquette University. She serves on the U.S. Lutheran–Roman Catholic dialogue, the U.S. Roman Catholic–Orthodox Theological Consultation, the conversation between the Roman Catholic Church and the Baptist World Alliance, and the International Lutheran-Catholic Dialogue. She has also participated in consultations on baptism, theological anthropology, and the nature and purpose of ecumenical dialogue sponsored by Faith and Order of the World Council of Churches and the Joint Working Group. She serves as a board member of the Center for Catholic and Evangelical Theology, is an associate editor of *Pro Ecclesia,* and serves on the editorial advisory board of the journal *Ecclesiology.* Most of her writing explores the connections between ecclesiology and sacramental theology. Her books include *Spiritual Exegesis and the Church in the Theology of Henri de Lubac* (Eerdmans, 1998), *Sacramental Orders* (The Liturgical Press, 2000), which has also been translated into Spanish, and *One Baptism: Ecumenical Dimensions of the Doctrine of Baptism* (The Liturgical Press, 2009). She is the editor of *Ordering the Baptismal Priesthood* (The Liturgical Press, 2003).

Index